SUPREME ANECDOTES

SUPREME ANECDOTES

Tales from the Supreme Court

BY
ROBERT S. PECK &
ANTHONY CHAMPAGNE

Rand-Smith Publishing

Copyright © 2024 by Robert S. Peck & Anthony Champagne

Paperback: 978-1-959544-53-0
Digital/Ebook: 978-1-959544-52-3
Library of Congress Control Number: 2024942512

Cover Illustration: Our overworked Supreme Court/ J. Keppler
Showing Justices Woods, Blatchford, Harlan, Gray, Miller, Field, Waite, Bradley, and Matthews trying to manage the court's caseload.
Published by Keppler & Schwarzmann, 1885 December 9
Library of Congress Prints and Photographs Division

All rights reserved.

No part of this book may be reproduced in any manner whatsoever without written permission except in the case of brief quotations embodied in critical articles and reviews.

First Printing, 2024

Rand-Smith Publishing
Rand-Smith LLC

Table of Contents

Reviews	vii
Preface	1
Acknowledgments	3
1. The Early Days	5
2. The Marshall Court	19
3. The Taney Era	39
4. The Post-Civil War Court	53
5. The First Third of the Twentieth Century	83
6. The New Deal Court	117
7. The Warren Court	155
8. The Burger-Rehnquist Courts	185
9. The Roberts Court	237
About the Authors	261
Endnotes	263

Reviews

"I cannot think of another book on the Supreme Court that I enjoyed reading more or that I learned more from. Robert Peck and Anthony Champagne have written a magnificent book presenting anecdotes about the justices, both the famous and the obscure. Most of all, the book shows us the human beings in the robes and reminds us that the law is a product of who is on the bench."

—**Erwin Chemerinsky,** Dean and Jesse H. Choper Distinguished Professor of Law, University of California, Berkeley School of Law

"The history of the Supreme Court traditionally has been treated as a long train of legal doctrines made by dour and serious justices taking the law, and often themselves, entirely too seriously. Peck and Champagne reveal, through a series of anecdotes and stories, that from the beginning, justices of the Supreme Court are anything but dour—indeed, they were people of flamboyant personalities who led interesting lives. This book not only will give the reader an appreciation of the history of the Supreme Court from the days of John Jay to the present Roberts Court but will also induce a chuckle a page. Readers will not so accidentally gain an appreciation for the honor and wisdom of people who have served but also endure puns about basketball games played on 'the highest court in the land.' Warning—put aside a couple of hours when you open this book because you won't be able to set it down!"

—**James Riddlesperger, Jr.,** Professor of Political Science, Texas Christian University

"An apt anecdote can reveal the character of a prominent person. That is especially the case for judges robed in neutral black. This charming book peeks beneath those robes at the foibles, follies, and the occasional withering wit of the Supremes who have populated the most solemn branch of government, proving that justices are human."
—**Royce Hanson,** Research Professor, George Washington University Institute of Public Policy

"The authors paint a refreshing and unprecedented portrait of the men and women who have profoundly shaped American history through their service on the Court. Superbly researched, evocative, and inspiring, *Supreme Anecdotes* is a must-read for all who care about the majesty and frailty of the rule of law."
—**Hon. Wallace B. Jefferson,** former chief justice of the Texas Supreme Court

"*Supreme Anecdotes* shows the reader a very different side of the Justices, including the fact that many of them did not come close to fitting our ideal of members of our Highest Court."
—**Alan B. Morrison,** Lerner Family Associate Dean for Public Interest and Public Service Law, George Washington University Law School

Preface

In 1990–1991, the authors served together as U.S. Supreme Court Fellows. At that time, they discovered a shared affinity for Supreme Court history. They traded numerous stories that each had learned over the years about the Supreme Court. They thought then that those anecdotes about the Court would prove to be interesting to lawyers, judges, and students of constitutional law. Fast forward to today, where the recent media attention on not only the rulings but the judges themselves makes these anecdotes even more relevant.

After their terms as Supreme Court Fellows ended, Peck gave numerous lectures to legal groups in which he incorporated stories about the Court and the justices. Champagne returned to university teaching and frequently spoke to community groups about the Court, and, like Peck, discovered that anecdotes about the Court were popular with audiences. Champagne even had a yearly contest for undergraduate pre-law students called "Supreme Court Trivia," where students prepared for the contest by studying the justices and then attempted to answer questions about them from a panel of three professors.

Peck and Champagne concluded that anecdotes about the justices could be collected in book form and made available to a wide audience interested in the Court and its justices. Supreme Court justices are often viewed as oracles separated from ordinary human ambitions, flaws, and foibles. These stories about the justices convey the Court's history and the humanity of those who sit on the bench.

Acknowledgments

We are especially grateful to Janice Herridge, an undergraduate student at the University of Texas at Dallas, who did an independent student research project where she explored judicial biographies and found a substantial number of anecdotes about the justices, which further persuaded us that there was value in such a book. We are also grateful to the many biographers and students of the Court who have chronicled stories about the Court, sparking our own interests and providing sources for many of these stories.

I

The Early Days

The Supreme Court began its existence with just six seats. Many potential nominees found the idea of sitting on Supreme Court unappealing. Several nominees declined the appointment in favor of state offices that they regarded as more prestigious.[1]

Although the justices originally appointed to the Court were distinguished lawyers and judges, many of whom had played important roles during the nation's formative period, none dominated the Court or notably defined its jurisprudence. During this period, the Court had three chief justices: John Jay, John Rutledge, and Oliver Ellsworth.

John Jay, Chief Justice (1789–1795)
John Rutledge, Associate Justice (1770–1791); Chief Justice (1795)
Oliver Ellsworth, Chief Justice (1796–1800)
Associate Justices:

John Blair, Jr. (1790–1795)
Samuel Chase (1796–1811)
William Cushing (1790–1810)
James Iredell (1790–1799)

Thomas Johnson (1791–1793)
William Patterson (1793–1806)
James Wilson (1789–1798)

The Chief Justices

John Jay

Born December 12, 1745, in New York, New York; died May 17, 1829; chief justice, 1789–1795. Jay served in both the First and Second Continental Congresses, drafted the first New York Constitution, served as his state's chief justice, became president of the pre-Constitution Continental Congress, represented the U.S. to Spain, was a primary negotiator of the peace treaty with England, and contributed to the "Federalist Papers" that helped win ratification of the U.S. Constitution. While chief justice, he was elected governor of New York in absentia and promptly quit the court.

John Jay studied law in the office of Benjamin Kissan. At some point afterward, Jay and Kissan wound up as opposing counsel. Jay did an exceptional job in the case, which led Kissan to exclaim, "Have I brought up a bird to pick out mine own eyes?"

Jay responded, "Not to pick out your eyes, but to open them."[2]

Following the Treaty of Paris in 1783, which resolved the Revolutionary War, many difficult issues remained between the new United States and Great Britain, with both countries claiming the other had violated the treaty. Jay accepted the assignment to resolve those issues, successfully negotiating a 1795 agreement that became known as the Jay Treaty. Critics argued Jay was too pro-British, that officials should not hold two offices, and that the separation of powers was violated.[3] Still, Jay's service in that diplomatic role established a precedent for other justices to take extrajudicial assignments.

The treaty also drew intense opposition from Thomas Jefferson's Democratic-Republican Party, which focused its opprobrium on Jay.

Anti-Federalist Party newspapers published couplets replete with crude language that expressed this disapproval. One imagined Jay's approach to negotiating with Britain's king:

> May it please your highness, I, John Jay
> Have traveled all this mighty way,
> To inquire if you, good Lord, will please,
> To suffer me while on my knees,
> To show all others I surpass,
> In love, by kissing of your [ass]...[4]

An analogous theme was evident in a short rhyme that appeared in Kentucky:

> I think Jay's treat is truly a farse,
> Fit only to wipe the national [arse].[5]

Newspapers were not the only place where Jay could see the hatred his treaty engendered. The fence of one of Jay's friends was once adorned with the words: "Damn John Jay! Damn everyone that won't damn John Jay! Damn everyone that won't put lights in his windows and sit up all night damning John Jay!"[6]

Still, Jay took the criticisms in stride, joking that he would have no trouble finding his way at night along the route from Boston to Philadelphia because those roads would be lit by all the people burning him in effigy.[7]

Although he became the nation's first chief justice, Jay's judgment about the national offices he was offered and rejected could be questioned. George Washington asked him to serve as Secretary of State, but Jay declined. The post then went to Thomas Jefferson, who continued to climb the available national offices until he reached the presidency.[8] Although he accepted his appointment as chief justice and served six years, Jay left the office to become New York's governor, an office to which he was elected without his knowledge while out of the country negotiating what became the Jay Treaty. The Court had little to do during that period. From February 1790–February 1793, the Supreme Court only heard five cases, and from 1790–1801, only fifty-five cases. The gubernatorial election was a redemption for Jay, who had previously sought that office while serving on the Court and lost.[9]

After John Adams became president, he attempted to entice Jay back to the Supreme Court, sending Jay's nomination to the Senate without consulting the nominee. Jay was quickly confirmed by the Senate, and Adams wrote Jay on December 19, 1800, to inform the then-New York Governor: "I have nominated you to your old station."

Jay declined the office, writing that the Supreme Court was "so defective it would not obtain the energy, weight, and dignity which was essential to its affording due support to the national government; nor acquire the public confidence and respect which, as the last resort of the justice of a nation, it should possess."[10] Again, Jay appears to have missed the boat. John Marshall was appointed chief justice instead, ushering in an era in which the Supreme Court took on an importance that remains to this day.

Jay's original appointment as the first chief justice of the United States was expected to help establish the Supreme Court's high place in the new American government. The Court did not, however, get off to an auspicious start. Convening for the first time on February 1, 1790, Jay was joined by only two other justices, James Wilson and William Cushing. Without a quorum, as well as no real business to conduct, the Court adjourned until the next day when Justice John Blair and Attorney General Edmund Randolph joined them.

Two original appointees, John Rutledge and Robert Harrison, never attended a single session of the Jay Court. Harrison, suffering from ill health, resigned just days after his appointment. Rutledge resigned his seat to accept what appeared to him to be a meatier post-chief justice of the South Carolina Court of Common Pleas.

With little more to do than admit attorneys to the Supreme Court Bar, the Court completed its first session in ten days and limited its second, in August, to two. Nevertheless, the opening of the Court attracted more press coverage than "any other event connected with the new Government."[11]

John Rutledge
Born September 1739, in Charleston, South Carolina; died June 21, 1800; associate justice, 1789–1791; chief justice, 1795. Rutledge was a member of the Stamp Act and Continental Congresses, served his home state as governor, and was a delegate at the federal Constitutional Convention. As governor, he was so autocratic that he was known as "Dictator John."

John Rutledge was seriously considered by George Washington for service as the first chief justice, an office to which he truly aspired. He wrote:

> Several of my Friends were displeased at my accepting the Office of an Associate Judge, (altho' the senior) of the Supreme Court... conceiving (as I thought, very justly,) that my Pretensions to the Office of Chief Justice were, at least, equal to Mr. Jay's in point of Law-Knowledge with the Additional Weight, of much longer Experience, and much greater Practice.[12]

Despite his absence as senior associate justice, Rutledge continued to covet the chief justiceship. Upon Chief Justice John Jay's election to New York's governorship, Rutledge wrote to President George Washington, saying, "I take the liberty of intimating to you *privately*, that if [Jay should accept his new office], I have no objection to take the place which he holds... [When] the office of Chief Justice of the United States becomes vacant, I feel that the duty which I owe to my children should impel me to accept it, if offered, tho, more arduous and troublesome than my present station, because more respectable and honorable."

Washington responded favorably to this self-nomination.[13]

Rutledge succeeded Jay as chief justice as a recess appointment because the Senate was not in session when he was named. He held the office, though, only until the Senate met to vote on his confirmation.

His nomination hit the skids because of his outspoken attacks on the Jay Treaty. Rumors also circulated that the nominee had lost his mind and had become a drunkard. When Rutledge learned that the Senate had refused to confirm him, he attempted to drown himself in Charleston Bay. Only the intervention of two enslaved men saved his life. He did go mad in the last five years of his life and died in 1800.[14]

Rutledge left virtually no mark from his service on the Court. His written legacy consists of a short seriatim opinion[15] that some commentators consider "so trivial that it is sometimes said that he wrote nothing at all."[16]

Oliver Ellsworth

Born April 29, 1745, in Windsor, Connecticut; died November 26, 1807; chief justice, 1796–1800. Ellsworth served in the Continental Congresses and on the Connecticut Supreme Court. He was a prime mover in the Connecticut Compromise that created the different standards for representation in the House and Senate during the Constitutional Convention (though he was absent when the delegates signed the final document) and, as a U.S. Senator, of the 1789 Judiciary Act. He undertook his own version of the Federalist Papers to support ratification of the Constitution under the title "Letters of a Landholder."

Oliver Ellsworth was a prominent New England family scion, who wanted him to become a minister. He was enrolled at Yale College for that purpose but did not fit the ministerial mold. After two years, he was asked to leave the school because he acted wildly "and Halloed in the College Yard." He completed his college education at Princeton, where his behavior was apparently better tolerated.[17]

Ellsworth cut an impressive figure as a U.S. Senator, and his views often prevailed. His influence there was so great that Aaron Burr once opined, "If Ellsworth had happened to spell the name of the Deity with two d's, it would have taken the Senate three weeks to expunge the superfluous letter."[18]

As chief justice, Ellsworth lost his patience with Justice Samuel Chase's constant badgering of advocates before the Court. Once, after Chase interrupted one lawyer a third time, the lawyer gave up and took his seat. Ellsworth invited the lawyer to resume his argument, making plain that the Court had taken no view of the case and "when it does, you will hear it from the proper organ of the Court." He pledged his word that there would be no further interruptions and "then turned his face towards Judge Chase with a withering look of rebuke, under which the judge, with all his nerve and daring, fairly quailed."[19]

The Associate Justices

John Blair Jr.

Born April 17, 1732, in Williamsburg, Virginia; died Aug. 31, 1800; associate justice, 1789–1795. Blair had served as a member of Virginia's House of Burgesses, a delegate at the Constitutional Convention, chief justice of Virginia's General Court, Chancellor of the High Court of Chancery, and a member of the state's first court of appeals, where he wrote that the court had the authority to declare a statute unconstitutional.

Despite prior distinguished service as a judge, John Blair was one of only four delegates to stay throughout the entire Constitutional Convention, vote regularly, and yet never speak a single word during the debates.[20]

Blair's service on the Court was cut short by the onset of what he described as "a rattling, distracting noise in my head." His resignation described the affliction as a "strange disorder of my head, which has lately compelled me to neglect my official duties."[21]

Samuel Chase

Born April 17, 1741, in Somerset County, Maryland; died June 19, 1811; associate justice, 1796–1811. He was a signer of the Declaration of Independence and served in the Revolutionary War Congress. As a Maryland judge, Chase was considered a brilliant and charismatic figure. As a circuit rider, he wrote opinions giving the courts the power of judicial review, which allows the judiciary to declare statutes unconstitutional. He was the only justice to be impeached. Chase had a brownish-red complexion that led him to be called "Old Bacon Face."

Justice Samuel Chase was a hothead. As a young man and leader of the Sons of Liberty, Chase was described by the mayor and aldermen of Annapolis as "busy restless Incendiary—a Ringleader of Mobs—a foul mouth'd and inflaming son of Discord and Faction—a common Disturber of the public Tranquility, and a Promoter of the lawless excesses of the multitude." Chase, incidentally, never mellowed with age.

Still, Chase did not take the description bestowed upon him lying down. He gave as well as he got. To him, the city officials who called him names were "despicable Pimps, and Tools of Power, emerged from Obscurity and Basking in proprietary Sunshine."[22]

Even after becoming a judge, politics was Chase's lifeblood, making him an unabashed partisan. In May 1803, he charged a grand jury in a way that is unthinkable today:

> The late alteration of the federal judiciary...and the recent change in our state constitution, [supporting] the establishing of universal suffrage...will...take away all security for property and personal liberty...and our Republican constitution will sink into a mobocracy, the worst of all popular governments.

He showed bias in his court against Republicans being tried under the Alien and Sedition Acts[23] and attacked legislation passed by the Republican administration. During the election of 1800, he forced the Supreme Court to delay its August term so that he could campaign in Maryland for the re-election of John Adams.

On his way to the Supreme Court in Philadelphia from Maryland in February 1800, Chase found the Susquehanna River frozen so he could not take the usual ferry across. Cautious as a heavy man, he decided he could journey on foot because a wagon and horse had crossed before him. Just 150 yards before reaching shore, he fell through the ice but did not sink because of a boat hook his son had brought along. Valiant efforts were made to keep Chase above water, which was difficult because of the heavy and now-wet fur coat he was wearing. Chase told his wife, "I had just offered up a prayer to go to protect Me from the Danger, when I instantly fell in." While that prayer may have gone unanswered, Chase was soon saved from drowning.[24]

Luther Martin, a prominent advocate in the early days of the Supreme Court and a friend of Chase's, served as defense counsel for Chase when Congress tried to impeach him. After the team prevailed, Martin refused to accept any fee.

Many years later, Martin was counsel in a case in which Chase sat as a circuit judge. Martin appeared drunk at the time, causing Chase to comment, "I am surprised that you can so prostitute your talents."

"Sir," Martin responded, "I never prostituted my talents except when I defended you and Colonel Burr," adding in an aside to the jury, "a couple of the greatest rascals in the world."

Chase began to cite Martin for contempt but stayed the effort at the moment he was required to sign the document, recalling Martin's great service at the impeachment proceedings and stating, "Whatever may be my duties as a judge, Samuel Chase can never sign a commitment against Luther Martin."[25]

William Cushing
Born March 1, 1732, in Scituate, Massachusetts; died September 1, 1810; associate justice, 1789–1810. Cushing was the first appointment to associate justice status. President George Washington later nominated Cushing to the chief justice's post, and the Senate confirmed the nominee after John Rutledge's nomination was rejected. Cushing technically held the top spot for a week before declining the office for health reasons.

As in Britain, the first justices wore brightly colored robes and powdered wigs to court. The attire was not popular and seemed out of step with the new American ideals where royalty and pomp were passé. "For Heaven's sake," Thomas Jefferson advised, "discard the monstrous wig which makes the English Judges look like rats peeping through bunches of oakum."[26]

William Cushing, however, was a traditionalist and prized the dignity that went with the office. He walked through New York in a full-bottom judicial wig to make sure everyone knew who he was. New York, however, was not that different from today. Small boys would follow him with schoolyard taunts. It is said that as many as 100 boys shadowed him once. Still, Cushing was clueless as to why he had attracted such a crowd when a sailor, upon seeing the justice decked out as he was, called out, "My eye! What a wig!"

At that point, Cushing decided to abandon the full wig, favoring the peruke he had made instead. It did not relieve the criticism. Soon afterward, no justice wore wigs. Still, they continued to sport colorful robes until John Marshall joined the court, and black robes became standard wear.[27]

President Washington nominated Cushing to the office of chief justice, to which he was confirmed in 1796. However, Cushing turned down the post because of old age and poor health, though he remained on the Court as an associate justice. Perhaps he would have accepted if he knew he would continue serving on the court for 14 more years.[28]

According to one possibly apocryphal story, Cushing learned of his appointment as chief justice at a dinner party hosted by Washington, where Washington told him that he should take the seat on Washington's right because he was now the new chief justice.[29]

James Iredell
Born October 5, 1751, in Lewes, England; died October 20, 1799; associate justice, 1790–1799. Iredell had been North Carolina's attorney general, briefly a judge on the state's highest court, and a vociferous supporter of the ratification of the U.S. Constitution.

James Iredell came to the colonies on a purchased position as comptroller of customs at Edenton but used his spare time to study law. Iredell's uncle disapproved of his nephew's newfound profession, telling Iredell that his career was "dangerous to virtue" and included "pettifoggers," who were nothing more than "pickpockets" and who carried "contagion along with them."[30]

The position of Associate Justice on the U.S. Supreme Court also entailed circuit riding, an unpleasant task, but Iredell decided that he would give it a go. Still, he complained incessantly. Iredell wrote his wife that he was once forced to share a bed at an inn with a man "of the wrong sort" and frequently had to sleep through loud, drunken carrying on at various taverns where he received overnight accommodations. His transportation left much to be desired. His coach once swerved into a tree, dumped the justice, and then plowed over his leg. He valiantly continued his journey for ten miles more before the pain forced him to stay "very inconveniently at a house on the road."

Iredell had the good fortune of having a mentor and brother-in-law, Samuel Johnston, a U.S. Senator. Iredell drafted at least two pieces of legislation modifying the circuit court system, and those proposed laws were introduced by Johnston. He also drafted a letter signed by all the justices protesting circuit-riding. The letter was sent to President Washington and forwarded to Congress.

He achieved some relief. In 1792, Congress passed a law that excused justices from riding the distant Southern circuit unless the justice agreed to undertake the arduous task.[31] Iredell also had some success in altering the times of holding some circuit courts and rotating circuit assignments. He went too far, however, when he devised a plan where each justice would give up $500 of his salary in exchange for an end to circuit-riding. Chief Justice John Jay convinced Iredell not to send that idea to Congress.[32]

Thomas Johnson
Born November 4, 1732, in Saint Leonard, Maryland; died October 26, 1819; associate justice, 1791–1793. Johnson holds the honor of having nominated

George Washington for Supreme Commander of the American forces in the Revolutionary War. He served in the First and Second Continental Congress, was a drafter of Maryland's first constitution, and served as the state's first governor. His death wish was to "meet Washington beyond the grave."

Thomas Johnson could have been a founding-era Forrest Gump, present at many of the historic events of his time, but he always missed the opportunity. For example, he skipped the vote and the signing of the Declaration of Independence to head for Annapolis, where he was busy recruiting a militia. He pushed hard for both the Mount Vernon and Annapolis meetings that were precursors to the Constitutional Convention but did not attend either. He was offered a chance to serve as a Maryland delegate to the Constitutional Convention but again found something else to do.[33]

During the Revolutionary War, Johnson served as a brigadier general. In January 1777, he arrived at General George Washington's camp to report on the reinforcements he had led through an arduous trek. When he arrived, he didn't look like a general. A short man, caked in mud, Johnson was stopped by a sentinel, who refused to let Johnson see Washington. Appearance was not the only reason to bar Johnson; the guard had instructions not to disturb Washington. Johnson would not let the soldier keep him from making his report. He launched a series of expletives that so unnerved the young guard that he relented. Appearing before Washington, the guard announced, "There was a filthy red-headed little man who demanded to see him and that [the man said] the general's orders could be damned but he intended to see him."

Washington did not hesitate to respond: "Oh! It is Johnson of Maryland! Admit him at once!"[34]

As a justice, Johnson participated in just six decisions. He wrote just one, which ran only seventeen lines.[35] Despite the paucity of his effort on the Court, Johnson resigned as a justice 14 months into his tenure, stating that he would rather not "undertake the labor."[36]

William Paterson

Born December 24, 1745, in County Antrim, Ireland; died September 9, 1806; associate justice, 1793–1806. Paterson was a drafter of New Jersey's first constitution, the principal proponent of the New Jersey Plan at the federal Constitutional Convention, and an author of the Judiciary Act of 1789. He also served as New Jersey's governor. As a U.S. Senator, Paterson was such a vigorous supporter of central economic planning that an opponent described him as a member of Alexander Hamilton's "gladiatorial band."

During the Court's early period, the justices spent only about two months out of each year in Washington. Until about 1845, they lived together in the same boardinghouse but had little to do with the rest of Washington or the government. This anonymity was so great that on one occasion, William Paterson traveled in a carriage for a full day with Thomas Jefferson, but neither man was aware of who the other was![37]

On October 26, 1803, Paterson's carriage went off the road and down an embankment. His son and wife were not seriously hurt, but Paterson was injured and confined to home. His injuries were bad enough that it was several weeks before he could change positions in bed or rise from his chair. He did attend the next session of Court, but he could do little on the circuit. He wrote his wife that he was "almost worn out" and never recovered.[38]

James Wilson

Born September 14, 1742, in Fife, Scotland; died August 21, 1798; associate justice, 1789–1798. Wilson served in the Second Continental Congress, signed the Declaration of Independence, and was second only to James Madison in influence at the Constitutional Convention. His radical political opponents, who found him too much a Tory, dubbed him "James the Caledonian, Leut. Gen. of the Myrmidons of power."

James Wilson desperately wished to be chief justice, suggesting himself for the post in 1789, 1795, and 1796, only to be turned down each time.[39] Some have speculated that President George Washington denied him this plum assignment as payback for a hefty fee Wilson charged Washington in 1782 to tutor nephew Bushrod Washington, who later became a Supreme Court justice himself.[40]

While other justices complained about the burdens of circuit-riding, Wilson found a rare benefit: love. While serving as a judge in Boston, Wilson met the woman who would become his second wife. The couple had a considerable age gap. Wilson was 51 with children from his first marriage ranging in age from 8 to 21. His new bride was 19. Within ten days of meeting Hannah Gray, Wilson, though traveling on his circuit, pined for an answer to his proposal. One note that he sent back read, "Do let that Answer be speedy and favorable. Let it authorize me to think and call you mine."

Wilson's courting of Miss Gray did not go unnoticed. John Quincy Adams wrote to his brother about what had transpired:

> He came, he saw, he was overcome...smitten at a meeting with a first sight love—unable to contain his amorous pain, he breathed his sighs about the Streets; and even when seated on the bench of Justice, he seemed as if teeming with some woeful ballad to his mistress eye brow. He obtained an introduction to the Lady, and at the second interview proposed his lovely person and his agreeable family to her acceptance...[41]

Wilson engaged in risky financial speculations that ruined him. While riding circuit, he was "[h]unted like a wild beast" by creditors who threatened to have the justice thrown in debtors' prison. Wilson was actually jailed in Burlington, N.J., bailed out by his son, and then jailed again in North Carolina shortly before he died while hiding from his creditors.[42]

2

The Marshall Court

John Marshall, known as the "Great Chief Justice," is the dominant personality in Supreme Court history. The Court's stature, which had been so low that several proposed appointees turned down what they considered the dubious honor of being appointed chief justice, rose tremendously during this period. Under Marshall's leadership, the Court solidified its standing as the branch of government with the authority to be the final expositor of the meaning of the Constitution and the power to declare statutes unconstitutional. During his tenure as chief justice, Marshall began the practice of written opinions by a single justice and wrote 547 of the 1,100 decisions issued by the Court during his tenure, dissenting only eight times.

John Marshall, Chief Justice (1801–1835)

Associate Justices:
Henry Baldwin (1830–1844)
Gabriel Duvall (1811–1835)
William Johnson (1804–1834)
Brockholst Livingston (1807–1823)

John McLean (1829–1861)
Alfred Moore (1800–1804)
Joseph Story (1812–1845)
Smith Thompson (1823–1843)
Thomas Todd (1807–1826)
Robert Trimble (1826–1828)
Bushrod Washington (1798–1829)

The Chief Justice

John Marshall

Born September 24, 1755, in Germantown, Virginia; died July 6, 1835; chief justice, 1801–1835. For an eloquent speech made during the Revolutionary War at Valley Forge, Marshall acquired the nickname "Silver Heels," though some say that he earned the sobriquet as a young man because of the colorful socks he wore. Marshall served as a delegate to Virginia's convention to ratify the Constitution, as an American diplomat, a U.S. congressman, and secretary of state. As chief justice, Marshall so towered over his colleagues in prestige and reputation that the Court was popularly known as "John Marshall and the six dwarfs." Even today, Marshall is remembered as "the Great Chief Justice."

John Marshall's appointment to the Court was hardly foreordained. As Secretary of State, Marshall was tasked with the responsibility of delivering John Jay's letter declining reappointment as chief justice to President John Adams.

"Who shall I nominate now?" Adams asked him.

Marshall was perplexed and had no response.

"I believe I must nominate you," Adams suddenly replied.

Marshall later recalled, "I was pleased as well as surprised (sic), and bowed in silence."[1]

Marshall's nomination was not met with the universal acclaim he now receives as a historical figure. Senator Jonathan Dayton of New Jersey, who was the youngest signatory on the Constitution and one of the early speakers of the U.S. House of Representatives, reluctantly voted to confirm Marshall as chief justice, explaining that, if the nomination did not go through, it "might induce the nomination of some other character more improper, and more disgusting." Despite misgivings like that, Marshall was unanimously confirmed.[2]

Though a grand statue of Marshall, heroic in appearance, sits on the first floor of today's Supreme Court, he is said to have had a somewhat crude appearance. One description of this titan of the law described him as "tall, meager, emaciated; his muscles relaxed, and his joints so loosely connected, as not only to disqualify him, apparently, for any vigorous exertion of the body but to destroy everything like harmony in his air and movements. Indeed, in his whole appearance and demeanor; dress, attitudes, gesture, sitting, standing or walking; he is as far removed from the idolized graces of Lord Chesterfield, as any other gentleman on earth."

Marshall was also no fashion plate, usually adorned with a plain black suit. Unorganized, he tended to misplace or lose important papers. As secretary of state, it was Marshall who failed to deliver the justice of the peace commissions in a timely fashion which ultimately led to his famous decision in *Marbury v. Madison*.[3] Even Marshall's voice was jarring, described as "dry and hard," and he affected an "extremely awkward" posture when speaking.[4]

In fact, Marshall usually made a bad first impression based on appearances. His clothing invariably looked like it came from "some antiquated slop-shop of second-hand raiment ... the coat and breeches cut for nobody in particular." He tended to wear "dirty boots," and his "large head of hair ... looked as if it had not been lately tied or combed."[5]

Still, when "[c]lad in the robes of his great office, with the Associate Justices on either side of him, no king on a throne ever appeared more majestic than did John Marshall," even though he chose to wear plain black judicial robes, rather than the colorful garb of English judges.[6]

Marshall frequently began an argument by stating his assumptions with the words, "It is admitted..." One of the Supreme Court's great advocates, Daniel Webster, told Justice Joseph Story that "When Judge Marshall says, 'It is admitted,' sir, I am preparing for a bomb to burst over my head and demolish my points."[7]

When word leaked out that during their private conferences the justices enjoyed a nice bottle of Madeira and the public reacted badly to the revelation, the Court was forced to adopt a rule of compromise. After all, the justices understood that it would not go over well if the public thought the nation's most important judicial decisions were being made under an alcoholic haze. The new rule stated that the justices would not imbibe unless it were raining. Who, the justices reasoned, could begrudge them a beverage on a dreary day in Washington, DC, which was still largely a swamp?

On the first day the new rule was in effect, Marshall began the conference by asking the junior justice, Joseph Story, to determine whether it was raining. Story dutifully went to the window but only saw sunshine. Knowing that the chief justice liked his drink, Story craned his neck in hopes of spying a threatening cloud that could lead to an ambiguous report, but to no avail. He returned to the table to report, dejectedly, that there was no chance of rain today.

Marshall eyed him sternly: "Mr. Justice Story, I have long admired your careful and well-reasoned approach to the law, but on this matter, I must disagree with you. I point out that our jurisdiction is nationwide, and somewhere it must be raining. Bring on the wine."[8]

Years later, when the reporter of decisions heard the justices recall this story, he questioned its veracity. Justice David Brewer answered, "Why, Mr. Reporter, the story is not only true but you ought to know that the Court sustained the constitutionality of the acquisition of the Philippines so as to be sure of having plenty of rainy seasons."[9]

While circuit riding was often hazardous, sometimes legal research proved just as dangerous. Once, climbing a stepladder to retrieve a law book, Marshall took a spill. An attendant rushed to help the chief justice, who quipped, "I was floored."[10]

Marshall's circuit-riding duties often brought him to Raleigh. In one case, Marshall was prepared to deliver his charge to a grand jury, only to find that the new crier had fallen asleep and thus could not caution the audience to remain silent. Marshall decided to skip the warning and began to read the charge anyway. However, the chief justice's voice woke the crier, who demanded that Marshall, "Stop, sir! Stop, sir!"

Marshall dutifully did as he was bid. The crier then shouted, the irony of which was entirely lost on him, "Oyez! oyez! oyez! All manner of persons are required to keep silence upon pain of imprisonment while the honorable judge is giving his charge to the grand jury!"

The crier then informed the chief justice, "You may go on, sir." People in the courtroom fully expected that Marshall would jail the crier for violating the rule he had just announced, but instead, Marshall began his grand jury charge anew and acted as if nothing unusual had happened.[11]

Once, a young lawyer arguing before Marshall while riding circuit sought to butter up the chief justice by declaring Marshall "the acme of judicial distinction." Marshall responded, without missing a beat: "Let me tell you what that means, young man...the ability to look a lawyer straight in the face for two hours with closed ears."[12]

While shopping, Marshall saw a fashionably dressed young man, complaining loudly about having no one to carry home the turkey he had just bought. Overhearing that the man lived enroute to where Marshall himself was headed, Marshall offered to carry the bird. When they reached the man's home, Marshall was offered a tip, but refused it, stating, "It was on my way, and no trouble."

The young man later asked a neighbor about the identity of the "old gentlemen who brought home my turkey for me?"

No doubt the reply took him aback: "That is John Marshall, the Chief Justice of the United States."

"Why then did he bring home my turkey?" the man asked.

"To give you a deserved rebuke," the neighbor said, "and to teach you to conquer your silly pride."[13]

Marshall was notoriously careless in dress and was well aware of that trait. On one occasion, he was invited to a dinner party and some of the diners made a wager with him. The other diners would pay for the entertainment if he came to the party flawlessly dressed. If Marshall were disheveled, he would pay. At the party, it looked as if Marshall was the winner of the bet, and he was thrilled. Then, one of the diners dropped his napkin, bent down to retrieve it, and noticed that one of Marshall's stockings was wrong side out. It was said that "...amidst the uproarious laughter of his companions, the chief justice acknowledged his defeat."[14]

Following the 1835 term of the Court, Marshall, who was 79, was injured in a stagecoach accident. In early June, he collapsed from exhaustion during his weekly 1.5-mile trek from his home to visit the grave of his beloved wife, Polly. He died shortly afterward, on July 6, 1835, in Philadelphia.[15] The Liberty Bell was rung in his honor and cracked when it tolled. It was never rung again.[16]

The Associate Justices

Henry Baldwin

Born January 14, 1780, in New Haven, Connecticut; died April 21, 1844; associate justice, 1830–1844. A former congressman who was rewarded with a seat on the Supreme Court for his support of Andrew Jackson's presidential bid, Baldwin was known for telling racy jokes. His reputation was nonetheless impeccable, and he was known as the "Idol of Pennsylvania" and the "Pride of Pittsburgh."

Pittsburgh had a reputation as a rough town when Henry Baldwin lived there. Disputes were often settled by a duel. Tarlton Bates, a political supporter of Baldwin's, died in a duel. Baldwin, too, found himself challenged to a duel and very nearly died himself. Only a silver dollar kept in his breast pocket saved him, as it stopped the bullet that might have spelled his demise.[17]

Baldwin suffered financial problems and decided he could make money by writing a book. The book was titled "A General View of the Origins and Nature of the Constitution and Government of the United States." In order to pay the costs of printing the book, he held an auction of 100 copies of the book. Unfortunately, that auction only netted him $70 or about $.70 a book. The low selling price of the first hundred copies also forced him to lower the price of additional copies of the book.[18]

Baldwin did not age gracefully and was given to such unpredictable and occasionally violent behavior that some believed him mad.[19] One Philadelphia judge said Baldwin was obviously insane because the justice required that coffee and cakes be delivered to him even while court was in session. Once, he was spotted dragging a ham by its hock, causing people to see him as more than a bit eccentric.[20] In December 1832, there were reports that "the Honorable Judge Baldwin was seized today with a fit of derangement." Two weeks later, Daniel Webster wrote about "the breaking out of Judge Baldwin's insanity." There was still another report that said, "Judge Baldwin is out of his wits." Baldwin missed the entire 1833 term and was hospitalized with "incurable lunacy."

Justice Joseph Story wrote in May 1833, "I am sure he cannot be sane. And, indeed, the only charitable view, which I can take of any of his conduct, is, that he is partially deranged at all times." In 1838, the Reporter of Decisions for the Court, Richard Peters, said, "I have heard on one day not less than five persons...say 'he is crazy.'"

Baldwin, however, was on the Court until his death in April 1844.[21] He died a pauper, having squandered his money and having spent his later years plagued by paralysis.[22]

An 1856 volume noted that Baldwin had a terrible tobacco habit and suggested that he smoked so much that it killed him.[23]

Gabriel Duvall

Born December 6, 1752, in Prince Georges County, Maryland; died March 6, 1844; associate justice, 1811–1835. Duvall, whose name is also spelled Duval in official reports of the Court, declined appointment as a delegate to the Constitutional Convention but did serve as chief justice of Maryland's General Court, a member of Congress, and Comptroller of the U.S. Treasury under President Thomas Jefferson. His most notable action while on the Supreme Court was to dissent without opinion in the famous case of Dartmouth College v. Woodward.[24]

Justice Gabriel Duvall is at least two scholars' candidate for the most insignificant justice.[25] Senility struck him in old age, and Duvall was supposedly denied any writing implements by Chief Justice John Marshall to discourage him from memorializing his thoughts.[26] Nonetheless, Duvall remained on the Court for 23 years.

Duvall is credited with precisely three words about constitutional disputes in his 23 years on the Court. In the *Dartmouth College* case, it states: "Duvall, justice, dissents."[27] His total output during his tenure consisted of 15 opinions.[28]

During his final decade of service, he was so ill and deaf that historian Carl Brent Swisher reported that arguments "meant little or nothing to him."[29] In fact, Senator Benjamin Tappan confirmed that Duvall could not hear a word that had been spoken in Court during that period of time.[30] Another author described the octogenarian Duvall as striking a strange figure on the bench, with "his hair, white as a snowbank, gathered into a long cue reaching to his waist."[31]

Duvall remained on the Court despite his infirmities, thinking that he was the most likely to be appointed as Marshall's successor as chief justice.[32] Even after he understood that his ambition to be chief justice would not be realized, he sought to influence the appointment by campaigning against a chief justice who would be "too much of a politician." He finally resigned once he was assured that fellow Marylander Roger B. Taney would be appointed to his seat. Taney, instead, won confirmation to John Marshall's seat as chief justice, Duvall's desired office.[33]

William Johnson
Born December 27, 1771, in Goose Creek Parish, South Carolina; died August 4, 1834; associate justice, 1805–1833. Johnson served as speaker of South Carolina's House of Representatives and in the Constitutional Court before President Thomas Jefferson named the 33-year-old to the U.S. Supreme Court. His initial actions as a justice angered members of the Jefferson Administration, who suggested that Johnson had caught "leprosy of the Bench." While later opinions were more in line with his Jeffersonian roots, his presence on a largely Federalist Court made him the first of the "great dissenters."

Politics were harsh between the parties, even back then. Still, an occasional sense of "respect" was accorded to opposing factions, such as when William Johnson was considered by the Senate for confirmation to the Supreme Court. Senator William Plumer of New Hampshire, then a Federalist, wrote that Johnson was a "democrat, but I am assured, a man of moral character, & not destitute of talents."[34]

Even in retirement, former President Thomas Jefferson resented the influence his cousin, Chief Justice John Marshall, wielded on the Supreme Court. He wrote Johnson, whom he had appointed to the Court, urging a return to seriatim opinions, by which each justice expressed his own view, instead of there being a single opinion for the Court. He told Johnson that the majority of opinions written by Marshall benefited only "the lazy, the modest, and the incompetent" justices.

Johnson, in response, admitted that serving on the Marshall Court was no "bed of roses" and took up Jefferson's cause after some further prompting. The best he could do, though, was to write separately in dissent or concurrence with some frequency.[35]

Johnson shared Jefferson's resentment over Marshall's influence and wrote negatively about his brethren:

> While I was on our state bench, I was accustomed to delivering seriatim opinions in our appellate court and was not a little surprised to find our chief justice in the Supreme Court delivering all the opinions in cases in which he sat, even in some instances when contrary to his own judgment and vote. But I remonstrated in vain; the answer was he is willing to take the trouble and it is a mark of respect to him. I soon, however, found out the real cause. Cushing was incompetent. Chase could not be got to think or write – Patterson was a slow man and willingly declined the trouble, and the other two judges you know are commonly estimated as one judge.[36]

Brockholst Livingston

Born November 25, 1757, in New York, New York; died March 18, 1823; associate justice, 1807–1823. Brockholst Livingston dropped his first name, Henry, to avoid confusion with two cousins of the same name. He was a veteran of the American Revolution and a Princeton classmate of James Madison. He wrote an epic poem about democracy, which he published using the pseudonym "Aquiline Nimble-Chops." As a result of his Revolutionary War service, his sister called him "the Colonel."

Brockholst Livingston was short-tempered, taking to the fields of honor with some frequency. In 1798, he killed a man in a duel at "Hobuck in New Jersey." When Livingston traveled to Spain in 1779 as an aide to his brother-in-law, John Jay, whom he detested, a relative asked his sister to: "Tell Harry to beware of engaging in a quarrel with the Dons in Spain. This dueling is a very foolish way of putting oneself out of the world."[37]

Livingston did not bring his penchant for brawling to his service in the judiciary. In fact, he was not exactly a major presence on the Supreme Court. Instead, it was said that he "maintained a tomblike silence throughout his seventeen years in Washington."[38]

John McLean
Born March 11, 1785, in Morris County, New Jersey; died April 4, 1861; associate justice, 1830–1861. The politically ambitious McLean won a seat as a "War Hawk" to the U.S. House of Representatives at the age of 27. He served on the Ohio Supreme Court until President James Monroe made him commissioner of the General Land Office. After ascending to the Supreme Court bench, McLean entertained presidential ambitions and courted virtually every political party that came along during his long tenure on the Court. For these electoral ambitions, he was known as the "Politician on the Supreme Court."

Justice John McLean's presidential ambitions knew no bounds. He was appointed Postmaster General under President James Monroe and remained in the post during the administration of President John Quincy Adams. McLean saw an opportunity to switch sides by supporting the candidacy of Andrew Jackson. Adams was outraged. He wrote, "McLean plays his game with so much cunning and duplicity that I can fix upon no positive act that would justify the removal of him." He added that McLean's "words are smoother than butter, but war is in his heart."[39]

John Quincy Adams said of McLean that he "thinks of nothing but the Presidency by day and dreams of nothing else by night."[40]

McLean hoped that he would follow Jackson to the presidency but was only rewarded in the Jackson presidency with the making of the Postmaster General position he held into a Cabinet office.[41] That was apparently insufficient to satisfy McLean, who later pursued his presidential ambitions by throwing in with the anti-Jackson Democrats. In later years, he pursued the Anti-Masons, Whigs, Free Soilers, the Constitutional Union, and even the Republicans, who accorded him 12 votes on the first ballot of their 1860 convention.[42]

McLean was an outspoken opponent of slavery and dissented notably in *Dred Scott v. Sandford*. His dissent, however, may have brought about the decision that now lives in infamy. Justice Samuel Nelson was writing an opinion for the Court in that case that avoided the constitutional issue on procedural grounds. McLean's planned dissent, along with that of Justice Benjamin Robbins Curtis, prompted Chief Justice Taney to write a broader decision that struck down the Missouri Compromise as unconstitutional and contributed to greater tensions between North and South.[43]

Age was unkind to the 76-year-old McLean. Justice Archibald Campbell wrote, "Judge McLean became wholly incapable of business at that term (December 1859) though he attended court with resolute will to the last. He was unable to defend any conclusions...."[44]

Alfred Moore

Born May 21, 1755, in New Hanover County, North Carolina; died October 15, 1810; associate justice, 1799–1804. Moore was a leader in North Carolina's ratification of the Constitution. He served his state as a state senator, attorney general, and a judge on its highest court. Moore was known for his biting wit and his logical mind. He left the Court due to ill health and became a founding father of the University of North Carolina.

Justice Alfred Moore holds the distinction of being the most diminutive justice. He was "only four-and-a-half feet tall and weighed between eighty and ninety pounds."[45] It was said that he was so slight that people often took him for a child. One of his acquaintances described him as having a head too large for his body "after the manner of dwarfs."[46]

As a Southerner, Moore was assigned the extensive and exhausting Southern circuit to ride as a judge. Transportation was always problematic. As a result, Moore was late when the Supreme Court heard the seminal case of *Marbury v. Madison*.[47] All but one witness had already testified in the case, which involved the Court's original jurisdiction. For that reason, Moore did not participate in the most momentous case in the Court's history.[48]

In his four-year tenure on the Court, Moore wrote a single, short opinion. According to Judge Frank Easterbrook, who has written a survey of insignificant justices, Moore "showed every promise of setting a standard of passive irrelevance for centuries to come; only his resignation prevented him from fulfilling his pledge."[49]

Joseph Story
Born September 18, 1779, in Marblehead, Massachusetts; died September 10, 1845; associate justice, 1811–1845. Story was briefly a member of the U.S. House of Representatives but found practicing law a far more congenial endeavor. While on the bench, he also served as a member of the Harvard law faculty and wrote an influential commentary on the Constitution. Despite his subsequent reputation as a great jurist, Story was President James Madison's fourth attempt to find a confirmable and willing successor to Justice William Cushing. Story was called "the poet of Marblehead" for his literary aspirations.

Joseph Story felt enormous parental pressure to succeed. He reported that his mother had told him as a young man: "Now Joe, I've sat up and tended you many a night when you were a child, and don't you dare not be a great man."[50]

Story was recognized as a legal talent even before he was 30 years old. When he was formally admitted to Supreme Court practice, he wrote that he had gone to "the wilderness of Washington," and he found "[t]he scene of my greatest amusement, as well as instruction, is the Supreme Court." He spent several hours a day at the Court "and generally, when disengaged, dine and sup with the judges." Three years later, he joined the Court.[51]

Ethical standards were considerably different in Story's day. For example, during his service on the Supreme Court, Story also served as president of one bank and vice-president of another.[52] He also regularly advised Daniel Webster about congressional policy proposals and advised John Quincy Adams on both domestic and foreign policy.

Story even drafted national bankruptcy legislation while he was sitting on the Court that was twice unsuccessfully introduced in Congress.[53]

Story had an encyclopedic knowledge of the law. Not long after he joined the Court, Chief Justice John Marshall assigned him *United States v. Crosby*,[54] a case that dealt with conflict of laws. Marshall explained he assigned the case to Story because "[B]rother Story, here ... can give us the cases from the Twelve Tables down to the latest reports."[55]

The election of President Andrew Jackson alarmed Story. He wrote: "The reign of 'King Mob' seemed triumphant." Jackson returned the favor by describing Story as "the most dangerous man in America."[56]

Story was a lover of anecdotes and believed that everyone should laugh an hour each day. He found comfort in composing verse, even while sitting through a trying presentation by a lawyer. He once wrote a short poem he entitled "Lines Written on Hearing an Argument in Court":

> How sad to find our time consumed by speech,
> Feeble in logic, feebler still in reach.
> Yet urged in words of high and bold pretense,
> As if the sound made up the lack of sense.[57]

Story had "an unquenchable capacity for talking." His recreation was described as "talking, not walking." Story's verbosity likely led to tensions in the court conferences that required Marshall's diplomatic skills to resolve.[58]

Story wrote his autobiography for his son, apparently concerned about what Thomas Jefferson would say about him after his death. He wrote, "You are too young to know the real facts: and when I am dead, you may feel an interest not to have your father's character sullied by the pen of Mr. Jefferson."[59]

During much of the 1842 term, Taney was ill. As senior associate justice, Story presided in his stead. During the same time period, a political issue arose concerning whether John Tyler had become President upon the death of William Henry Harrison or whether he was just Acting President. Story compared his situation to that of Tyler.

Story said: "Was Tyler President or Acting President at the demise of Gen. Harrison? A nice question, gentlemen, and hard to solve. The question was debated in cabinet meeting, and on Mr. [Daniel] Webster's opinion, Tyler was addressed as President. On one occasion, when Chief Justice Taney was ill, I took his place as Chief Justice and was thus addressed. At first, I felt nervous, but soon becoming used to it, found it, like public money to new members of Congress, 'not bad to take.' And this was probably the feeling with Mr. Tyler."[60]

Smith Thompson
Born January 17, 1768, in Amenia, New York; died December 19, 1843; associate justice, 1823–1843. Thompson served as an Antifederalist delegate to New York's convention that, despite his efforts, ratified the U.S. Constitution. He was a former chief justice of New York's Supreme Court and secretary of the navy when President James Monroe placed him on the U.S. Supreme Court.

Thompson was incredibly ambitious and certain that those ambitions would be realized. He hesitated at the offer of an appointment to the U.S. Supreme Court, hoping that he might instead start a stampede in his own favor for the presidency. He lied to President Monroe in initially rejecting the offer by claiming to be in poor health. When it became clear that Thompson would not be President, he accepted Monroe's offer.

Even after he ascended the bench, he kept his presidential ambitions alive. He considered but rejected an offer to be appointed mayor of New York City, while a Supreme Court justice. While on the bench, though, he ran unsuccessfully for governor of New York.[61]

Thompson sat as the circuit judge and heard the initial appeal of the criminal charges in the famous *Amistad* case. The *Amistad* was a Spanish slave ship that, in 1839, was transporting captured Africans from Africa to Cuba. The Africans took over the ship and killed some of the crew. The ship ended up off the coast of the northern United States. It was a major case at the time that involved slavery as well as U.S. relations with Spain. The story became a major movie in 1997 in which Justice Harry Blackmun had a cameo role as Justice Joseph Story, with a total of three lines from the Court's opinion.[62]

Thompson ruled that the capture and transport of the Africans violated treaties against the international slave trade and that the captives could not be tried on criminal charges because the murders of the crew and piracy that they were charged with did not occur in U.S. waters. Additionally, as free men, the Africans were entitled to take whatever measures were necessary to secure their freedom. Thompson further held that the Africans be returned to their homelands at government expense.[63]

President Van Buren ordered the case be taken to the Supreme Court,[64] where former president John Quincy Adams argued the defendants' cause. The Supreme Court affirmed most of Thompson's decision, though reversed the order of repatriation, insisting instead that they be freed.

Thomas Todd

Born January 23, 1765, in King and Queen County, Virginia; died February 7, 1826; associate justice, 1807–1826. Todd is mostly remembered for his highly readable handwriting as a clerk at virtually every level of Kentucky government, where his records made historical work easier to research. He was chief judge of Kentucky before being placed on the U.S. Supreme Court.

Thomas Todd spent remarkably little time at the Court during his tenure as a justice. He explained his absence from the Court's 1808 Term in a letter to his son Charles:

> I set out last winter for the Federal City, but owing to the extreme high freshlets, which had removed every bridge between

Levington & Chillicothe & almost every bridge & causeway between the latter place and Wheeling. I went no farther than to Chillicothe. Your Mama's ill health when I left her had also considerable influence to induce me to return.[65]

A long tradition honors a late justice with the publication of a eulogy in the official reports of the Court. Todd, who is not remembered with distinction for his service on the Court, has such a eulogy, but oddly it was delivered by an anonymous "judicial friend" and did not appear until fourteen years after his demise. This oddity caused one legal scholar to wonder: "Did no one notice his absence?"[66]

It is entirely possible that no one noticed. During his years of service, Todd missed the Court's 1808, 1819, and 1825 Terms, as well as considerable portions of the 1809, 1813, and 1815 Terms.[67] His absences caused Judge Frank Easterbrook to designate Todd as the Supreme Court's most insignificant justice.[68]

Robert Trimble
Born November 17, 1776, in Berkeley County, Virginia; died August 25, 1828; associate justice, 1826–1828. Trimble, a former chief justice of the Kentucky Court of Appeals, holds the distinction of being the first federal judge to be elevated to the Supreme Court.

Appointment to the Supreme Court has long seemed to have had a fountain-of-youth effect on the person named. Even justices who are senior in years seem to be rejuvenated and serve for many years, sometimes into their nineties. Trimble, however, proved an exception to this rule. He was appointed at the age of 50 and was described as "robust and strong" at the time of his appointment. He died 27 months later of a "malignant bilious fever."[69]

Bushrod Washington
Born June 5, 1762, in Mount Holly, Virginia; died November 26, 1829; associate justice, 1798–1829. A Revolutionary War veteran and a delegate to the Virginia

convention that ratified the U.S. Constitution, Bushrod Washington was a nephew of George Washington and inherited his uncle's estate, Mount Vernon. Though historians dispute the description, Senator Albert J. Beveridge described the justice as the "slow-thinking Bushrod Washington" in his magisterial multi-volume biography of Chief Justice John Marshall.

Washington Irving reported that once Bushrod Washington and his close friend, John Marshall, were on their way to visit Mount Vernon, attended by a black servant who had charge of a large portmanteau containing their clothes. As they passed through a wood near Mount Vernon, they stopped to make a hasty toilet, being covered with dust. They undressed while the servant opened the portmanteau. Out flew cakes of soap and fancy articles of all kinds but no clothes. By mistake, the man had changed portmanteaus with a Scottish peddler at their last resting place. Gen. Washington happened to be near and, attracted by the noise, came up and was so overcome by their strange plight and the servant's dismay that he is said to have actually rolled on the grass with laughter.[70]

Another version of the story was conveyed by Senator Albert Beveridge, the biographer of Marshall. Bushrod and Marshall used the same pair of saddlebags to pack their clothing. Arriving at Mt. Vernon in drenching rain, they unlocked the saddlebags to discover a bottle of whiskey. Each claimed the whiskey belonged to the other. They then found tobacco, cornbread, and a wagoner's worn clothing. Somehow, at a tavern along the way, their saddlebag was exchanged with the driver's. George Washington found their misfortune hilarious.[71]

George Washington died in 1799. In his life estate, Washington left Mt. Vernon to his wife, Martha, and a remainder to Bushrod. That led to problems in the Washington family. For example, George's brother, Lawrence, cared for Mt. Vernon during the Revolutionary War and expected to inherit the property. Perhaps Martha sought to remedy family tensions by willing all her personal property that included the furnishings and supplies at Mt. Vernon to others, even though Bushrod had managed Martha's legal affairs after she was widowed.

When Bushrod attended Martha's funeral, Lawrence and Eleanor Lewis (Lawrence was George Washington's nephew, and Eleanor was Martha's granddaughter) were so upset that the estate did not pass to their family, they did not invite Bushrod to stay for refreshments.

Although Bushrod inherited the house and 4,000 acres, he had no furniture, no farm implements, and no supplies. He had to go into debt to manage the plantation which turned out to be a very unprofitable enterprise for him.[72]

3

The Taney Era

The Taney Court earned history's opprobrium for its decision in *Dred Scott v. Sandford*,[1] which denied that African Americans could ever be U.S. citizens, declared the Missouri Compromise unconstitutional, and likely precipitated the Civil War.

While that decision overwhelms whatever the Court accomplished, the justices otherwise took a pragmatic approach to the law. Near total turnover in personnel moved the Court beyond the nationalistic preoccupation that characterized the Marshall era to a more cooperative approach between the federal and state governments. Even so, tensions plagued the Court. Justice Joseph Story, who had served on a largely harmonious Marshall Court with fewer justices, noted the contrast:

> You may ask how the Judges got along together? We made very slow progress, and did less in the same time than I ever knew. The addition to our numbers [from 7 to 9] has most sensibly affected our facility as well as the rapidity of doing business. 'Many men of many minds' require a great deal of discussion to compel them to come to definite results; and we found ourselves often involved in long and very tedious debates. I verily believe, if there were twelve judges, we should do no business at all, or

at least very little. So far as my personal comfort and personal intercourse were concerned, everything went well.[2]

Roger Taney, Chief Justice (1836–1864)

Associate Justices:
Phillip P. Barbour (1836–1841)
John A. Campbell (1853–1861)
John Catron (1837–1865)
Benjamin Curtis (1851–1857)
Peter Daniel (1842–1860)
Robert Grier (1846–1870)
John McKinley (1838–1852)
Samuel Nelson (1845–1872)
James Wayne (1835–1867)
Levi Woodbury (1845–1851)

The Chief Justice

Roger Brooke Taney
Born March 17, 1777, in Calvert County, Maryland; died December 12, 1864; chief justice, 1836–1854. Taney served President Andrew Jackson as Attorney General and then moved over to Treasury as a recess appointment to help Jackson drain federal funds from the Second Bank of the United States. The unpopular action resulted in Senate rejection of Taney's formal nomination for Treasury Secretary and, subsequently, as an associate justice of the U.S. Supreme Court. Still, he was later confirmed as chief justice. Although he carved out a meticulous jurisprudence that enabled him to be ranked by historians among the greatest to serve on the Court, his tenure is overshadowed and most remembered for his opinion in Dred Scott v. Sandford, *which marked the demise of his influence on the Court and stands as one of the worst errors in the Court's history, famously termed a "self-inflicted wound." Early in his political career Taney led a dissenting Federalist Party faction known as the*

"Coodies" that supported the Madison Administration during the War of 1812. For his role in this faction, Taney was called "King Coody."

Roger B. Taney had a legendary fondness for cigars, which he spelled as "segars." The association between the chief justice and his smokes was so well known that he once signed a promissory note, sending his son-in-law to the bank to retrieve some funds. Taney's signature, however, was unreadable. Taney reassured his son-in-law, though, that the bank would recognize the validity of the note because it was imbued with the unavoidable odor of Taney's cigars.[3]

Taney was no Nostradamus. Although the *Dred Scott* decision proved disastrous for the Court and the country, Taney resisted critics of his decision. He wrote former President Franklin Pierce that he had "an abiding confidence that this act of judicial life will stand the test of time and the sober judgment of the country."[4]

Taney suffered from poor eyesight his entire life. He would walk down the street and ignore acquaintances because he had never gotten a good enough look at them. His vision was so bad that he wrote, "I sometimes pass my own children in the street without knowing them until they speak to me."[5]

For his decision in the *Dred Scott* case, for his views on the national bank, and for a suspicion that he was sympathetic to the Confederates, Republicans hated the Jackson-loyalist Taney. Radical Republican Senator Ben Wade of Ohio claimed that for years he prayed that Taney would live until a Republican president could replace him. That eventuality, however, was long in coming, and Wade feared that he had prayed too hard. Taney lived to be 87 and was chief justice for 28 years.[6]

When Taney died, Senator Charles Sumner said, "the name of Taney is to be hooted down the page of history. Judgment is beginning now and an emancipated country will fasten upon him the stigma of which he deserves."[7] Another critic said Taney "was, next to Pontius Pilate, perhaps the worst that ever occupied the seat of judgment."[8] Taney did earn history's opprobrium, although some historians had regarded him as a very good chief justice if the *Dred Scott* decision was put aside.[9] Still, Taney was honored with a statue in the U.S. Capitol Building. In 2020, however, the U.S. House of Representatives voted to remove the Taney statue from that august placement because he was a defender of slavery, substituting in its place another native of Maryland, Justice Thurgood Marshall, the first African American to serve on the Supreme Court.[10]

The Associate Justices

Philip P. Barbour

Born May 25, 1783, in Orange County, Virginia; died February 25, 1841; associate justice, 1836–1841. Barbour, whose brother served as a U.S. senator, was Speaker of the House of Representatives and closely aligned with President Andrew Jackson's policies. He was first appointed to the federal trial bench in Eastern Virginia. When he was nominated to the Supreme Court, a Richmond newspaper called Barbour "the pride of the Democracy of Virginia."

Justice Philip Barbour was a devoted Jacksonian who was promoted by Southern interests for the 1832 vice presidency. Barbour was also the poster boy for those who thought Andrew Jackson so irresponsible that he would appoint justices to the Supreme Court solely on the basis of their opposition to Chief Justice John Marshall's decisions. In fact, John Quincy Adams opined that he feared "some shallow-pated wild-cat like Philip P. Barbour, fit for nothing but to tear down the Union to rags and tatters, would be appointed" to succeed the venerated Marshall.[11]

John A. Campbell

Born June 24, 1811, in Washington, Georgia; died March 12, 1889; associate justice, 1853–1861. A prodigy, Campbell attended the University of Georgia when he was eleven and graduated in three years at the top of his class.

He was admitted to the Georgia bar by special act of the legislature at the tender age of 18. His advocacy before the Supreme Court was so acclaimed that, after President Millard Fillmore sent three nominations to the Senate in vain and was succeeded by Franklin Pierce, the Supreme Court itself unanimously suggested that Campbell, then 41, be nominated. He resigned his seat out of loyalty to his home state and was made the Confederacy's assistant secretary of war. After the war, he argued cases before the Supreme Court once again.

In 1877, there was an effort to persuade President Rutherford Hayes to put John A. Campbell back on the Supreme Court, from which he had resigned to become assistant secretary of war in the Confederacy. Campbell, however, was 66 years old, and Justice Samuel Miller made it clear that he thought Campbell was too old. He told the Attorney-General, "... if an old man was appointed, we should have within five years a majority of old imbeciles on the bench."[12]

When the then-ancient Campbell argued his last case before the Court he once served on, he was described by a Washington reporter:

> He is a very old man. His form is thin and bent, his skin is in the parchment state, and his hair is as white as the driven snow; but a great mind looks out through his keen eye and a great soul controls his fragile body. He is a lawyer to the core – in some respects one of the wisest, broadest, deepest, and most learned in the United States. He has neither the presence, voice, nor tongue of the orator, but when he speaks in his thin, measured tones, never wasting a word, the Supreme Court of the United States listens as it listens to almost no other man.[13]

John Catron

Born January 7, 1786, in Pennsylvania; died May 30, 1865; associate justice, 1837–1865. Catron, who served under General Andrew Jackson during the War of 1812, was a justice and later chief justice of Tennessee's Court of Errors and Appeals. After his court was abolished, Catron directed Martin Van Buren's

1836 presidential campaign in the state. Before he left office, Jackson rewarded his old military buddy with a seat on the Supreme Court, though he was confirmed after Van Buren became president.

Apparently not the prize student in deportment, John Catron described his education as little more than having been "flogged through the common schools in Western Virginia and Kentucky."[14]

Before joining the Supreme Court, Catron had served on the Tennessee Supreme Court for twelve years. With considerable humor, he wrote his friend, James K. Polk, about the first time he rode circuit in Kentucky. Catron wrote that he "Met with a cool reception, under a belief ... that [I] wanted legal skill—wanted lawyership in Kentucky! Where the most important causes are heard and decided without reference to a single book, and knowledge where the law is to be found."[15]

Matilda Catron, John's wife, seems to have had a major role in his appointment to the Supreme Court. She read in the paper that there was a vacancy on the Supreme Court and, the next morning, arranged for a carriage to take the couple to Washington. Her goal was to meet with President Jackson, a friend of Catron with whom he had served in the Battle of New Orleans during the War of 1812, and ask him to appoint John to the Court. Upon arriving at the White House, she forced her way past the usher to find Jackson in his gown and slippers. Jackson was having breakfast and smoking when she asked that John be appointed. Jackson's response was, "By the eternal, he shall have it."[16]

Benjamin Robbins Curtis
Born November 4, 1809, in Watertown, Massachusetts; died September 15, 1874; associate justice, 1851–1857. Curtis, a former student of Justice Joseph Story at Harvard, was promoted for a seat on the Supreme Court by Daniel Webster. He resigned from the Court after his dissent in the Dred Scott case strained his relations with other justices. Curtis nonetheless argued numerous cases before the Court subsequent to his resignation and served importantly as

a counsel for President Andrew Johnson during the impeachment trial in the Senate. As a circuit court judge, he upheld the constitutionality of the Fugitive Slave Act, even though he hated the law. For this decision, the Northern press christened him "the slave-catcher judge."

Justice Benjamin Robbins Curtis may have had a hidden financial reason for resigning from the Court. In 1854, he wrote that the justices' salaries "... are so poor that not one judge on the bench can live on what the government pays him." After he resigned, Curtis wrote Millard Fillmore that he had done so due to an inadequate salary. Within a week after his resignation, he received seven retainers in important cases, and in his post-court years, his legal fees amounted to $650,000.[17]

After Curtis resigned from the Court on September 1, 1857, he practiced law for the next 17 years, during which he argued 54 cases before the Supreme Court and many more before other federal and state courts. He was also highly sought for providing advisory opinions and arbitrating disputes. Curtis was regarded as an exceptional advocate, most famously as one of the lawyers for President Andrew Johnson in his impeachment trial. Curtis made the opening argument where he spoke for five hours over two days. President Johnson was so grateful for Curtis's representation that he offered to make him Attorney General.[18]

Peter V. Daniel
Born April 24, 1784, in Stafford County, Virginia; died May 31, 1860; associate justice, 1841–1860. A protege of Edmund Randolph, whose daughter he married, Daniel benefited his entire career from well-placed political connections. He was a long-serving lieutenant governor of Virginia. On the Supreme Court, he was out of step with most of the justices, often finding himself alone in dissent. Historian Don Fehrenbacher dubbed Daniel a "brooding proslavery fanatic."

With the advent of abolitionism, Justice Peter V. Daniel became passionate about the Southern cause. By 1851, he was even blaming bad weather on the North. When it was cold, he said, "Ah! That vile north. It infects and spoils even the very atmosphere we breathe." When oranges were sent to him from the South, Daniel wondered aloud, "When the North...would ever produce anything like these oranges! or indeed anything else that is good and decent."[19] Daniel's hostility reached the point that he became deeply offended that respectful funeral rights were given to anti-slavery advocate and former President John Quincy Adams.[20] Daniel refused to even acknowledge the retirement of anti-slavery Justice Benjamin Robbins Curtis. He associated with the Democrats on the Court and seemed to have nothing to do with the others. He noted with pleasure that he and Justice James Wayne were invited to a dinner at which no Whigs were present.[21]

On another occasion, he was introduced to the highly celebrated Supreme Court advocate Daniel Webster. Daniel said afterward, "My hand was actually contaminated by contact with his."[22] He referred to Webster as a "most depraved and immoral creature."[23]

His enmity carried over to Washington, DC itself, which he called a place of "profligacy, roguery, and humbug."[24]

Though disagreeable on many things, Daniel shared the revulsion of his brethren for circuit-riding. He wrote:

> The discomfort of being about in immediate contact with all sorts of people, some of the most vulgar and filthy in the world, women more disgusting if possible by their want of cleanliness than the men; with squalling children and being required to use in common, two tin basins encrusted with filth, and one long towel for the whole male establishment, is a misery beyond which my imagination can scarcely picture any earthly evil. My washing therefore was limited to wiping my eyes and mouth with my linen handkerchief, but I neither took off my clothes nor slept during this purgatory.[25]

The death of Daniel's first wife profoundly depressed him, but in 1853, when Daniel was 67, he married Elizabeth Harris who was 31. Elizabeth gave birth to two more children—Daniel had three children with his first wife who were as old as Elizabeth. Unfortunately, on the evening of January 3, 1857, the Daniels had returned home from a dinner. Daniel went to his library and Elizabeth went to her room. Somehow the flame from a candle touched her robe which caught fire. Screaming, she ran into the hallway where a burst of air caused the robe to become engulfed in flames. Daniel tried to rescue Elizabeth, but hours later Elizabeth died from her burns. Daniel and Elizabeth had been married a little more than three years. John Frank, Peter Daniel's biographer, wrote, "Daniel never had any real happiness again."[26]

Robert Cooper Grier

Born March 5, 1794, in Cumberland County, Pennsylvania; died September 25, 1870; associate justice, 1846–1870. Grier was virtually unknown when nominated to the Court, making his confirmation utterly uncontroversial. He tipped off President James Buchanan as to the result in the Dred Scott case, leading Buchanan to make mention of it in his inaugural address – two days before the decision was announced. Grier was known as a "doughface," a Northerner with Southern sympathies.

Once, Justice Robert Cooper Grier commended an advocate, Philip Phillips, on the skill he demonstrated in his oral argument.

Phillips was surprised by the compliment: "I thought you were asleep, Judge."

"Oh," Grier replied, unwilling to be the loser in what was now a battle of wit, "you see, Phillips, when I have seen where you go in, I know where you are coming out; but with some of these fellows I have to keep awake and watch them all the time."[27]

In 1867, Miller wrote that Grier was "getting a little Muddy," and by 1869, he was sleeping on the bench. In spite of Grier's physical and mental decline, his daughters wanted Grier to stay on the Court to maintain their social status.[28]

John McKinley

Born May 1, 1780, in Culpepper County, Virginia; died July 19, 1852; associate justice, 1837–1852. McKinley served one term in the U.S. Senate, representing Kentucky, but did not win reelection. He later made a comeback, winning election once again to the Senate, but had to decline the seat to take another… on the Supreme Court.

Justice John McKinley is perhaps best remembered for his frequent absences from his judicial duties. Illness was responsible for his failure to participate during the 1840, 1843, and 1848 Terms. He also, remarkably, missed numerous arguments even when he was in Washington. By the January 1850 term, the reporter of decisions felt compelled to record McKinley's absence for reasons of illness in the report of the Court's decisions.

Duly chastised for doing so, the reporter declared in the next year's volume: "ERRATUM. The note in the eighth volume, stating that 'Mr. Justice McKinley was prevented, by indisposition, from attending the Court during the January term, 1850,' is incorrect; as Mr. McKinley was engaged during that period in holding an important session of the U.S. Circuit Court at New Orleans."[29]

When McKinley was riding circuit, he was involved in an embarrassing incident in Jackson, Mississippi. In 1839, a fight broke out in the Mississippi capital between the governor and the son-in-law of the recently deceased state treasurer. It spilled over into the courtroom that McKinley was using in the Capitol. Though there are different stories about what happened, one commonly circulated stated that McKinley asked the court crier to get the Marshal and, when the crier failed to get help, McKinley insulted him. That led to the crier grabbing McKinley's nose.

When due to illness McKinley did not return to Mississippi the following year, he was accused of neglecting his circuit duties, and there was an effort to first cut his salary and then to impeach him.[30]

McKinley stayed away from the Court for several years not only because of illness and his travels on circuit, but also because he wanted to keep an eye on his hemp business.[31]

Samuel Nelson
Born November 10, 1792, in Hebron, New York; died December 13, 1873; associate justice, 1845–1872. An associate justice and chief justice of the New York Supreme Court, Nelson won appointment to the U.S. Supreme Court after President John Tyler had failed in several prior attempts to fill the court vacancy.

Justice Samuel Nelson heard an admiralty case in New York while riding circuit where the issue was whether a light had been displayed on the "port" side of the ship. It was evening, and Nelson was seated between two large globe lights. Suddenly, Nelson brought his hand down on the desk so hard that one of the lights shattered.

His clerk exclaimed, "There goes your port light, Judge!" The remark broke up the courtroom. Nelson initially appeared not to be amused, but then he smiled and ordered the port light to be removed. Nelson told the story for years afterward, always laughing heartily when he did.[32]

James M. Wayne
Born 1790, in Savannah, Georgia; died July 7, 1867; associate justice, 1835–1867. Wayne had served as a judge in the Savannah Court of Common Pleas and Superior Court. He then was elected to Congress, where he came to the attention of President Andrew Jackson, who placed him on the Supreme Court.

Even when he commenced his legal practice in Georgia, Justice James M. Wayne was less than diligent about his work. Learning that Wayne had taken to Savannah's society with great relish, Judge Charles Chauncy of New Haven, who had been one of Wayne's teachers, wrote his protégé that one does not become a good lawyer by wasting time at balls and dinners. Wayne later conceded that his teacher was "more than half right."[33]

As a first-term congressman, Wayne successfully called for an investigation into a project designed to make the Savannah River more navigable. The leader of the project, Dr. William C. Daniell, was so incensed by Wayne's implications that he challenged Wayne to a duel. Wayne, who was opposed to dueling, cleverly insisted on his right to choose the weapons. He chose to use broadswords until one of the duelers was disabled, and then he said the fight would resume with rifles. A horrified Daniell called the choices inhuman and refused to proceed with the duel, ending the challenge.[34]

Wayne was not highly regarded when he was appointed to the Supreme Court. The Georgia Messenger reacted to Wayne's appointment by writing, "aye, a seat besides Judge Marshall! Friends, imagine Judge Blackstone on the bench, and a ring-tail monkey grinning at his side."

Chief Justice Roger Taney withheld assignments when he could, having little respect for Wayne's judicial abilities.[35]

Levi Woodbury

Born December 22, 1789, in Francestown, New Hampshire; died September 4, 1851; associate justice, 1845–1851. Woodbury had served as an associate justice of the New Hampshire Superior Court and later as governor. After losing reelection, he was eventually elected to the U.S. Senate. He left the Senate to become, successively, Secretary of the Navy and Secretary of the Treasury, before returning to the Senate. Woodbury succeeded Justice Joseph Story on the Court. For his careful and sound views on all subjects, he was known as "the Rock of New England Democracy."

Many would accuse Levi Woodbury of being a very confused college student who matched irreconcilable subjects as though they were harmonious. After all, it was while attending college that he declared that he would seek a career in the "study of law and politics and politeness."[36]

Woodbury was among the many justices who hated his circuit-riding duties. In a letter to his wife, he complained, "The 'villainous sea-sickness which generally afflicts me in a Stage[coach] has yielded, in some degree, to my suffering from the extreme cold."

He added, "I think I never again, at this season of the year, will attempt this mode of journeying. Beside the evils before mentioned I have been elbowed by old women – jammed by young ones – suffocated by cigar smoke – sickened by the vapours of bitters and whiskey – my head knocked through the carriage top by careless drivers and my toes trodden to a jelly by unheeding passengers."

If absence made the heart grow fonder, that appeared to be the condition favored by his wife. He once returned from such an unpleasant sojourn to discover his wife away on vacation. He dashed off a plaintive message to her: "Why do you talk of regret at my necessary absence on the Circuit to support my family and object to my going to Washington and still so unwilling to stay with me when at home?"[37]

4

The Post-Civil War Court

The Court's decision in the *Dred Scott* case has been called a "self-inflicted wound" and helped precipitate the Civil War. Respect for the Court dropped perilously low after it. When the Court reversed itself during the post-Civil War era in one year's time in the *Legal Tender Cases*, Charles Evans Hughes later wrote it administered a second self-inflicted wound. Nonetheless, the Court's prestige slowly rose again during this period. Salmon Chase, Morrison Waite, and Melville Fuller served as chief justices. The Court also boasted a colorful set of figures, including Joseph Bradley, Stephen J. Field, and John Marshall Harlan.

Of note as well is the fact that most of the justices lived in the same Washington, DC hotel during the term, giving them ample opportunity to dine together. Members of the Supreme Court bar often joined them for these meals, providing further opportunities to supplement their arguments in court, a practice that would raise significant ethical questions today.

Salmon Chase, Chief Justice (1864–1873)
Morrison Waite, Chief Justice (1874–1888)
Melville Fuller, Chief Justice (1888–1910)

Associate Justices:
Samuel Blatchford (1882–1893)
Joseph Bradley (1870–1892)
David Brewer (1890–1910)
Henry Brown (1891–1906)
Nathan Clifford (1858–1881)
David Davis (1862–1877)
Stephen J. Field (1863–1897)
Horace Gray (1882–1902)
John Marshall Harlan (1877–1911)
Ward Hunt (1873–1882)
Howell Jackson (1893–1895)
Lucius Q. C. Lamar (1888–1893)
Stanley Matthews (1881–1889)
Samuel Miller (1862–1890)
Rufus Peckham (1896–1909)
George Shiras (1892–1903)
William Strong (1870–1880)
Noah Swayne (1862–1881)
William Woods (1881–1887)

The Chief Justices

Salmon P. Chase

Born January 13, 1808, in Cornish, New Hampshire; died May 7, 1873; chief justice, 1864–1873. Chase long entertained presidential ambitions that were never realized. Before sitting on the Supreme Court, Chase served as governor of Ohio, a U.S. Senator, and Secretary of the Treasury. He also unsuccessfully advocated a view of the Thirteenth Amendment, which abolished slavery, that he said made both the Declaration of Independence and Bill of Rights applicable against all violations, federal, state, or private. As a young lawyer, for his legal representation of abolitionists and fugitive slaves, he was called "Attorney General for Runaway Negroes." He earned a less well-intentioned nickname when, as Treasury Secretary, after he ordered his image placed on one-dollar bills: "Old Mr. Greenbacks."

Growing up in New Hampshire, Salmon Chase continued his education at the most natural place in the world, Dartmouth College. He found the oral examination for admission a cinch and had prepared so well that he was accepted into the third-year class.

He later said: "One of the questions by the learned professor of mathematics amused me. He undertook to fathom my geographical attainments and asked, 'Where do the Hottentots live?' I was tempted to answer in 'Hanover,' but prudence restrained me."[1]

In 1829, Chase submitted to the oral exam for admission to the bar before Judge William Cranch of the District of Columbia Court. Although most of Chase's answers were correct, Chase did not have the requisite three years of legal training. Cranch, after consulting other bar examiners, said, "We think, Mr. Chase, that you must study another year and present yourself again for the examination."

Chase pleaded, "Please, your honors, I have made arrangements to go to the Western country and practice law."

Cranch again consulted with the others and then shouted to the court's clerk, "Swear in Mr. Chase." Chase was sufficiently prepared to practice in Ohio.[2]

With an opportunity to appoint a chief justice, Lincoln said that he wanted someone who would "sustain what has been done in regard to emancipation and the legal tenders."[3] Legal tenders referred to the adoption of greenbacks in place of silver or gold coins as currency, which, as treasury secretary, Chase had proposed and won the necessary congressional approval as an emergency war measure. Knowing that the Legal Tender Act's constitutionality was going to the Supreme Court, Lincoln perhaps felt Chase was a sure vote to preserve what was the Treasury Secretary's own handiwork. The calculation proved wrong. Chase led a slim and questionable majority in declaring the Act unconstitutional.[4]

As a member of the Cabinet, Chase had felt that he had the obligation to do his best in securing financing for the war. As a member of the Court, he apparently determined his best was not good enough.

When Chase's daughter, Kate, gave birth to a son, she proposed to name him Salmon Portland in honor of her chief justice father. Chase would have none of it. One "Salmon" was plenty. To inflict such a name on anyone, let alone an innocent child, was too much, he mused.[5]

As chief justice, Chase was not above chauvinist tendencies. Once he was introduced to a beautiful Southern belle. She told him, "I must warn you that I am a rebel who has not been reconstructed."

He reputedly replied, "Madam, reconstruction in your case – even in the slightest degree – would be nothing short of sacrilege."[6]

Chase was not fully dedicated to being chief justice or seeking the presidency. In 1866, he sought the presidency of the Union Pacific Railroad. He wrote that business was preferable to the "monotonous labors and dull dignity of my judicial position." In 1869, he turned to his friend, wealthy businessman and banker Jay Cooke, and asked that Cooke make him president of Northern Pacific Railroad. Cooke did not give Chase the job, but he did loan Chase $22,000 and thereafter provided for Chase's financial needs.[7]

Shortly before his death, Chase took communion at the Metropolitan Church in Washington, DC. He was a church board member and faithfully attended services, but he had explained that he felt unworthy to take communion. Taking communion had a powerful effect upon Chase, and when in the Court's robing room, he told Justice Miller, "Oh, I want to tell you to-day [sic] what the Lord has done for my soul! He came very near me yesterday."

Miller did not seem impressed and responded, "Well, we will talk of that some other time, now we have the wages of sin and not righteousness before us."[8]

Morrison R. Waite

Born November 29, 1816, in Lyme, Connecticut; died March 23, 1888; chief justice, 1874–1888. Waite was one of the founders of the Republican Party in Ohio. A successful lawyer, he was summoned to Washington to serve as one of three lawyers for the U.S. at the Geneva Arbitration Tribunal, which resolved claims against Great Britain for damages inflicted on Northern shipping by the Confederate raider "Alabama" during the Civil War. After winning $15 million in damages, the three lawyers returned to the U.S. as heroes. When Chief Justice Salmon Chase died in 1873, President Ulysses S. Grant's scandal-plagued administration eventually turned to one of the heroes of Geneva, Waite, for the job. Waite believed his appointment so unlikely that he first assumed it to be a practical joke. As Grant's seventh choice for the position, Waite was called "His Accidency."

Before Chief Justice Morrison R. Waite's appointment and confirmation, Justice Nathan Clifford performed the tasks of the chief justice. Upon Waite's arrival, Clifford patronizingly advised him to take a back seat, observe, and learn. Waite felt like an intruder in a private club. His friend, Benjamin Cowan, advised otherwise: "Gather up the reins and drive."

The next day, Waite returned to visit Cowan, very pleased with himself. He reported, "I got on the box as soon as I arrived there this morning, gathered up the lines and drove, and I am going to drive and these gentlemen know it."[9]

As a member of the Court, Waite was something of a plodder. The brilliant Justice Samuel Miller, who believed he should have been named chief justice, wrote of Waite: "I can't make a great chief justice out of a small man."[10]

Melville W. Fuller

Born February 11, 1833, in Augusta, Maine; died July 4, 1910; chief justice, 1888–1910. Fuller served at the Illinois Constitutional Convention in 1861, in the state House of Representatives, and was a successful Chicago lawyer. He argued frequently before the U.S. Supreme Court before being tapped for the chief justice slot. While on the Court, Fuller also served on the Venezuelan Boundary Commission and on the Permanent Court of Arbitration at The Hague. While a member of the Illinois legislature, colleagues considered him such a solemn presence that he acquired the nickname "Judge," though none of those who served with him foresaw it as prophesy.

At the age of 23, Melville Fuller left his home state of Maine to seek his fortune in Chicago, going to work for the law firm of Pearson and Dow. Within a year, Fuller became Dow's partner by successfully suing Pearson on behalf of a boardinghouse operator for back rent. Pearson left town, giving the youthful Fuller an early promotion.[11]

Fuller was not enamored of Chicago's food. He wrote: "The soup was like the refuse from a tanyard; the roast beef was like a side of sole leather; the potatoes, like a dozen boiled cobblestones; and the mince pie, like steeped tea leaves between two sheets of blotting paper."[12]

In a case in Superior Court, Fuller had the misfortune of representing a man whose only defense was ignorance of the law. When this plea was met with the response that everyone is presumed to know the law, the witty Fuller, knowing that he had nothing to lose at this point and that his salvation lay in an appeal, responded: "I am aware of that, Your Honor. Every shoemaker, tailor, mechanic, and illiterate laborer is presumed to know the law. Every man is presumed to know it, except judges of the Superior Court, and we have a Court of Appeals to correct their mistakes."[13]

During the time he was in Maine, Fuller once discovered hams missing from his smokehouse. Since it was but a petty theft, he elected not to report the crime. Some days afterward, a neighbor visited and said, "I heard yew had some hams stole t'other night?"

Realizing his thief had identified himself, Fuller replied, "Yes, but don't tell anyone. You and I are the only ones who know it."[14]

As Justice David Brewer described it when the justices sat at conference to discuss the cases, "The tug of war commences. They are all strong men and do not waste a word. They lock horns and the fight is stubborn; arguments are hurled against each other, the discussion grows animated and continues so for hours." Another witness to the aftermath of the events described the exodus from the conference as a "worn and fatigued" group, "as if they had been on rides on bicycles or had just returned from participating in a game of football in the most approved modern style."[15]

To overcome the hard feelings that were sometimes evident, Fuller instituted the practice of having the justices greet and shake hands with every other justice, a tradition that continues to this day.[16] Still, knowing the justices' propensity to take issue with one another at that time, it might have been described as: "Shake hands and come out fighting."

Fuller was a modest man of great charm. When he came onto the Court, he knew there were several members who felt that they rather than he should have received the appointment as chief justice. Fuller deflated the situation when he told his colleagues that after his appointment, he went to his childhood hometown of Augusta, Maine and rode the bus from the train depot to the Augusta House. He knew the bus driver from his childhood and engaged him in conversation:

Fuller: "Have the boys heard that I have been appointed chief justice?"
Bus Driver: "Oh, yes."
Fuller: "What did they say?"
Bus Driver: "Oh – they laughed."[17]

Once, while presiding at a church-sponsored conference, Fuller was surprised when a speaker lambasted higher education and went on to thank God that he had not been subjected to university training. Fuller asked the man, "Are we to understand that the speaker is thanking God for ignorance?"

"Well, yes," came the reply. "I suppose you could put it like that."

"In that case," advised Fuller, "the speaker has a very great deal to thank God for."[18]

Fuller had been appointed by President Grover Cleveland, and the two men had a strong friendship. In 1890, the then-former president argued his only case before the Supreme Court.[19] It was a complex case that involved drainage warrants in New Orleans. Still, the Court was a stickler for adjourning on time. When Cleveland realized that it was approaching the witching hour with only two minutes remaining, he said he would only need a few minutes to finish his argument.

Fuller was not prepared to play favorites, even for a former president. He stated, "Mr. Cleveland, we will hear you tomorrow morning," and the Court adjourned.[20]

The Associate Justices

Samuel Blatchford

Born March 9, 1820, in New York, New York; died July 7, 1893; associate justice, 1882–1893. Blatchford gained attention as a publisher of admiralty and Second Circuit opinions. He served as a federal district and appellate judge before his elevation to the Supreme Court. He was considered a workhorse during his tenure, outwriting his brethren during a period when the Supreme Court considered more than three times as many cases as today.

Samuel Blatchford was considered unusually courteous to advocates who came before the Supreme Court. He achieved this distinction by choosing not to read cases while a lawyer was addressing the Court. His colleagues apparently felt no similar compunction.[21]

Blatchford was a steady but uninspired expositor of the law. Upon his death, few reached for hyperbole to describe his service. U.S. Attorney

General Richard Olney, at the Court's own memorial service, declared, "If he was not brilliant, he was safe."

The editor of the *American Law Review*, Seymour D. Thompson, put it this way: "It is no great disparagement of him to say that he was probably a better reporter than judge."[22] That is no great compliment, either.

Joseph P. Bradley

Born March 14, 1813, in Berne, New York; died January 22, 1892; associate justice, 1870–1892. Bradley rose to attention as a railroad lawyer and active Republican. While on the Court, he served on the electoral commission that awarded Rutherford B. Hayes the 1876 election over Samuel Tilden.

At Rutgers College, Joseph P. Bradley was described as "a desperately serious young man." Nonetheless, he did have at least one acknowledged weakness, obvious in an oath he took: "I will not, by any means, or on any account whatever, except it be from absolute necessity, call at any of the public houses of this city for the purpose of getting refreshment, refectory, or trash of any kind except oysters, during my collegiate course."[23]

Bradley was so orderly that he became furious when his schedule was interrupted. Once, when he wanted to catch a train, his wife, Mary, insisted he wear newer pants. So, Bradley changed pants, which caused him to miss the train. He went home, had Mary stand in front of him, and began cutting his pants with a knife while saying, "You will never compel me to miss another train."

On another occasion, he hailed a carriage to take him to church, but the driver took him to the wrong one. He was so upset that not only did he not attend church that Sunday, he did not attend for several weeks afterward.[24]

Bradley's incredible breadth of interests led the first Justice John Marshall Harlan, when talking about what the other justices were doing during the Court's recess, commented, "Bro. Bradley, I take it, is somewhere studying the philosophy of the Northern lights...."[25]

When Bradley consulted the Bible, he did so in its "original Greek" translation.[26]

Bradley cut a colorful and curious figure. One of his best friends described him as "amusingly petulant – naturally eccentric." Another justice described Bradley as full of "vinegar." When he was elderly, one Court watcher wrote that Bradley was "a little dried-up anatomy of a man... His skin hangs in wrinkles and all of his fat has long since gone to figures and judicial decisions. He is 77 years old, but there is a fair chance for his lasting at least twenty-three years longer. There is not much of him to die, and when his soul is disembodied, it will not be much freer than it is now."[27]

David J. Brewer

Born January 20, 1837, in Smyrna, Asia Minor [now Turkey]; died March 28, 1910; associate justice, 1890–1910. A nephew of Justice Stephen J. Field, with whom he served on the Court, Brewer had previously been a judge on the Kansas Supreme Court and the U.S. Court of Appeals for the Eighth Circuit. As a member of a close-knit group of justices, Brewer was described by Chief Justice Melville Fuller as "one of the most lovable of them all." He was, however, so conservative that one modern biographer described him as the "William O. Douglas of the Right."

In 1905, a lawyer appeared before the Court representing a drugstore operator who was arrested for selling alcohol to an "allottee." The advocate cut a strange figure to the Court. He didn't just lack a vest, which was the uniform of the day, but he wore a yellow tweed suit with a pink shirt and tan shoes, all of which were duly noted.

David Brewer, an acknowledged expert on the law relating to Native Americans, asked the advocate before the Court, "Mr. Counsellor, what do you think the status of an Allottee is?"

The baffled lawyer raised his palms upward and replied, "If you fellows up there don't know, how do you think us fellows down here should know?"

Silence filled the room as the Court reacted to being addressed as "you fellows," and the court reporter noted, "The shocked expression on the face of dear Chief Justice Fuller will never be forgotten." For his part, Oliver Wendell Holmes convulsed in laughter and buried his face in his arms in an unsuccessful effort to hide his amusement.[28]

President Theodore Roosevelt considered Brewer, along with Chief Justice Fuller and Rufus Peckham to be "upright well-meaning judges," who were nonetheless a "menace to the welfare of the Nation." He questioned Brewer's intelligence, saying the justice had "a sweet-bread for a brain."[29]

Henry B. Brown

Born March 2, 1836, in South Lee, Massachusetts; died September 4, 1913; associate justice, 1890–1906. Brown served as a state court judge and a U.S. district court judge. He taught law at the University of Michigan before his appointment to the Supreme Court. He is chiefly remembered as the author of the majority opinion in Plessy v. Ferguson, *which established the "separate-but-equal" doctrine that was overturned in* Brown v. Board of Education.

Although graduates of the law schools at Harvard and Yale have come to dominate the modern Supreme Court, Henry B. Brown holds the distinction of being the only Supreme Court justice to have dropped out of both schools.[30]

Brown authored the infamous *Plessy v. Ferguson*[31] decision, which upheld state-imposed racial segregation under the standard of "separate but equal." Oddly, in a letter to his close friend, Charles Kent, in 1903, he worried about decisions from his Court that were unjust to African Americans, seemingly oblivious to the significance of *Plessy* as the foundation for racial injustice. He wrote, "In some criminal cases against negroes, coming up from the Southern States, we have adhered to the technicalities of the law so strictly that I fear injustice has been done to the defendant."[32]

His friend, Charles Kent, described Brown as having "a grim sense of humor" and illustrated that point with a story about a university classmate of theirs. The classmate, wrote Kent, was always getting into financial difficulties and then quarreling with old classmates who had given him money on the grounds that they should give him more money.

Brown had contributed money several times to the man when suddenly the financially strapped classmate died. Brown was asked to contribute money to pay the classmate's hotel bill and funeral costs, but before doing so, Brown wrote, "To the object of which you speak I gladly contribute, but before sending a check I wish to receive a burial certificate to be sure that he is dead."[33]

Brown was a great believer in leisure to balance hard work. Nonetheless, he understood that his duties included the endurance of unpleasant and perhaps even unnecessary tasks. At his retirement dinner, he described his outlook on moving on, as well as how he approached his judicial labors, this way:

> I feel there is at least some compensation awaiting me in the absolute freedom from all cares not voluntarily assumed. There is no one to say, and no inner conscience even to suggest, that it is your duty to be in Court at twelve o'clock; to keep your ears, if not your eyes, open, howevermuch [sic] you may prefer a stealthy nap, until four thirty; to listen to arguments for four hours, when in fact, you made up your mind in four minutes; and to be prepared at the next Saturday's Conference to give an opinion, which your Associates will probably overrule.[34]

He also called his forthcoming retirement an opportunity to "wander in the land of the lotus eater where it is always afternoon."[35]

Nathan Clifford

Born August 18, 1803, in Rumney, New Hampshire; died July 25, 1881; associate justice, 1858–1881. A former speaker of the Maine House of Representatives, Clifford served in the U.S. Congress and as U.S. Attorney General before going on the Supreme Court bench. His nomination was strenuously opposed because, despite being a New Englander, he harbored Southern sympathies. He was confirmed by a close 26-23 vote. Clifford also headed the commission that settled the 1876 presidential election between Rutherford B. Hayes and Samuel Tilden.

The most striking thing about Nathan Clifford was his extreme partisanship. Justice Samuel Miller described Clifford as a "lifelong bitter Democrat." He had been President James Polk's Attorney General and was known as a pro-slavery Democrat. When Whig William Henry Harrison was elected President, he refused to attend the inauguration, calling Harrison "an imbecile old man." He thought President Rutherford Hayes was a "usurper," and he refused to enter the White House while Hayes was President.[36]

Clifford was a dedicated fisherman who would send parts of his catch to his colleagues on the Court. Unfortunately, by the time the justices got the fish, it would usually be rotten.[37]

Clifford took little interest in the Court's proceedings unless he noticed a large enough audience to make his efforts worthwhile. When that was the case, he would turn into a one-man hot bench, pummeling the advocate arguing that day with question upon question and leaving no time for answers to intervene. Then, certain that those watching understood his dominance, he would smile at the audience as though he shared with them the amusement of another tortured lawyer.[38] Clifford's efforts to dominate oral argument did not necessarily impress as he expected. He was known on the Court for "his preposterous irrelevancies and obstreperous posturing."[39]

David Davis
Born March 9, 1815, in Sassafras Neck, Maryland; died June 26, 1886; associate justice, 1862–1877. Davis had served in the Illinois legislature and at its constitutional convention before joining the state bench. His friend, Abraham

Lincoln, for whom he had served as campaign manager, placed Davis on the U.S. Supreme Court. During his tenure as a justice, Davis is best known as the author of Ex Parte Milligan, *which held that the Constitution did not permit military trials of civilians when the civil courts were available. After leaving the Court, Davis represented Illinois in the U.S. Senate and served as president pro tempore. Davis was known as "Lincoln's best friend."*

David Davis and Lincoln remained close friends after Lincoln appointed Davis to the Court in October 1862. Davis continued advising Lincoln after his appointment. For example, he advised Lincoln to fire Secretary of the Treasury (and future Chief Justice) Salmon Chase and Postmaster General Montgomery Blair, recommended military promotions, criticized Attorney General James Speed, and suggested a replacement for Chief Justice Roger Taney. Sometimes, however, Lincoln got frustrated with Davis's continual advice. Lincoln complained, "[Davis] bothers me nearly to death."[40]

As a former justice, Davis's advice to a young lawyer on handling questions from the justices would not be useful today, if it ever were useful. He told the lawyer:

> You need not be afraid to speak before the Supreme Court, and if one of those duffers in a toga interrupts you in the midst of an argument by some irrelevant question, don't get frightened and spoil your argument by stopping to answer him. Just say quietly: "Excuse me, your Honor, but I will reach that by and by," and if you don't reach it, it won't matter. You need not be afraid that you will be called up to answer it after you have taken your seat.[41]

Stephen J. Field

Born November 4, 1816, in Haddam, Connecticut; died April 9, 1899; associate justice, 1863–1897. After a single year in the California legislature, Field lost a bid for higher office and turned to law. He achieved great success and eventually was elected to the California Supreme Court. As a member of the U.S. Supreme Court, Field served on the commission that settled the 1876 presidential election between Rutherford B. Hayes and Samuel Tilden. Because he cast his lot with Tilden, Field refused to attend the Hayes inauguration. Field unsuccessfully sought the Democratic nomination for president in 1880 and 1884. Despite his return to electoral politics, Field remained on the bench, staying long after he was capable of discharging his duties. He did so because he wanted to break the record of 33 years set by Chief Justice John Marshall and to spite President Grover Cleveland, whom he had expected to appoint him chief justice in 1888.

As a young man, Stephen J. Field moved to California during the great "gold rush" to establish a legal practice. He settled in Maryville, a tent city at the time. When he arrived, he found people signing up for lots that cost $250 apiece. Field had only $20 to his name but learned that there were no consequences to signing up for a lot and then choosing not to take it. He promptly signed up for 65 lots. His action caused people to assume that he was a wealthy visitor, and the town honored him at a dinner. Field used the occasion to suggest that the town needed a local government.

The idea took root and enabled Field to run for the position of alcalde, which served as a combination of law enforcement officer and judge. The main objection to him was that he was a newcomer to the area. He had been there for only three days, whereas his opponent had been there twice as long – six days. Field still won the election by nine votes.[42]

Field was twice expelled from the California bar by the same judge. William R. Turner succeeded Field as a judge in Maryville, California. It was not a friendly passing of the torch. During Field's first appearance as a lawyer in Turner's courtroom, the two argued so angrily that Turner fined Field $500, imprisoned him for two days, and expelled him from the bar. The California Supreme Court reinstated Field, who promptly petitioned for Turner's removal and wrote impassioned editorials against the jurist.

Field then took to wearing a pistol in anticipation of a confrontation with the judge. He even shadowed the judge and let him know that he would be killed if he came at Field.

Turner reacted by ordering Field to appear before him under threat of a second bar expulsion. Field took that as a reason to question Turner's competence and character in front of him. Turner then ordered Field expelled from the California bar again, only to be overturned a second time by the state's highest court.

Field exacted his revenge by winning a seat in the state assembly and shepherding through legislation that exiled Turner to a judicial seat in the state's far northwest region. The feud continued though and in 1851, nearly resulted in a shoot-out on the assembly floor.[43]

Field was both opinionated and obstinate. As one person who knew him wrote, "When Field hates, he hates for keeps."[44]

Field provided newly elected President Grover Cleveland with a list of Californians whom Field said should never be appointed to federal office. When Cleveland nonetheless appointed several of the people from that list, Field swore off functions held at the White House for the remainder of Cleveland's presidency.[45]

In one unusual case that came before the Supreme Court and garnered national attention, in part for its salacious qualities, Field was a participant in the underlying facts. The tale began with Nevada Senator William Sharon and his mistress, Sarah Althea Hill, whom he housed in a San Francisco hotel with a generous monthly stipend for her expenses. Sharon eventually abandoned her and had her evicted from the hotel. Hill sued, claiming a wife's share of Sharon's fortune that was largely derived from ownership of some silver mines. She claimed to have a written marriage contract. California courts held the contract valid, but a federal court ruled it a forgery.

The federal court based its ruling, in part, on information that Sarah Hill had secreted herself in the Senator's hotel room and reported the Senator's intimacies with another woman. The court felt that her behavior was disqualifying because that was not something a wife would do.

Hill was represented by David Terry, "a six-foot, three-inch giant [who] customarily carried a bowie knife tucked in his bosom." Terry had served as chief justice on the California Supreme Court at the same time Field was on that court. Terry had also killed Field's friend, Senator David Broderick, in a duel years earlier.

Sharon died, but Hill, represented by Terry, continued to pursue the case. Terry also married Hill at that point. The appeal came before Justice Field, sitting as a circuit judge, who, in open court, rejected the alleged marriage contract between Hill and Sharon. Mrs. Terry hurled accusations of bribery at Field before being ejected from the courtroom. Judge Terry then took over his wife's harangue, brandishing his bowie knife to protect his wife. Both Terrys were held in contempt.

After being jailed, the Terrys threatened to horsewhip Field. The Attorney General dispatched Marshall David Neagle to protect Field when he rode circuit. It proved fateful. One day, Field and Neagle were eating in a railroad dining room in California at the same time as the Terrys. After recognizing Field, Terry came up from behind Field and struck him on the side of his face twice. Neagle pointed a gun at Terry to stop the attack. Terry moved his hand to his pocket, which Neagle took as an action to retrieve the famous bowie knife. Neagle fired two shots, killing Terry.

The sheriff arrested both Field and Neagle, though Field was quickly released on a federal writ of habeas corpus, which was available for "an act done or omitted in pursuance of a law of the United States." Neagle's eligibility for the writ was unsettled, and it was that question that went to the Supreme Court.[46]

The Court held Neagle was entitled to habeas corpus because his action was within the authority of his federal assignment to protect Field, an assignment that was within the executive authority of the president.[47] Justice Lucius Quintus Cincinnatus Lamar dissented, joined by Chief Justice Melville Fuller. Lamar wrote: "If the act of Terry had resulted in the death of Mr. Justice Field, would the murder of him have been a crime against the United States?" They answered their own question with an emphatic "no."[48] Field, of course, did not participate in the decision.

Field's experience as a Westerner and an ornery individual led to an unusual requirement that he placed on his outerwear. He was the "only justice to wear a coat specially tailored so that he could fire pistols through both pockets at once."[49]

Field's mind began to fail by the early 1890s, and Fuller assigned a diminishing number of cases for Field's authorship. In his prime, Field had written 25-30 opinions a year, but in 1893, he wrote only 9, in 1894, just 6, and in 1895, but 4. One report has it that Fuller sent two justices to Field's home to discuss a case with him. Field received them but was found in an armchair with his head drooping and his eyes closed. He initially did not appear to recognize his visitors and spoke little to them. One justice began to read a memorandum on the case, but Field remained silent throughout the exposition. At one point, though, he suddenly opened his eyes and said, "Read that again." After he heard what had been written a second time, Field said, "That is not right. That is not good law. You err when you say..." Field then proceeded to take the justices through an extensive and impressive legal argument, entirely on point, before he lapsed again into his previous state.[50]

Justices often fear that they overstay their capacity to do the job, but some linger on well past the time that retirement should occur. As a young justice, Field was dispatched to inform Justice Robert Grier that his colleagues thought that it was time for Grier to leave the bench.

When Field seemed to no longer have the capacity to perform, the task fell to Justice John Marshall Harlan. When Harlan approached Field, he found the elder justice sitting by himself in the Robing Room in something of a stupor. After rousing Field, Harlan took a gentle route by asking if Field recalled what he had told Grier when it was time for him to retire. As Chief Justice Charles Evans Hughes wrote of the incident, "The old man listened, gradually became alert and finally, with his eyes blazing with the old fire of youth, he burst out: 'Yes! And a dirtier day's work I never did in my life!'"[51]

Horace Gray

Born March 24, 1828, in Boston, Massachusetts; died September 15, 1902; associate justice, 1882–1902. Gray joined the U.S. Supreme Court after serving as chief justice of the Massachusetts Supreme Judicial Court, where future justice Louis D. Brandeis served him as a clerk. He had been the youngest person ever appointed to the state high court.

Justice Horace Gray always enjoyed the outdoors. While a member of the Massachusetts bench, he received a private note from John Quincy Adams II, who asked that his case be postponed "for the sake of Old Izaak Walton... [T]he smelts are biting and I can't leave."

Gray obviously sympathized and granted the continuance, telling the clerk that Mr. Adams "had been detained on important business."[52]

When Gray was nominated to the Supreme Court, the joke that made the rounds said that the Massachusetts bar was so tired of Gray's petulance on the bench that it recommended him for the Supreme Court just to get rid of him.[53]

On one occasion, a lawyer appeared before the Court wearing a gray coat rather than a dark one. Gray was outraged and said, "Who is that beast who dares to come here with a grey coat."[54]

Gray was a large man who chafed at the cramped and overheated quarters of the Court. He demanded that the window behind the screen be kept open when the justices were seated. Justice Henry Brown, who cut a much thinner and smaller figure, once asked a page to shut the window because he could feel the draft. Gray jumped up, apparently suspecting that the window had been closed at someone's request, and shouted at the page, "What damn fool told you to close that window?" When the page responded, "Mr. Justice Brown," Gray returned to his seat, muttering, "I thought so."[55]

Justice Oliver Wendell Holmes Jr. succeeded Gray, first on the Massachusetts Supreme Judicial Court and then on the U.S. Supreme Court. Still, Gray mystified Holmes, who told his law clerk, future U.S. Attorney General Francis Biddle, that Gray's opinions and the conclusions "stood forth like precipices, with a roaring torrent of precedents between, but he never quite understood how Gray got across..."[56]

John Marshall Harlan
Born June 1, 1833, in Boyle County, Kentucky; died October 14, 1911; associate justice, 1877–1911. Harlan embarked on a political career at an early age, but frequently changed his political stripes. He was elected a county judge on the Know Nothing ticket and Kentucky attorney general as a Constitutional Unionist but had two failed races for governor under the Republican banner. Justice Oliver Wendell Holmes Jr. described his colleague, Harlan, as "the last of the tobacco-spittin' judges." Harlan has also been called the "Great Commoner of the Supreme Court" and the "Great Dissenter."

Justice David J. Brewer said of John Marshall Harlan: "He goes to bed every night with one hand on the Constitution and the other on the Bible, and so sleeps the sweet sleep of justice and right conscience. He believes in the Constitution, as it was written...and the Constitution as it shall be, unless and until the American people shall, in the way they have appointed, amend its provisions."[57]

William Howard Taft loved to vacation in Murray Bay, where he enjoyed the outdoors and socializing with his family. A favorite activity of the future president and chief justice was golf. One day, he came across another vacationer at Murray Bay on the golf course – Harlan. When Taft happened upon him, Harlan was "jumping up and down to coax a ball that was hovering on the very edge of the first hole." Unfortunately for Harlan, the ball would not move, so he called over to Taft. Both were large men, but Taft was much heavier. Harlan instructed Taft, "Come on! You jump. That will do the business."[58]

A friend of Harlan's sent him a case of fine Kentucky bourbon, but Harlan did not see the friend until he went to church the following Sunday. Forgetting where he was for a moment, Harlan said, "That was fine–," and then realized where he was, "the sermon, I mean."[59]

In 1875, Congress passed the Civil Rights Act, an anti-discrimination law that applied to places of public accommodation. The Supreme Court declared the statute unconstitutional in *The Civil Rights Cases*,[60] leading to the enactment of Jim Crow laws.

Harlan planned to dissent but struggled to write it. Then, Harlan's wife, Malvina, had an inspiration. Sometime earlier, Harlan had instructed Malvina to get rid of an old inkstand he owned that had previously belonged to Chief Justice Roger Taney and had been used to write the *Dred Scott*[61] opinion, a decision Harlan detested. She had disobeyed and kept it in storage. To help her husband write the opinion, she cleaned the ink stand and placed it on Harlan's desk.

When he arrived home that day, she told him she "put a bit of inspiration on your study table." His wife later explained that

> the memory of the historic part that Taney's ink stand had played in the *Dred Scott* decision, in temporarily tightening the shackles of slavery upon the negro race in the antebellum days, seemed that morning, to act like magic in clarifying my husband's thoughts in regard to the law that had been intended by [Senator] Sumner to protect the recently emancipated slaves in the enjoyment of 'civil rights.' His pen fairly flew on that day and, with the running start he then got, he soon finished his dissent. She described the inkstand's role in helping Harlan write his dissent as an example of "poetic justice.[62]

Harlan's famous temper was on display in *Pollock v. Farmers' Loan & Tr. Co.*,[63] when he "delivered an extemporaneous dissent in which he banged his fist on his desk and glared at the Chief Justice." *The Nation* described Harlan's action as "the most violent political tirade ever heard in a court of last resort."

Another report described Harlan's actions this way: he "pounded the desk, [shook] his finger under the noses of Chief Justice [Melville Fuller] and Mr. Justice [Stephen] Field" and "several times ... turned his chair" to glare at Field, Fuller and Horace Gray.

Harlan later blamed Field for his anger because he said that Field was whispering and shuffling papers while Harlan was reading his dissent and that Field "acted like a mad man" throughout the case.

Harlan also saw things differently. He claimed he merely showed "a good deal of earnestness."[64]

Harlan chose to interpret the Constitution as would a layperson relying on common sense. Justice Oliver Wendell Holmes, who served with Harlan, was critical of this approach, saying that Harlan's mind was "a powerful vise the jaws of which couldn't be got nearer than two inches to each other."[65]

Harlan was a large man who was also strong and a good athlete. As a colonel in the army, he often joined his men when a wagon was stuck in the mud to push it forward or when a tree had to be taken down to effect a road repair.[66] At the age of 75, Harlan joined his colleagues in a baseball game against members of the Washington, DC bar. At bat, he cracked a deep drive into centerfield for a triple. He must have been quite a sight, running the bases with ideal posture, coattails visible behind him.[67]

Ward Hunt
Born June 14, 1810, in Utica, New York; died March 24, 1886; associate justice, 1873–1882. A founder of New York's Republican Party, Hunt declined political office, but won election as a justice of the New York Court of Appeals, where he later served as chief justice. Hunt was the judge, sitting on the circuit, who fined Susan B. Anthony $100 for voting in a New York election before women could vote in that state.

Ward Hunt, sitting as a circuit judge, presided at the trial of Susan B. Anthony. Since women were not allowed to vote and Anthony did so, she was charged with fraudulent voting in violation of the Civil Rights Act of 1870. Hunt rejected the constitutional arguments in Anthony's defense and would not permit her to speak because he held that a woman was not competent to testify on her own behalf. He found her guilty as a matter of law, directed jurors to return a guilty verdict, and then refused to allow jurors to be polled. Prior to sentencing, Hunt asked Anthony if she had anything to say, and she vigorously attacked the constitutionality of her conviction while Hunt unsuccessfully sought to silence her. Then, by fining, but not imprisoning her, Hunt foreclosed Anthony's ability to have a writ of habeas corpus appeal to the Supreme Court.[68]

Howell Jackson
Born April 8, 1832, in Paris, Tennessee; died August 8, 1895; associate justice, 1893–1895. Jackson longed to become a judge, but a single attempt – a failed bid for the Tennessee Supreme Court – refocused his attention on political office. He won election to the state House of Representatives and then to the U.S. Senate. He realized his real dream when President Grover Cleveland appointed him to the U.S. Court of Appeals for the Sixth Circuit. He was later elevated to the Supreme Court by President Benjamin Harrison, with whom he had served in the Senate.

From Tennessee, Howell Jackson initially opposed secession. He was not in the military in the Civil War, but he did serve as the Confederate Receiver of Sequestered Property for West Tennessee. Basically, Jackson sat out the war, foreshadowing the nature of his tenure on the Supreme Court.[69]

When Jackson was a judge on the Sixth Circuit, he participated in an advertisement for a brand of cigar.[70]

Jackson was appointed to the Supreme Court by Republican President Benjamin Harrison and might be called a "midnight judge." He was sworn in as a justice on March 4, 1893, at 11 am. An hour later, Grover Cleveland, a Democrat, was sworn in as President.[71]

Lucius Q. C. Lamar

Born September 17, 1825, in Eatonton, Georgia; died January 23, 1893; associate justice, 1888–1893. A cousin of Justice John Archibald Campbell, Lamar served in both houses of Congress and as President Grover Cleveland's Secretary of the Interior. Lamar was confirmed for a seat on the U.S. Supreme Court by a four-vote margin. He was controversial because he had drafted Mississippi's secession law that made the state part of the Confederacy and served as an aide to Confederate President Jefferson Davis. His later outspoken advocacy of reunification earned him the nickname the "Great Pacificator."

Lucius Q.C. Lamar came to the Court without prior judicial experience at the age of 62 and was immediately overwhelmed by the work expected by a justice. He wrote a friend in 1889 that he would be "an impostor...if I were to allow you to believe that I am doing anything useful or even with moderate ability."[72]

Lamar had a hard time mailing a letter at 15th and G St. in Washington, DC He was at a fire-alarm box and unsuccessfully tried to insert the letter. Finally, a young man shouted, "Hey, mister, that's a fire-alarm box. The letter box is on the opposite corner." "You are right, my lad," said the old gentleman. As a spectator commented to a friend, "Judicial honors have had no effect on Lamar. I see he is quite as absent-minded as ever."[73]

Stanley Matthews

Born July 21, 1824, in Cincinnati, Ohio; died March 22, 1889; associate justice, 1881–1889. Matthews served as a U.S. Attorney in southern Ohio, as a state court judge, and later as a U.S. senator. He was originally nominated by his old college friend, President Rutherford B. Hayes, whose case he successfully argued before the commission that determined the winner of the 1876 presidential election. When the Senate did not vote on the controversial nomination, the new president, James Garfield, renominated Matthews, who won confirmation by a single vote, 24-23.

Justice Stanley Matthews served as a Republican strategist and counsel during the dispute over the deadlocked 1876 presidential election. He displayed unrestrained confidence throughout. He searched the Louisiana vote count diligently for ballots cast for Rutherford B. Hayes. He wrote: "I seemed all day to walk through the valley of the shadow of death. I felt as if a great conspiracy of ignorance, superstition, and brutality had succeeded in overthrowing the hope of Christian civilization represented and embodied by the Republican party."[74]

Matthews had long represented railroad interests. The connection caused the Detroit Free Press to announce his nomination by writing that "Mr. Jay Gould [railroad magnate] has been appointed to the United States Supreme Court in place of Judge Swayne, resigned."[75] Railroad interests did assist Matthews in obtaining Senate confirmation. Jay Gould lobbied Kansas Senator Preston Plum for Matthews; railroad baron Collis P. Huntington also lobbied senators.[76]

Matthews's support by railroad entrepreneurs led to rumors that Gould had given large campaign contributions in 1880 in exchange for the opportunity, along with other railroad barons, to choose Garfield's Supreme Court nominees. Matthews claimed the rumor was "slander," and Rutherford Hayes was exasperated by the rumor and expressed the wish to "... be allowed to perform my public duties without further libels."[77]

Samuel Freeman Miller
Born April 5, 1816, in Richmond, Kentucky; died October 13, 1890; associate justice, 1862–1890. Miller earned a medical degree and spent a decade as a physician before turning to the law. Because his anti-slavery views made him a pariah in his native Kentucky, he moved to Iowa, where he helped promote Abraham Lincoln's presidential campaign. He was rewarded for these efforts with a seat on the U.S. Supreme Court. Miller served on the commission that determined the disputed Hayes-Tilden presidential race in 1876 and was considered by President Ulysses S. Grant for elevation to chief justice.

Despite his many achievements, Samuel Freeman Miller might accurately have been described as lazy. He adopted as his motto: "Never walk when you could ride, never sit when you can lie down."[78] He also quipped that "it was fortunate [I] was born poor, as otherwise [I] would never have worked."[79] Still, when he did work, Miller "worked in furious spurts, often sitting for four or five hours without breaking." He then became what one friend described as a "well-fed, well-contented steam engine."[80]

Miller did not tolerate fools. Holding court as a circuit judge in St. Louis one stiflingly hot summer day, collar loosened and waving a palm leaf as a fan, the sweating and uncomfortable Miller finally could take no more. He shouted at the lawyer before him, "Damn it, Brown, come to the point!"

"What point, your Honor?" Brown replied.

Miller responded, "I don't know; any point; some point."[81]

Miller enjoyed presiding in criminal jury trials, and the circuit clerk in Omaha scheduled cases accordingly to accommodate Miller's visits. Once, Miller gave the jury instructions that guaranteed a conviction. Defense counsel protested and asked that Miller remind the jurors that no adverse impression should be drawn from the defendant's decision not to take the stand.

Miller was annoyed but recognized his duty. He told the jury that counsel was correct. He added: "I have not charged you as I should have done that the circumstance that this accused did not take the stand on his own behalf, as he might have done, and did not explain the matters in evidence against him, as he might have done, is something that you are not to consider at all. Now, gentlemen, the law says you must entirely dismiss this from your mind, give it no consideration, forget it completely, but" as his eyes shot upward toward the ceiling, he whispered, "It's a mighty strange rule of law, isn't it?"[82]

Not long after Justice L.Q.C. Lamar went on the Court, the justices heard a patent case about a pump. After the justices voted on the case,

Lamar commented to Miller, "I must confess, Judge, that one thing I did not understand. When you questioned the counsel so sharply about the spout of the pump, I did not quite catch its bearing on the patent."

"Oh," replied Miller, "I had dropped into a doze and was afraid someone had noticed it. So, I went for the counsel and made him explain all about the spout again so that he would think I had been following his argument."[83]

Miller suffered a stroke returning home from the Court on October 10, 1890. Doctors attending him at home urged him to remain quiet and "not strain his brain." Miller quipped that it was a "compliment for you must think that when I talk, I use my brains." Miller passed away three days after his stroke.[84]

Rufus W. Peckham
Born November 8, 1838, in Albany, New York; died October 24, 1909; associate justice, 1895–1909. Peckham had been a stalwart in the Democratic Party, a district attorney, and a state court judge before his appointment to the U.S. Supreme Court.

Like a number of justices, Rufus W. Peckham was not his nominator's first choice. President Grover Cleveland initially nominated William Hornblower to the Court, but Senator David Hill blocked his confirmation. Cleveland then nominated Wheeler Peckham, the brother of the future justice, but Senator Hill blocked Wheeler too, saying that if Cleveland had nominated "the other Peckham," he would have been confirmed. Frustrated with his failures to get his nominees confirmed, Cleveland nominated Senator Edward White, who had no problem being confirmed. However, when Cleveland had another seat on the Court to fill, he made sure "the other Peckham" was still satisfactory to Senator Hill and nominated Rufus to the Court. Rufus Peckham was confirmed by a voice vote.[85]

Peckham saw his appointment to the Court as if he had been consigned to a monastery. He said, "If I have got to be put away on the shelf, I suppose I might as well be on the top shelf."[86]

George Shiras, Jr.
Born January 26, 1832, in Pittsburgh, Pennsylvania; died August 2, 1924; associate justice, 1892–1903. Shiras joined the Supreme Court directly from a thriving private practice. He turned down an opportunity to run for the U.S. Senate to avoid association with the state's Republican machine. As the justice most associated with the fifth vote in striking down the income tax in Pollock v. Farmers' Loan and Trust Company,[87] the popular jargon held that when a reform law was undone, it was "Shirased."

When Justice George Shiras, Jr. joined the Court, its caseload was largely devoted to patent cases and other issues that were less than earth-shattering. In an oral argument during one patent dispute, Shiras tried to make the best of it by declaring, "I could sustain this patent [one involving a collar button] if this hump in the shank would prevent the button from rolling under the bureau."[88]

William Strong
Born May 6, 1808, in Somers, Connecticut; died August 19, 1895; associate justice, 1870–1880. Strong served two terms in Congress as a Democrat before returning home to Pennsylvania to take a seat on the state supreme court as a Republican. He also served on the commission that decided the 1876 presidential election while a member of the U.S. Supreme Court.

Illness had struck Justices Nathan Clifford, Ward Hunt, and Noah Swayne with such frequency in their later years that it seemed as though they were members of the Court in name only. To set an example and perhaps persuade them to retire, the still-vigorous octogenarian William Strong announced his retirement, hoping that others would follow. Several weeks later, a reluctant Swayne retired. Clifford died the following year, and Hunt finally retired more than a year after Strong.

When he retired, Strong said that it was better to leave when people would ask, "Why does he?" rather than "Why doesn't he?"[89]

Noah Swayne

Born December 7, 1804, in Frederick County, Virginia; died June 8, 1884; associate justice, 1862–1881. Swayne's nomination to the U.S. Supreme Court by President Abraham Lincoln was the result of an extensive campaign orchestrated by Swayne himself. When the chief justice's position became vacant in 1864, Swayne again mounted a campaign – this time unsuccessfully. Upon Chief Justice Salmon Chase's death in 1873, Swayne, then 68 years old, again promoted himself for the position. He finally resigned his seat under pressure from President Rutherford B. Hayes only after being assured that his friend, Stanley Matthews, would be his successor. For championing the interests of the railroads, one historian dubbed Swayne the "judicial patron of the bondholding class."

Even today, it is not unusual for a nervous advocate to call a justice by the name of a different justice. In the cases of Justices Noah Swayne and David Davis, the confusion might have been understandable. The two were seated side-by-side at the far right of the bench. Both were large men, both in girth and in height. Both justices were known to have a sweet tooth, sending pages for stick candy, which they might crunch during an argument. Both also were a bit on the antsy side, not infrequently standing and leaning against one of the pillars behind the seats.[90]

William B. Woods

Born August 3, 1824, in Newark, Ohio; died May 14, 1887; associate justice, 1881–1887. After the Civil War, Woods moved to Alabama, where he served on a state chancery court. He was later appointed a judge on the U.S. Court of Appeals for the Fifth Circuit before being elevated to the U.S. Supreme Court.

Court messengers were employees of the Marshal's Office. They were essentially personal attendants to the justices with their primary duty being the delivery of court correspondence. Depending on the justice, they could function as well as chauffeurs, valets, cooks, or even barbers. William B. Woods, however, had a difficult time adjusting to having a messenger.

He wrote, "My body-servant is the most annoying thing I have experienced. The fellow is the first man I see in the morning and the last man I see at night. He forces his way into my bedroom in the morning and orders me down to breakfast; taking my order himself to the cook. I cannot get rid of him in any way. He haunts me all the time. I try to think of places to send him, but he is back again as quick as lightning. That fellow will be the death of me. I have this satisfaction, however; the other justices are tortured in the same way."[91]

5

The First Third of the Twentieth Century

The Supreme Court was considered extremely conservative at the beginning of the twentieth century. Representative of the views in this era was the decision in *Lochner v. New York*,[1] where the Court struck down a New York law that limited the number of hours for workers in bakeries. That social legislation was found to be an unconstitutional intrusion into the free marketplace, prompting Justice Oliver Wendell Holmes, in dissent, to criticize the majority for reading "a particular economic theory" into the Constitution. Justices Pierce Butler, James McReynolds, George Sutherland, and Willis Van Devanter formed the ultraconservative core of the Court and were collectively known as the "Four Horsemen," derived from the Four Horsemen of the Apocalypse. The group rode home together each day from the Court and was also a frequent golf foursome. William O. Douglas described their golf "as slow as molasses, taking many shots and consuming what seemed like hours in putting."[2]

During this period, Edward Douglas White and former president William Howard Taft served as chief justices. Two associate justices from this era, Charles Evans Hughes and Harlan Fiske Stone, covered in the succeeding chapter, later became chief justices.

Edward White, Chief Justice (1910–1921), Associate Justice (1894–1910)
William Howard Taft, Chief Justice (1921–1930)

Associate Justices:
Louis Brandeis (1916–1939)
Pierce Butler (1923–1939)
John H. Clarke (1916–1922)
William Day (1903–1922)
Oliver Wendell Holmes, Jr. (1902–1932)
Joseph P. Lamar (1911–1916)
Horace Lurton (1910–1914)
Joseph McKenna (1898–1925)
James McReynolds (1914–1941)
William Moody (1906–1910)
Mahlon Pitney (1912–1922)
Owen Roberts (1930–1945)
Edward Sanford (1923–1930)
George Sutherland (1922–1938)
Willis VanDevanter (1911–1937)

The Chief Justices

Edward Douglas White

Born November 3, 1845, in Lafourche Parish, Louisiana; died May 19, 1921; associate justice, 1894–1910; chief justice, 1910–1921. During the Civil War, White was held as a prisoner by Union forces. Afterwards, he eventually won appointment to the Louisiana Supreme Court, but lost his seat after his political patron went down to defeat two years later. When his sponsor retook the governor's seat, White was appointed to a vacancy in the U.S. Senate, where he emerged as a fierce defender of Louisiana's sugar interests. White was the first sitting justice to be elevated to the chief justice's seat.

Edward Douglas White served in the Confederate army during the Civil War and was captured during the siege of Port Hudson in Louisiana.[3] His colleague on the Court, Oliver Wendell Holmes, served with the Union forces. As a result, Holmes noted that "the C.J. & I had been enemies."[4]

Still, every year, on the anniversary of the Battle of Antietam, White would give a rose to Holmes.[5] One of the three wounds Holmes suffered during the Civil War was at Antietam, but it was that particular wound that made Holmes famous as a war hero because Holmes' father wrote a memorable account in the *Atlantic Monthly* about searching for and finding his wounded son.[6]

Typically, Southerners did not support protective tariffs which raised costs for Southern consumers and benefited Northern industry. Though a senator from Louisiana, White did support the protective tariff, however. He explained that, during the Civil War, his mother had to made him a suit out of a piano cover and he believed a tariff would have encouraged the growth of the clothing industry so no one would have to suffer a similar indignity.[7]

White was fond of telling the story of being a young lawyer in New Orleans and having a judge ask him to defend a man who could not afford counsel. He did so, and his client got two years of hard labor. As they were leaving the courtroom, a friend of the client asked, "Say, Jim, have you got any money?"

Jim replied, "If I had had any money, don't you suppose I would have employed a lawyer?"[8]

On one occasion, while a lawyer was arguing before the Court, it appeared as if White was asleep. The lawyer incorrectly cited a precedent, and White suddenly sat up in his chair and corrected the dumbfounded lawyer.[9]

No one could criticize White's work ethic. He once explained to a lawyer friend that he was so occupied with Court business that "Since the court sat last October, I have not read a book, I have not read a magazine, and I have hardly glanced at the daily papers." He then added, "I want to say to you, sir, it is a dog's life; it is a dog's life."[10]

Cordiality was not the watchword on the White Court. White's predecessor as chief justice, Melville Fuller, had started the tradition of the justices shaking hands with each other before ascending the bench. During White's chief justiceship, legend has it "they actually shook fists at one another."[11]

Once, then-Professor Felix Frankfurter asked his Harvard law students why a particular Supreme Court opinion ran so long. The students valiantly offered a variety of plausible answers.

"No," Frankfurter thundered. "It's because Chief Justice White wrote it – that man is so long-winded he couldn't say anything in less than 50 pages."[12]

Holmes found that over time, White had mellowed, no longer acting in what Holmes believed was undignified fulminating from the bench. In conference, however, White's "roars [were] fit to shake the building."[13]

Hughes told Frankfurter that he thought White had been likable and well-respected, but he lacked executive ability.

Hughes said: "Whatever little success I may have achieved when I became chief justice, I think it was largely due to the lessons I learned in watching White during the years when I was an associate Justice and seeing how it ought not to be done. I am fond of saying that perhaps parents help their children most through their faults because children hate the faults and failings of their parents and are helped thereby. And so, if I had any virtues as chief justice, they were due to my determination to avoid White's faults."[14]

William Howard Taft

Born September 15, 1857, in Cincinnati, Ohio; died March 8, 1930; chief justice, 1921–1930. Taft served as a state court judge, U.S. Solicitor General, and a judge on the U.S. Court of Appeals for the Sixth Circuit before being appointed civil governor of the Philippines. He enjoyed the work abroad so much that he twice refused offers of appointment to the Supreme Court. He then became President Theodore Roosevelt's Secretary of War, which became the launching pad for his own successful presidential race. After he lost his bid for reelection, he became a professor at Yale Law School. President Warren Harding appointed Taft to the post he coveted most – Chief Justice. His size resulted in the nickname, "Big Chief," after he joined the Court.

When William Howard Taft taught at Yale Law School as the Kent Chair in Constitutional Law, he made fun of his own legendary girth by suggesting that a chair in law might not be enough. Instead, he suggested that the school consider "a sofa of law."[15]

Others were not above joking about Taft's size. Once, when he was president and vacationing in Atlantic City, New Jersey, a woman commented, "No swimming. President Taft is using the Atlantic."[16]

Once awaiting a train at a rural station, Taft learned the express train only stopped if it was picking up several passengers. Taft wired the conductor: "Stop at Hicksville. Large party waiting to catch the train." The train stopped, Taft boarded, and, trading on his considerable girth, announced, "I am the large party."[17]

A quirk of fate and conflicting personal ambitions were among the factors that made Taft the President of the United States. In 1906, as a cabinet member, he was preoccupied with "the War Department, the Panama Canal and the Philippine business," and did not want appointment as Justice Henry Brown's successor. Mrs. Taft was also adamant that her husband not take the judicial job.

While the possibility of nomination was pending, a close friend of the Taft family asked the War Secretary's son whether his father was going to be a Supreme Court Justice. "Nope," the boy answered firmly. To the further query, "Why not?" came the knowledgeable reply, "Ma wants him to wait and be President."[18]

One year after leaving the presidency, Taft was a svelte 270 pounds, having lost 70 pounds. When people asked how he did it, he explained that the weight of the presidency had lifted.[19]

President-elect Warren Harding met with Taft on December 26, 1920. In the course of a wide-ranging conversation, Harding suddenly said, "By the way, I want to ask you, would you accept a position on the Supreme Bench?"

Taft responded that "…it was and had always been the ambition of my life." He then told Harding that since he had been president and had appointed members of the Court along with opposing Wilson's nomination of Louis Brandeis to the Court, he could only accept an offer to be chief justice. Surprisingly, he explained to Harding that Chief Justice Edward White, a Democrat whom Taft had elevated to chief justice from associate justice, had told him many times that "he was holding the office for me and that he would give it back to a Republican Administration."[20]

Taft announced that he had joined the Court with the express purpose of repelling "socialistic raids on property rights." At his first conference as chief justice, he said he "had been appointed to reverse a few decisions."

He later said with some obvious glee, "I looked right at old man Holmes when I said it."[21]

Although Taft had opposed Brandeis's nomination to the Court, and they remained ideological opponents during their joint tenure, the two became quite friendly after Taft became chief justice. Brandeis considered Taft a much better chief than White had been. That puzzled Brandeis, though. He noted that "it's astonishing he should have been such a horribly bad president, for he has considerable executive ability."[22]

Taft was very personable as Holmes explained to his friend Harold Laski: "How can you help loving a man with such a kind heart? I must tell you that the moment he heard of my wife's death, the Chief Justice at once communicated with Arlington and made sure that everything was ready."[23]

Taft wanted to stay on the Court as long as he possibly could "in order to prevent the Bolsheviki from getting control...the only hope we have of keeping a consistent declaration of constitutional law is for us to live as long as we can... The truth is that [Herbert] Hoover is a Progressive just as [Harlan] Stone is, and just as Brandeis is and just as Holmes is."[24]

The Associate Justices

Louis D. Brandeis

Born November 13, 1856, in Louisville, Kentucky; died October 5, 1941; associate justice, 1916–1939. Despite his brilliance, seven former presidents of the American Bar Association, who were said to have the "courage of their retainers," opposed Brandeis's nomination. As a dedicated reformer, Brandeis earned the nickname "the People's Attorney." One of the most quotable of writers ever to serve on the Court, Brandeis had an extraordinary role in influencing both President Woodrow Wilson's "New Freedom" and Franklin Roosevelt's "New Deal." Presidents, admirers, and law clerks came to call him "Isaiah" for his reputation as a visionary prophet.

Louis Brandeis enrolled in Harvard Law School at the age of 18 without an undergraduate degree after studying two years in Germany. When he graduated from law school two years later, he had the highest record in the school's history with an average of 97 on a scale of 100.[25]

As a lawyer, Louis Brandeis was the author of what became known as "the Brandeis Brief," a written legal argument that used the social science and common knowledge of the period rather than legal precedent to justify a maximum-hour law for women. Although the brief contained two pages of legal citation, more than one hundred pages were devoted to labor statistics that showed the experience of excessive working hours on women to justify the imposition of safety and health measures. The brief was favorably received by the Supreme Court, which complimented Brandeis for it in the opinion.[26] Yet Brandeis was not impressed with the research that he cited. He told Dean Acheson, when the future secretary of state served as Brandeis's law clerk, that the title of the brief should have been "What Any Fool Knows."[27]

Evidence of the controversy sparked by the Brandeis nomination comes from a letter that then ex-president Taft received from a friend: "When Brandeis' nomination came in yesterday, the Senate simply gasped…There wasn't any more excitement at the Capitol when Congress passed the Spanish War Resolution."[28]

Although serving as a justice, Brandeis also advised President Woodrow Wilson and members of his administration. One example occurred in December 1917 when Wilson was concerned that the railroads were unable to move raw materials and that war supplies could not be moved to the Atlantic ports. Accompanied by two Secret Service agents, Wilson went to Brandeis and asked him about the legitimacy of government seizure of the railroads and for advice on whom should be the administrator of the railroads if they were seized. Brandeis replied that the railroad seizure was legitimate and that William McAdoo should be in charge of the railroads. Wilson followed that advice.[29]

It was rumored, particularly in light of Taft's vocal opposition to the nomination of Brandeis, that the two were not on speaking terms. Few knew of the chance meeting that Brandeis described to his wife on December 4, 1918:

> Had an experience yesterday which I did not expect to encounter in this life. As I was walking toward the Stoneleigh about 1:00 p.m., Taft and I met. There was a moment's hesitation and when he had almost passed, he stopped and said in a charming manner, 'Isn't this Justice Brandeis? I don't think we have ever met.' I answered, 'Yes, we met at Harvard after you returned from the Philippines.' He, at once, began to talk about my views on regularity of employment. After a moment, I asked him to come in with me. He spent a half hour in 809, talking labor and War Labor Board experiences – was most confidential. I told him of the great service he had rendered the country by his action on the Labor Board and we parted with his saying in effect – he hoped we would meet often.[30]

Brandeis had a passion for saving money that colored everything he did. Judge Julian Mack used to tell friends that whenever he dined at the Brandeis home, he would eat both before and afterward.[31]

His law clerks found themselves spending endless hours in libraries; not only in the Court library, seeking legal precedents, but also in the Library of Congress, where they sought out the innumerable citations to sociological material that Brandeis demanded be part of opinions. His memory always astounded them.

While working on a patent case, he told one clerk, "There is a book in the Library of Congress published about 1870; a small volume with a green cover; and in chapter three the point in this case is discussed." The amazed clerk found the book, the green cover, and the point in chapter three.[32]

Brandeis had his law clerk, Dean Acheson (later Secretary of State under President Truman), collect footnotes in a minor prohibition case; when published, the footnotes covered fifteen pages. Two of them referred to two particular state cases. Brandeis looked at the footnotes, had a page bring him the relevant volumes, and demanded of Acheson, "Did you read all the cases cited in the footnotes?" When Acheson replied that he had, Brandeis said, "Suppose you read these two again," and walked out.

Acheson discovered, to his horror, that he had made an error in his notes and that the two cases were totally irrelevant. He apologized and was told by Brandeis, "Please remember that your function is to correct my errors, not to introduce errors of your own."[33]

Acheson once commented that Brandeis was tolerant of "a large segment of humanity – which did not include his law clerks."[34]

Brandeis could be quite critical of his fellow justices. Justice George Sutherland, he felt, was "a mediocre Taft;" Justice Edward Sanford was "thoroughly bourgeois," and James McReynolds was "lazy" and moved by the "irrational impulses of a savage." In fact, McReynolds was a man, Brandeis opined, who "would have given Balzac great joy" and who looked at times like "an infantile moron." Justice Mahon Pitney, he thought, was "much influenced by his experience and he had had mighty little." Justice Pierce Butler, Brandeis said, gave "no sign of anything except a thoroughly mediocre mind." The worst, he believed, was the elderly Justice Joseph McKenna."[35]

Brandeis joined the Court when it still met in the Capitol Building. There was no space for offices for the justices or their clerks, and the Court's library was in the basement. Brandeis felt that a wing should be added to the Capitol for court offices, although Taft prevailed and received authorization for a new building across the street.

The building, to Brandeis's mind, was too opulent and somewhat isolated from Congress and the White House. He refused to move into it and ignored his right as senior justice to have his choice of chambers. He said that he would just take whatever chambers was left over, since he had no plans to use the offices anyway.[36]

Brandeis disliked the size and centralization of government under Franklin Roosevelt's New Deal. In reference to one anti-New Deal decision of the Court, he told Thomas Corcoran, one of Roosevelt's key aides, "This is the end of this business of centralization, and I want you to go back and tell the President that we're not going to let this government centralize everything. It's come to an end. As for your young men, you call them together and tell them to get out of Washington – tell them to go home, back to the States. That is where they must do their work."[37]

Pierce Butler
Born March 17, 1866, in Northfield, Minnesota; died November 16, 1939; associate justice, 1923–1939. Butler came to the Court after a prosperous career defending railroads in trouble for transgressing government regulations. On the Court, he was a reliable conservative and was thus dubbed one of the "Four Horsemen," conservative justices who voted consistently against the constitutionality of New Deal legislation. Still, he wrote a notable dissent in 1928 in which he supported individual privacy interests against government wiretap authority.

Pierce Butler was a farm boy with a muscular build and who "became the foremost wrestler and bruiser of [his] neighborhood."[38]

As a lawyer, Butler employed the same skills he had honed as a wrestler. Fellow lawyers described his technique as "bullying" and "shredding." One described him admiringly as "the most ruthless cross-examiner practicing in the court of that day."[39]

President Warren Harding tended to defer to Chief Justice William Howard Taft's judgment about judicial appointments. With the prospect of Justice Joseph McKenna retiring, the Court's only Catholic member,

Taft set about searching for a Catholic replacement. However, there were few Catholic Republicans who fit the bill, and, at any rate, Taft wanted a Catholic Democrat to shore up Harding's relations with congressional Democrats because Republican conservative strength in the Senate had weakened in the 1922 elections. Butler fit the bill. He was Catholic, a Democrat, and he was favorably recommended by people like trusted Taft ally Willis Van Devanter.[40]

When it looked like President Harding was going to appoint Butler to the Court, Butler's son expressed worry that, although Butler wanted the job, he could not afford it. The salary for an associate justice was then $12,000 a year. That was far less than Butler made practicing law. In fact, wrote Butler's son, "Father spends more than that now and could not live on twice that sum."

Butler's son thought Butler could get money from the family construction business, which would raise his yearly income to $25,000. If money continued to be a problem, the son's idea was that his father could serve on the Court four or five years, resign, and like Charles Evans Hughes, make a great deal of money practicing law.[41] As it turned out, Butler served on the Court from 1923 until his death so money turned out not to be the overwhelming problem that was feared.

Rarely did anyone get the best of Justice Oliver Wendell Holmes Jr. Once, Butler, who usually disagreed with Holmes, achieved a majority in a case over his rival. He rubbed in the defeat by saying, "Well, I'm glad we have arrived at a just decision."

Holmes treated the line like that of a straight man. "Hell," he said, "is paved with just decisions."[42]

When Harlan Fiske Stone once praised a Butler opinion by saying, "There is something in what you say," Butler responded gruffly, "I am not interested in your sympathy except it be expressed in a vote."[43]

Butler once told Justice William O. Douglas that he considered wiretapping an utterly pernicious practice. Still, recalling the difficulties he had had as a prosecutor in certain kinds of crimes, he added, "Wiretapping is unconstitutional. But if I were prosecutor and had a kidnapping case, by God, I would tap the wires!"[44]

At the end of Butler's service on the Court, Douglas wrote, "He is a powerful advocate of all vested interests and of laissez-faire. When you cross swords with him, you have a worthy opponent. He knows what he wants and how to get it. He has thought through your side from the major premise on and knows its every weakness."[45]

Perhaps no one mourned the death of Butler more than his great friend on the Court, Justice James McReynolds. As Douglas put it, "McR being by nature the laziest person I ever knew got Butler to write most of the dissents."[46]

John H. Clarke

Born September 18, 1857, in New Lisbon, Ohio; died March 22, 1945; associate justice, 1916–1922. Clarke was a two-time candidate for the U.S. Senate, failing to win the election both times. He was on the verge of a third attempt when he was offered and accepted an appointment to a federal district court seat. Clarke's tenure on the Court ended when he could no longer stomach the ill humor of Justice James McReynolds, whose animosity toward Clarke was so great that McReynolds refused to sign the note from the Court expressing regret at the resignation.

John H. Clarke was appointed by Woodrow Wilson to replace Justice Charles Evans Hughes, who had resigned from the bench to accept the Republican presidential nomination. Clarke resigned after only two years on the Court in order to devote himself to the cause of American entry into the League of Nations. Privately, however, Clarke told friends that the real reason for his early resignation was his feelings about Justice James McReynolds, who had been extremely hostile to Clarke, as he was with just about everyone.[47]

Clarke claimed he resigned from the Supreme Court to pursue world peace and the League of Nations. The press described Clarke as a "flaming liberal" and one who possessed "remarkable oratorical gifts."[48] He had been an early advocate of direct election of senators, supported low railroad fares, backed home rule for cities, supported independence for the Philippines, wanted political campaign expenditures reported publicly, and wanted the war debts of our allies in World War I to be forgiven. It was a radical political agenda for the early 20th century.[49]

The problem for Clarke was that he was terribly unhappy on the Court, which he did not think was involved in the really important issue of the day—working to ensure world peace. As a dedicated Wilsonian, that meant working for American involvement in the League of Nations.

Instead, Clarke explained to his friend Louis Brandeis, as a justice, "I continued to devote my time to determining whether a drunken Indian had been deprived of his land before he died or whether the digging of a ditch in Iowa was constitutional or not." He explained to colleagues on the Court that he wanted to read more than constitutional law, and he wanted to be involved in the great questions of the day. He could not do these things while on the Court. Chief Justice Taft, who saw his position on the Court as the fulfillment of his dreams, could not understand Clarke. He wrote to him, "Few men have laid down power as you are doing."[50]

William Rufus Day

Born April 17, 1849, in Ravenna, Ohio; died July 9, 1923, associate justice, 1903–1922. Day had been a close personal confidant of President William McKinley and served as secretary of state. He had briefly served as a state court judge and as a judge on the federal appellate bench. He was a moderate who also wrote some very liberal decisions. He was widely known by his nickname, "Good Day."

William Rufus Day was a small man, mild of manner and puny of appearance. He did not strike his opponents as an adversary for whom they might have to brace. Nothing, however, could have been further from the truth. When a group of lawyers attempted a takeover of one of Day's railroad clients, they found that at the initial stages of the trial, Day appeared as browbeaten, just as they might have hoped. Yet, as the trial proceeded, "the country lawyer [Day]...[put] the lights of the Boston bar in a semi-comatose condition and wondering what had happened to them."[51]

Day had been President William McKinley's neighbor in Canton, Ohio. They were good friends, though Day was clearly the better lawyer of the two. When McKinley became President, for political reasons, he made John Sherman Secretary of State. Sherman, however, was senile, and Day actually ran the State Department.

Day was always known for being direct with people, even in this post where diplomacy reigns. When the Cuban junta intercepted a message from the Spanish minister to the United States that insulted McKinley, rather than going through diplomatic channels, Day went directly to the Spanish minister. Day handed the minister the insulting message and asked if it was genuine. It was, and the Spanish minister knew what he had to do. He asked to be relieved of his position in Washington and, within hours, was out of the United States, never to return.[52]

Day is remembered for his very important, though now overruled, opinion in *Hammer v. Dagenhart*,[53] a decision that declared a federal law prohibiting interstate commerce in products produced by child labor unconstitutional.

One of the arguments Day used in striking down the law was based on the Tenth Amendment, where he wrote that: "In interpreting the Constitution it must never be forgotten that the nation is made up of states to which are entrusted the powers of local government. And to them and to the people the powers not *expressly* [our emphasis] delegated to the national government are reserved."[54] The problem with Day's point is that the term "expressly" is not found in the Tenth Amendment, and the national government is not so limited in its law-making powers. He seems instead to be relying on language that appeared in the Articles of Confederation rather than the Constitution—the Articles did use the term "expressly."

Day was so devoted to the memory of President McKinley that he gave each justice a carnation to wear each year on the anniversary of McKinley's birth.[55]

Day's devotion to McKinley must have been tested when litigation developed over McKinley's estate. Day and George Cortelyou were the administrators of President McKinley's estate, and, unfortunately, McKinley's niece, nephew, and his two sisters sued the children of McKinley's brother, claiming that they were in unlawful possession of estate property.[56]

Day, a tiny man, once sat as a justice on a case argued by his son, W. A. Day, who was a large man. During the argument, the justice passed a note to Justice Oliver Wendell Holmes that read "a chip off the old block." Holmes sent the note back, indicating that it was more like a "block off the old chip."[57]

Oliver Wendell Holmes, Jr.
Born March 8, 1841, in Boston, Massachusetts; died March 6, 1932; associate justice, 1902–1932. Holmes served as chief justice of the Massachusetts Supreme Judicial Court immediately prior to his appointment to the U.S. Supreme Court. A polished and literary figure, Holmes is universally considered one of the Supreme Court's greatest justices. He so captured the popular imagination that he was the subject of a well-received play and movie entitled after a sobriquet he earned, "The Magnificent Yankee." He was also called "the last Puritan."

President Abraham Lincoln visited the front lines during the Civil War and stood upon a parapet to get a better view of the battle. A young Oliver Wendell Holmes, Jr., then a soldier on the battlefield, saw the easy target and yelled at the president, "Get down, you damn fool."

Lincoln was not taken aback even if Holmes was apologetic once he recognized the object of his ire. The president responded, "Captain, I am glad you know how to talk to a civilian."[58]

After the Civil War had left him thrice wounded, Holmes resolved to go to law school and promptly informed his writer-physician father. Dr. Holmes replied as the justice recalled at age 90, "What's the use of that, Wendell? A lawyer can't be a great man."[59]

While on the Massachusetts Supreme Judicial Court, he despaired at what passed for oral argument, as lawyers seemed to practice a particularly protracted style of speech. He suggested that they might be better off if they spent time reading some risqué novels, where "they might learn to say things by innuendo."[60]

The Boston Bar sponsored a reception to see their native son, Holmes, off to the U.S. Supreme Court. One lawyer toasted Holmes by saying, "Finally, justice will be done in Washington."

"Don't be too sure," Holmes replied, knowing that the laws are written by legislators rather than judges. "I am going there to administer the laws."[61]

An example of Holmes's willingness to enforce even silly laws came in the antitrust cases. After Solicitor General John W. Davis argued one before the Court, Holmes walked out with Davis.

"How many more of these economic policy cases have you got?" Holmes asked. "Quite a basketful," Davis replied.

"Well," Holmes continued, "bring 'em on, and we'll decide 'em. Of course I know, and every other sensible man knows, that the Sherman [Antitrust] law is damned nonsense, but if my country wants to go to hell, I am here to help it."[62]

After meeting for the first time when President Theodore Roosevelt was considering Holmes for appointment to the Supreme Court, a great friendship developed between Holmes and Roosevelt. Holmes rented a house across from Lafayette Park, very near the White House. He and his wife, Fanny, were frequent guests of Teddy and Edith Roosevelt for dinner at the White House or visits to the theater. TR liked Fanny and enjoyed Holmes's war stories. Both men were excellent conversationalists. The friendship was a close one that Holmes thought developed because neither he nor Fanny wanted anything from TR.

The friendship chilled, however, as a result of Holmes's dissent in the *Northern Securities* case.[63] The case involved a dispute over the Chicago, Burlington, and Quincy Railroad. James Hill owned the Great Northern Railroad, and Edward Harriman owned the Union Pacific. Both men saw the Chicago, Burlington as providing the ideal connection for their railroads with the city of Chicago. Hill joined his banker, J. Pierpont Morgan, who owned the Northern Pacific Railroad, to outbid Harriman for control of the Chicago, Burlington. As a result, Harriman's railroad was cut off from Chicago, so he launched a raid on Northern Pacific shares that sent the stock market into turmoil.

To avoid an economic debacle, Morgan convened a conference where he proposed a "community of interest." Morgan, Hill, and associated stockholders would form a holding company that would own Hill's Great Northern and Morgan's Northern Pacific. Harriman would be protected by having a seat on the board. This created the Northern Securities Company.

TR saw this combination as a violation of the Sherman Antitrust Act and challenged the arrangement. The Court agreed this was a violation of the act, but Holmes joined the dissenters. This "disloyalty" infuriated TR, who wrote that Holmes "has been a bitter disappointment."[64] TR also labeled Holmes a coward for his stand and claimed he "could carve out of a banana a judge with more backbone."[65]

Holmes wrote that their relationship was never again the same after that. He and Fanny attended White House dinners, and sometimes it seemed Holmes's relationship with TR was like it was in the old times, but at other times, there was tension. TR let it be known to Holmes that he was unhappy with him, arranging a private dinner with Holmes so he could express his displeasure. After TR's death, Holmes wrote that Roosevelt "was very likable, a big figure, a rather ordinary intellect, with extraordinary gifts, a shrewd and I think pretty unscrupulous politician. He played all his cards – if not more."[66]

A series of cases aimed at the oil and tobacco trusts tested the reach of the Sherman Antitrust Act. In the tobacco case, a lawyer told the justices that foreign companies were of no consequence in determining the level of competition. To drive his point home, he said, "no body but dudes and fools smoke foreign cigarettes."

"Are you sure?" Holmes asked. "I have smoked them, and I am sure I am not a dude."[67]

Holmes cherished the 30 young men who had served him at the Supreme Court as his law secretaries, as law clerks were called then. When he was first appointed to the Court, he relied on Harvard law professor John Chipman Gray, the brother of his predecessor on the Court, to make the annual selection. Later, another Harvard law professor, Felix Frankfurter, took over the chore.

Gray had strict criteria for these recruits. Of course, they had to be honor students. More importantly, though, to serve Holmes well, they had to be sufficiently talented to "deal with the *certiorari*, balance his checkbook, and listen to his tall talk."[68]

Holmes instructed each secretary about his "philosophy," which was "divided into two parts, each equally important: the first – keep your bowels open; and the second – well, the second is somewhat more complex and a part of your duties is to hear it during the next nine months."[69]

Holmes also made a contract with each of his law secretaries in which the young man promised not to marry during his year of service. In the interests of full disclosure, as his years advanced, Holmes added a clause reserving to himself a right to die or resign.[70]

On one occasion, Felix Frankfurter spoke to Holmes about his colleagues and said, "Mr. Justice, I suppose if your brethren talked the same kind of nonsense in the conference, at the conference table, that they put in their opinions, don't you get bored?"

Holmes responded, "No, because I've got a remedy against it. Whenever they begin that kind of stuff, I try to compose my mind and think of all the beautiful women I've known."[71]

When Holmes was assigned an opinion, he was despondent until he finished it. Assignments were usually made on Sunday following the Saturday conference, and Holmes would work with such intensity that he would often have proof sheets of his opinions ready to distribute within three days of getting an assignment. That left him free to indulge his passions in philosophy, social theory, and fiction.[72]

Holmes was known for his rapid production of opinions. He described how he would write an opinion: "My way of writing a case is to get into a spasm over it. At the end of each week a case is assigned to me and by Monday morning I am in a delirium, if as is often true the case is important and interesting, and work until I go to Court and then walk back and work again until dinner time. It is dyspeptic but thrilling."[73]

Chief Justice Charles Evans Hughes also explained how Holmes was able to produce opinions very quickly. When Hughes was an associate justice, he wrote that "Holmes had the most fascinating personality." Holmes, he further noted, disliked administrative detail but took meticulous notes in cases. He was the only justice who took comprehensive notes during oral arguments. Then, Holmes could take his notes and at once prepare an opinion. That was important to Holmes because he was miserable until he was done with an opinion.[74]

When Holmes agreed to delete some language from an opinion at the urging of his colleagues, he said that "the fizz" had been removed from the opinion.[75]

The other justices thought Holmes gave little import to the arguments of the parties. Holmes tended to hear arguments, read the briefs, think for a day or two, and then write his opinion. To counteract this criticism, Holmes continued his routine but then filed the opinion in a desk drawer for a month or two before sharing it with the Court. As a result, Holmes claimed, the brethren called the opinions thoughtful instead of glib and tempered rather than offhanded.[76]

It was said that "[Justices Horace] Gray, [John Marshall] Harlan, and [Edward] White could make good ideas uninteresting: Holmes made the dullest case a literary adventure."[77]

Once, a secretary suggested that Holmes should not employ the word "afflatus"[78] in an opinion since it was not a term that was generally understood.
Holmes, who enjoyed word games, replied, "Yes, I felt myself that it was rather a cabriole word."[79]

Holmes's admirers included the highly regarded (and future justice) Benjamin Cardozo, who, while a New York Court of Appeals judge, wrote, "I gnash my teeth with mixed feelings of admiration, jealousy and despair. What is the use of toiling and struggling, painfully giving birth to some commonplace statement of the obvious...when this man [Holmes] is able in a flash and without any bother or fuss to say something that lifts you up to the summit, bathed in eternal light."[80]

A lawyer was arguing that his client's income from a trust fund constituted a gift and thus was not taxable as income. Holmes had a particular interest in the case since he derived similar income from a trust, which he revealed during oral argument.
In closing, the lawyer said, "I hope, Mr. Justice Holmes, that the Statute of Limitations will not have run against you, so you will not be foreclosed from getting back the tax you have mistakenly paid out."

Indicating his view of the lawyer's argument, Holmes replied, "Nothing, nothing you have said leads me to hope."[81]

When Holmes had worked out a case to his satisfaction, he would relax. On the bench, he liked to nap after lunch and tried to hide it by resting his head in his hands as if he were in deep study. Once he awoke from a nap to discover a lawyer continuing on with an uninteresting argument. Holmes loudly exclaimed, "Jesus Christ!" and went back to sleep.[82]

Holmes frequented a burlesque show in Washington, DC, but found on one occasion the fare was unexpectedly racy even for his broadminded ways. Nonetheless, he turned to the stranger sitting beside him and exclaimed, "I, thank God, I am a man of low tastes."[83]

Holmes had a weakness for racy French novels. He told Albert Einstein that he often needed "some French indecency to restore the tone of my mind."[84]

Brandeis was appalled at Holmes's affection for French dime novels. To encourage more appropriate reading, Brandeis had the Library of Congress ship a large box of books to Holmes for summer reading. Upon seeing that they covered such non-scintillating subjects as worker's compensation and economic regulation, Holmes ordered the box placed in the basement until the fall when it would be returned to the library as though it had been read."[85]

After his retirement, a friend called upon Holmes and found him deep into Plato at age 90. "Still studying at your age?" the surprised friend inquired.

"I'm preparing for the final examination," Holmes answered.[86]

Joseph P. Lamar
Born October 14, 1857, in Ruckersville, Georgia; died January 2, 1916; associate justice, 1911–1916. A cousin of Justice Lucius Q.C. Lamar, Lamar served as a law revision commissioner and state legislator in Georgia, as well as a state supreme court justice before joining the U.S. Supreme Court. A friend from youth of President Woodrow Wilson, Lamar represented the president in a diplomatic mission in South America even though he was serving as a justice at the time.

Joseph P. Lamar's competence and hard work as a legislator was very apparent. When summer heat suggested that the legislature recess until cooler weather even though important work remained to be done, one of Lamar's colleagues suggested that they "let the Clerk and Joe Lamar finish the business of the session" while the rest of them went home.[87]

As a member of the Georgia Supreme Court, which met at that time in Atlanta, Lamar was nearly run over on a busy street while walking to work. He did not blame the incautious driver. He quipped that to live in Atlanta "was contributory negligence." He resigned from the Court shortly thereafter to return to his home in Augusta.[88]

It was claimed that Lamar died from overwork.[89] He was, however, active on the Washington social scene. He belonged "to all the best clubs in Washington," and he attended "many social functions" with Mrs. Lamar. He was an avid golfer, and he and his wife lived in "a comfortable, handsome home on New Hampshire Avenue, where they entertain a great deal...."[90]

Horace H. Lurton
Born February 26, 1844, in Newport, Kentucky; died July 12, 1914; associate justice, 1910–1914 Lurton had served as one of Tennessee's chancellors before winning election to the state supreme court. He briefly served as chief justice of that court before being appointed to the U.S. Court of Appeals for the Sixth Circuit, where he served with then-judge and later Supreme Court justices William Howard Taft and William Rufus Day.

Harold Lurton and Justice John Marshall Harlan became close friends. Harlan was a Union soldier in the Civil War, and Lurton was a Confederate. Once, they were summering together in Murray Bay, and Harlan began talking of some of his experiences in the Civil War. He described a march that he made through Tennessee and Kentucky chasing the Confederate raider John Morgan. As he told of nearly overtaking Morgan and his men near Hartsville, Tennessee, Lurton suddenly reacted: "Harlan, is it possible I am just finding out who it was that tried to shoot me on that never-to-be forgotten day?"

A shocked Harlan answered, "Lurton, do you mean to tell me that you were with Morgan on that raid? Now I know why I did not catch up with him, and I thank God I didn't hit you that day."[91]

Lurton had been held as a Union POW during the Civil War, and when Taft nominated him, it was said he was "the only man appointed to the Court who has served time in prison."[92]

Joseph McKenna

Born August 10, 1843, in Philadelphia, Pennsylvania; died November 21, 1926; associate justice, 1898–1925. McKenna rose from an impoverished beginning to become a district attorney and state legislator in California before winning a seat in the U.S. House of Representatives. He served on the U.S. Court of Appeals for the Ninth Circuit and then as President William McKinley's Attorney General before moving on to the Supreme Court bench.

As a practicing lawyer, Joseph McKenna was noted for sizing up the situation quickly and making all necessary adjustments to his arguments. He was described by contemporaries as being "nimble as a cat" and "never at a loss and never get[ting] rattled." McKenna, however, was not a well-educated man. One biographer noted that "syntax and punctuation were always a problem, and he found it difficult to craft a sentence with precision." As a justice, nevertheless, he authored 659 opinions.[93]

To address concerns that he was unqualified for the Court, McKenna enrolled in classes at Columbia Law School after being confirmed but before taking his seat on the Supreme Court.[94]

By 1921, poor health had taken a toll on McKenna. His mind was largely gone, and he could not be entrusted with even the most straightforward opinions. Still, McKenna refused to retire. After all, he was two years younger than Oliver Wendell Holmes. Moreover, he asserted that "[w]hen a man retires, he disappears and nobody cares for him."[95]

Chief Justice Taft wrote his brother, "I don't know what course to take with respect to him, or what cases to assign him. I had to take back a case from him last Saturday because he would not write it in accordance with the vote of the court." [96]

In one instance, McKenna circulated an opinion, but Taft could not figure out what case it addressed. The chief justice described language in McKenna's opinions as "a fog." "He does not know what he means himself. Certainly, no one else does."[97]

When Taft could not get McKenna to retire, he called the other justices to his home, and they reached an agreement that if there was a 4-4 vote with McKenna as the tie-breaking vote, they would not allow the case to be decided. That practice went on for a couple of years, and a few cases were carried over. Finally, Taft persuaded McKenna to retire in November 1924.[98]

While McKenna still served, Justice Louis Brandeis observed that the "only way of dealing with him is to appoint guardians for him."[99]

James C. McReynolds
Born February 3, 1862, in Elkton, Kentucky; died August 24, 1946; associate justice, 1914–1941. McReynolds served as an assistant to then-U.S. Senator and later Justice Howell E. Jackson before beginning private practice and a

professorship at Vanderbilt University. He served as an assistant attorney general under President Theodore Roosevelt and later as U.S. Attorney General under President Woodrow Wilson. McReynolds became known as one of the "Four Horseman" on the Court for his conservative opposition to the New Deal. Journalist Drew Pearson found his misanthropic and miserly ways to make him the perfect "Scrooge."

Even before he was a member of the Supreme Court, James C. McReynolds freely showed his contempt for its members when they disappointed him. When the Court handed down its opinion in *Standard Oil Co. v. United States*,[100] McReynolds was a special assistant to the Attorney General. He was so disappointed with Chief Justice Edward White's opinion for the Court that he wrote a note to the chief indicating that the opinion was unsatisfactory and hoping that the pending case of *United States v. American Tobacco Co.*,[101] which raised similar antitrust issues, would be better. White grew enraged at the effrontery of McReynolds's *ex parte* letter.[102]

When serving as Attorney General, McReynolds would often reject the candidates for judgeships that were recommended by party leaders and would do so for the most trivial of reasons. It was claimed he rejected one candidate for a judgeship because he had no chin. Two candidates for U.S. Marshal were rejected because they were fat. Colonel Edward House, President Woodrow Wilson's chief of staff, joked that he would like to suggest a candidate for a judgeship but that the man had a mole on the back of his ear, and he was afraid McReynolds would reject him![103]

Outspokenly anti-Semitic, McReynolds entertained an animosity for Justice Louis Brandeis that bordered on the unbelievable. In 1922, he declined Chief Justice William Howard Taft's invitation for the Court to ride a train together to a ceremony in which the justices were participating because Brandeis would be a fellow passenger. He told the chief justice: "I am not always to be found when there is a Hebrew aboard. Therefore, my 'inability' to attend must not surprise you."

He also turned down an invitation to a dinner that would have included Brandeis by saying, "I do not dine with the Orient." If Brandeis spoke in conference, McReynolds would walk out. In 1923, his anti-Semitism caused him to refuse to sit with the Court for its annual picture, and the photograph had to be canceled. He explained, "I have absolutely refused to go through the bore of picture-taking again until there is a change in the Court and maybe not then."[104]

McReynolds's sting was felt by other brethren than Brandeis. Once, Chief Justice Charles Evans Hughes sent a messenger to assure that McReynolds would not be late for court. The messenger was polite and bowed as he passed on the chief justice's request that McReynolds "come at once and put on [his] robe." McReynolds coldly replied, "Tell the Chief Justice that I do not work for him." McReynolds did come to Court, but not for another half hour.[105]

McReynolds also held Chief Justice Harlan Fiske Stone in low regard. Once, Stone commented on how dull a brief had been. McReynolds, for a change, agreed: "The only duller thing I can think of is when you read one of your opinions."[106] In one case, after Stone circulated an opinion, McReynolds responded with a note: "Not one lawyer in a thousand would agree with your reasoning, but it's not important enough for me to dissent."[107]

McReynolds could also be difficult during oral arguments. Once, a lawyer lost track of time and asked the chief justice how much time he had. McReynolds answered first: "Give him ten years."[108]

McReynolds felt that he needed to stay on the Court to save the country from FDR, a man McReynolds called a "crippled jackass." It was only after Roosevelt was elected to his third term that McReynolds concluded the country "deserves no protection" and resigned.[109] After Douglas joined the Court, McReynolds would talk to his younger colleague about the president every day "with great emotion." Among the questions he asked the Roosevelt appointee is: "That man is really mad, is he not?" and "Do you think he'll have to be committed?"[110]

FDR similarly thought little of McReynolds. During one of his evening poker games in 1940, the president introduced a mean and dirty variety of poker that he dubbed "Justice McReynolds."[111]

William H. Moody
Born December 23, 1853, in Newbury, Massachusetts; died July 2, 1917; associate justice, 1906–1910. Moody, who had greatly impressed the Massachusetts bar examiners with both his youth and preparation, served successively as a school board member, city solicitor, city water board member, and U.S. Attorney, during which he successfully prosecuted the notorious Lizzy Borden. He was elected to the U.S. House of Representatives and then served President Theodore Roosevelt as Secretary of the Navy and Attorney General. His judicial career was cut short by a crippling form of arthritis.

Justice William H. Moody fondly recalled that he had sported a campaign badge for Abraham Lincoln during the 1860 election when he was but a boy. The influence was such that he concluded, "From childish impulse, I was then a Republican."[112]

As a justice, Moody kept a box of hard candy by his side, which, according to Justice Oliver Wendell Holmes, he ate "with a sort of methodical persistence."[113]

Mahlon Pitney
Born February 5, 1858, in Morristown, New Jersey; died December 9, 1924; associate justice, 1912–1922. Pitney served two terms in the U.S. House of Representatives before winning election to the New Jersey Senate, quickly becoming its president. His designs on the governor's seat were short-circuited by appointment to the state supreme court and eventual elevation to chancellor, the top judicial position in the state.

Mahlon Pitney was a controversial Supreme Court nominee, having been derided as anti-labor and anti-progressive. He was forced to announce, almost Nixon-like, "I am not an enemy of labor." Pitney also had to overcome the disability of having been accused of writing some anti-union opinions as a New Jersey judge that were actually written by his father, who was also a New Jersey judge.[114]

Pitney received a mixed reception from some of his colleagues on the Supreme Court bench. Justice Oliver Wendell Holmes wrote, "When he first came on the bench, he used to get on my nerves, as he talked too much from the bench and in conference, but he improved in that, and I came to appreciate his great faithfulness to duty, his industry and candor. He had not wings and was not a thunderbolt, but he was a very honest hard-working judge and a useful critic."[115]

Brandeis once observed that Pitney was "much influenced by his experience, and he had had mighty little."[116]

Owen J. Roberts
Born May 2, 1875, in Germantown, Pennsylvania; died May 17, 1955; associate justice, 1930–1945. Roberts won national attention as a special U.S. attorney during the Teapot Dome scandal. Roberts's vote in West Coast Hotel v. Parrish,[117] *to sustain New Deal legislation, even though it preceded the announcement of the court-packing plan, was dubbed "the switch in time that saved nine." Roberts chaired the committee that investigated U.S. preparedness in light of the Japanese attack on Pearl Harbor. After his judicial tenure, he was dean of the University of Pennsylvania's law school.*

The Supreme Court moved into its current building in 1935, but the justices insisted on bringing with them the very different chairs each had sat on in their old quarters inside the Capitol building. Despite the discomfort that the high-seated chair caused Justice Benjamin Cardozo, he insisted on keeping it, saying, "if Justice Holmes sat in this for twenty years, I can sit in it for a while."

During the first term in their new building, Owen Roberts leaned back in his chair only to hear a loud crack as one of the legs broke. He grabbed the bench to keep from going down. That turned out to be the final straw. New chairs were purchased, and the old chairs were sold to a dealer for the magnificent sum of $35.[118]

Justices have long had very clear opinions about proper attire when arguing before the Court, and Roberts was among that number. In the 1930s, formal cutaways remained the proper wear. Once, a youthful red-haired lawyer from Oklahoma argued a case before the Court, wearing a brown suit, white shirt, and colorful tie. Roberts leaned over to Justice Pierce Butler to ask, "Where does the SOB think he is, police court?"[119]

Being a swing vote on a divided Court can exact a price. When Roberts retired in 1945, Stone drafted a letter on behalf of the Court that contained the usual flowery praise for a departing colleague. Convinced that Roberts would use the letter's praises to bolster the Felix Frankfurter forces against the Court's liberals, Justice Hugo Black refused to sign the letter and urged Justice William Douglas to follow suit. Black particularly objected to a sentence that read: "You have made fidelity to principle your guide to decision."

Douglas saw the letter as Frankfurter "looking for trouble" but still called the whole incident "a goddam tempest in a teapot." The result was a statement, with no letter sent by the Court.[120]

Edward T. Sanford

Born July 23, 1865, in Knoxville, Tennessee; died March 8, 1930, · associate justice, 1923–1930. Sanford served as both a special assistant to the U.S. Attorney General and as an assistant attorney general before receiving an appointment to the federal trial bench. Sanford was elevated to the Supreme Court after Chief Justice William Howard Taft lobbied for the Tennessean's nomination.

After graduating from Harvard Law School and serving as one of the founding editors of the Harvard Law Review, Edward Sanford toured Europe. On his return, he sought admission to the Tennessee bar and appeared before Tennessee Supreme Court Justice Horace Lurton (later U.S. Supreme Court associate justice) for his oral bar exam. Lurton asked him just one question based on a case Lurton had recently decided. When Sanford gave a "proper" answer, Lurton said, "Young man, you are splendidly equipped; I am not going to ask you another question."[121]

Sanford was a golfing fanatic. No matter how inundated he was by the press of his docket as a district court judge, he found time to golf. He owned 200 golf clubs.[122]

Sanford voted so often with Chief Justice William Howard Taft that one biographer opined that it was a "fitting irony for the two to die on the same day."[123]

George Sutherland
Born March 15, 1862, in Buckinghamshire, England; died July 18, 1942; associate justice, 1922–1938. Sutherland was a member of the Utah territorial legislature and a state senator before going on to first the U.S. House of Representatives and then the U.S. Senate. His conservatism earned him membership in the Court's anti-New Deal "Four Horsemen."

George Sutherland had wanted to retire well before Franklin Roosevelt proposed packing the Court in order to weaken the influence of conservative justices such as Sutherland. He was having such high blood pressure that he was forced to write most of his opinions while he was lying in bed. However, he would not retire because Oliver Wendell Holmes had done so in 1931 and then faced the reduced retirement pay for justices contained in the 1933 Economy Bill passed by Congress. Sutherland did not want to be in the same situation as Holmes was.[124]

Despite his conservatism, George Sutherland got along well with the Court's liberal wing. Holmes would implore his raconteur colleague, "Sutherland, J., tell us a story." Justice Louis Brandeis was sometimes critical of Sutherland but respected his colleague even though they differed. On one occasion, after reading a circulated Sutherland dissent, wrote back: "My Dear Sutherland: This is perhaps the finest opinion in the history of American constitutional law. Regretfully, I adhere to my error. Brandeis."[125]

Sutherland was, at best, a reluctant photographer's subject. Once, two photographers called upon Sutherland at home, asking if they might shoot his picture. Sutherland reacted angrily, telling the photographers to go and slamming the door shut.

One, however, feigned his departure and hid behind some bushes. The other rang the doorbell again. Sutherland appeared at the door, threateningly holding up a cane. That image was snapped, and newspapers across the nation featured the picture of the angry, cane wielding justice.[126]

Willis Van Devanter

Born April 17, 1859, in Marion, Indiana; died February 8, 1941; associate justice, 1910–1937. After earning his law degree and working for his father's law firm in Cincinnati, Van Devanter set out for Wyoming, where he became city attorney of Cheyenne, a territorial legislator, and chief justice of the territory's court, later its state supreme court. He came to Washington, DC as assistant attorney general in the Interior Department before being appointed to the U.S. Court of Appeals for the Eighth Circuit. While on the Court, he helped draft the Judiciary Act of 1925. As a conservative consistently opposed to the New Deal, he was known as one of the "Four Horsemen."

Justice Willis Van Devanter was not a prolific writer on the Court, penning very few written opinions. In his last decade on the Court, he averaged only three a term. It was said that he suffered from chronic "writer's block," or what Justice George Sutherland called "pen paralysis."

Yet, this man, who has been described as "very remote and reserved" and "tightly disciplined," was able to build a powerful conservative coalition on the Supreme Court and serve as its ideological leader.[127] For his behind-the-scenes contributions to the Court, Chief Justice William Howard Taft termed Van Devanter "far and away the most valuable man in our court."

Even liberal Justice Louis Brandeis admired Van Devanter as a "master of formulas that decide cases without creating precedents."[128]

Van Devanter amazed his colleagues in conference with his ability to summarize a case. Justice William O. Douglas wrote, "If his words had been recorded, they would have made a perfect opinion. Yet Justice Van Devanter's mind froze the moment he picked up a pencil or pen, and therefore, he had the lowest record of any member of the Court in the number of opinions written."[129]

6

The New Deal Court

President Franklin D. Roosevelt's New Deal faced an extremely hostile, conservative Supreme Court, dominated by longtime members, who regularly struck down the new regulatory statutes passed by Congress. A.A. Berle, a member of FDR's Brain Trust, referred to the Court in passing as the "nine old men" in 1933, and the name stuck. A column in a Kentucky newspaper reflected a popular concept when it referred to the Court as "nine old back-number owls (appointed by bygone presidents) who sit on the leafless, fruitless limb of an old dead tree."[1] FDR attempted to overcome the obstacle that the Court posed by proposing in 1937 that up to six additional justices be appointed for each one over the age of 70. The proposal was quickly denounced as a "court-packing plan" and proved unpalatable to the Congress and the public.

Though the votes were taken before the issue was voted on in Congress, the switch of Justice Owen Roberts from a minimum wage opponent in one case to a supporter in another was popularly dubbed "the switch in time that saved nine." FDR's long service in the presidency presented him with the most Supreme Court appointments since President George Washington.

Charles Evans Hughes, Chief Justice (1930–1941), Associate Justice (1910–1916)
Harlan Fiske Stone, Chief Justice (1941–1946), Associate Justice (1925–1941)
Fred Vinson, Chief Justice (1946–1953)

Associate Justices:
Hugo Black (1937–1971)
Harold Burton (1945–1958)
James Byrnes (1941–1942)
Benjamin Cardozo (1932–1938)
Tom Clark (1949–1967)
William O. Douglas (1939–1975)
Felix Frankfurter (1939–1962)
Robert H. Jackson (1941–1954)
Sherman Minton (1949–1956)
Frank Murphy (1940–1949)
Stanley Reed (1938–1957)
Wiley Rutledge (1943–1949)

The Chief Justices

Charles Evans Hughes

Born April 11, 1862, in Glen Falls, N.Y.; died August 27, 1948; associate justice, 1910–1916; chief justice, 1930–1941. Hughes resigned from the Supreme Court to run a close race as the Republican candidate against President Woodrow Wilson. Although President Taft chose Edward White as chief justice over Hughes, the chief justiceship eventually came to Hughes anyway. During that period, he was considered a swing vote fitting between the Court's four conservatives and its liberals. As a result, one wag tagged him as "the man on the flying trapeze" after the popular song. His beard, which earned him the nickname "Whiskers" during his early political career caused Justice Felix Frankfurter to call Hughes "Bushy," though only behind the chief justice's back.

In 1887, Charles Evans Hughes was a young lawyer who decided to take a vacation to Block Island. As he sat in the hotel smoking room, he was approached by a man who asked if he played whist. When Hughes said he did, he was invited to be the fourth hand in a game in the stranger's room. That stranger turned out to be Justice Samuel Miller of the U.S. Supreme Court, and Hughes played cards with him every night of his stay. On the last night of Hughes's stay at the hotel, Miller told him, "Well, Hughes, if you will practice law as well as you play whist, I think you will get along."[2]

Hughes's remarkable memory feats are legendary. Once, when he was Secretary of State, as he was leaving his desk to hold a press conference, an official gave him a three-page memorandum that was ready to be announced. Hughes walked to the conference room while reading the announcement, then placed it in his pocket and made the announcement from memory. When the stenographic record of the conference was compared with the memorandum, it was found that Hughes had recited its contents perfectly, save for one insignificant word.[3]

Hughes usually came to conference with few notes, yet aided by his exceptional memory, he succinctly stated all the issues in a case, leaving little else to be said. Some resented this, especially his successor as chief justice, Harlan Fiske Stone. Felix Frankfurter later said that Hughes as chief justice conducted the Court the way Toscanini conducted an orchestra.[4]

Hughes was frequently discussed as a presidential candidate on the Republican ticket. Indeed, ultimately, he resigned from the Court to run for President in 1916 and was narrowly defeated by the incumbent, Woodrow Wilson. Wilson was sufficiently concerned about the Hughes threat before the then-justice became a candidate that Wilson used several emissaries to suggest that Hughes should stay on the bench and would be rewarded with the center seat.

Secretary of the Interior Franklin K. Lane once took Hughes aside at a dinner party and told him that if he stayed on the Court, he would be appointed chief justice. After the election, Lane approached Hughes and said, "You know what I told you and what might have been."

Still, shortly before the Republican National Convention, Chief Justice Edward White came to Hughes's home and told him, "Before you decide on what course you will take, I feel that you should know that I am going to retire and that if you do not resign, you will succeed me."

Hughes exclaimed, "Why, President Wilson would never appoint me chief justice!"

"Well," answered White, "he wouldn't appoint anyone else, as I happen to know."[5]

Hughes resigned from his first appointment to the Court to mount an ultimately futile electoral challenge against President Wilson. Still, in a precursor to the famous "Dewey Defeats Truman" headline, Hughes retired the evening of the election believing he had won. Long after Hughes was asleep, a reporter attempted to talk to him, but a Hughes aide answered insistently with, "The president cannot be disturbed."

"Well," the reporter replied, "when he wakes up, just tell him that he isn't president."[6]

Back in private practice after his presidential race, Hughes was in Washington to argue a case before the Court, but the justices did not reach the matter during the first session. After Court adjourned, Hughes started walking down the corridor, and, at the same time, the justices began to file across the hall from the old court chamber to the robing room. Chief Justice William Howard Taft rushed over to Hughes and slapped him on the shoulder: "Hughes, my boy, I am delighted to see you."

Hughes reacted coolly, responding, "Mr. Chief Justice, I am honored to see you."

An attorney with Hughes asked him later why he had treated Taft so coldly. Hughes replied, "I did it intentionally as I intend to win my cases on their merits and not through friendship with the judges."[7]

Hughes was an effective advocate before the courts. During one 28-month period, he argued 25 cases before the Supreme Court and other cases before lower federal and state courts. Benjamin Cardozo, then on the New York Court of Appeals, said that he "always reserved judgment for twenty-four hours in any case argued by Hughes to avoid being carried away by the force of his personality and intellect."[8]

For a few days after Hughes was appointed chief justice, his son still served as solicitor general, the office that presents the federal government's arguments before the Supreme Court. Hughes went to his son's home for dinner during that period and greeted both his son and his son's wife with a kiss.

"Well," said Hughes, "I suppose this is the first time the Chief Justice ever kissed the Solicitor General, and certainly, it is the first time the Chief Justice ever kissed the Solicitor General's wife."[9]

As chief justice, Hughes received more fan mail than any official other than the President and Senator Huey Long. Once, a fan simply drew a picture of Hughes's famous whiskers on a postcard without the name or address, and it was delivered correctly![10]

When Hughes was chief justice, Holmes continued his habit of taking catnaps on the bench. Once, a man in the front row of the Court fell asleep, and Hughes sent a page to wake the man up. He then whispered to Holmes, "We can't have that. Only Justices are allowed to sleep in this courtroom."[11]

It was once the practice of the Court to dispense with the reply argument if the first advocate had failed to convince the justices that his argument had merit. In one instance, after hearing the first argument, Hughes said, "The Court does not care to hear further argument."

Somehow missing this statement, the respondent stepped to the lectern and began to speak to the Court. Hughes repeated himself, this time somewhat louder. Counsel plodded ahead, also somewhat louder.

Hughes then asked the losing attorney, "Won't you please tell counsel that the Court does not care to hear further argument?"

Whereupon, the petitioner's counsel loudly told opposing counsel, "They say they would rather give you the case than listen to you."[12]

On January 20, 1941, Hughes administered the oath to Roosevelt for a third time. Hughes later confessed to Roosevelt that, "I had an impish desire to break the solemnity of the occasion by remarking, 'Franklin, don't you think this is getting to be a trifle monotonous.'"[13]

Harlan Fiske Stone

Born October 11, 1872, in Chesterfield, New Hampshire; died April 22, 1946; associate justice, 1925–1941; chief justice, 1941–1946. Stone was dean of Columbia Law School, where one of his students, William O. Douglas, was to later join him as a member of the U.S. Supreme Court. He was tapped for U.S. Attorney General by President Calvin Coolidge to restore the Justice Department's reputation after the Teapot Dome and related scandals. Stone was the first Supreme Court nominee to testify at his confirmation hearing before the Senate Judiciary Committee. Stone also holds the distinction of being the only justice to have gone from junior justice to senior justice and then be elevated to chief justice, thereby occupying each of the seats behind the bench. To his neighbors, Stone was known as "Doc."

When Harlan Fiske Stone received word that Amherst College would admit him, Stone was pitching horse manure on his parents' farm. He jumped for joy, throwing his pitchfork down, never to lift one again. He later said, "Had I realized what I'd be doing later in my career, I'd have hung on to that pitchfork."[14]

Stone was awed by the new marble temple that was to house the Supreme Court. On one occasion, he remarked, "Whenever I look at that building, I feel that the justices should ride to work on elephants."[15] He went on to say that upon entering the building, he felt like a beetle crawling into the Temple of Karnak.[16] He wrote his sons, "It is a very grand affair, but I confess that I returned from my visit with a feeling akin to dismay. The place is almost bombastically pretentious, and thus, it seems to me wholly inappropriate for a quiet group of old boys such as the Supreme Court of the United States."[17]

When Stone became chief justice, he learned how difficult the position could be as his colleagues were "so busy disagreeing with each other." At the end of the 1942 term, he wrote, "I have had much difficulty in herding my collection of fleas."[18]

To help the conviviality of conference, Stone would bring a variety of cheeses to the Court. During one case discussion, Frankfurter challenged Stone's lengthy review of a case: "I suppose you know more than those who drafted the Constitution."
Stone responded, "I know some things better than those who drafted the Constitution."
Frankfurter conceded that point: "Yes, on wine and cheese."[19]

Stone's penmanship was so bad that the justices joked that if a fly was dipped in ink and walked across a page, one had a fair replica of his handwriting.[20]

Stone beamed about his accomplished mathematician son, Marshall. At a dinner at his home, Stone brandished a copy of his son's book, *Linear Transformation and Helbert Space and Their Applications to Analysis*, for his guests to see. He said, "I am so proud because there's not a sentence in this book I can understand."[21]

Fred Vinson

Born January 22, 1890, in Louisa, Kentucky; died September 8, 1953; chief justice, 1946–1953. Vinson served successively as city attorney, district attorney, and a Member of Congress. He joined the U.S. Court of Appeals for the District of Columbia but resigned to direct President Franklin Roosevelt's economic stabilization program. He then became the Federal Loan Administrator and Director of War Mobilization and Reconversion, before becoming President Harry Truman's Secretary of the Treasury. Vinson was appointed chief justice of a divided Court that contained some bitter rivalries. For his pro-Establishment stands, Vinson was known as the "great oak."

Chief Justice Fred Vinson was fond of telling people that he "had been born in jail." His father was a jailer who lived in a home attached to the jail, which is where Vinson was born.[22]

At the end of his first day at the Court, Vinson summoned his secretary to "Send for the Court car" since he had a formal dinner to attend. Vinson had had a car available to him as Secretary of the Treasury and expected the chief justice would certainly command a similar privilege.

William Douglas, curious to see what would transpire, accompanied Vinson down to the garage. After a considerable wait, a rusty Ford pickup roared to a halt before them.

"What's this?" Vinson asked.

"The Court car," Douglas explained.

Embarrassed, Vinson nonetheless stepped into the pickup and zipped off to his engagement.[23]

Justice Felix Frankfurter displayed great expertise in getting under Vinson's skin. In conference, Frankfurter once criticized Vinson's views rather bluntly and personally. Vinson shot up from his chair, brandishing his fist and shouting, 'No son of a bitch can ever say that to Fred Vinson!"[24]

Although Vinson had an impressive career prior to becoming chief justice, he was looked down upon by his colleagues on the Court as having a second-rate mind. Justice Stanley Reed, one of the least impressive of President Franklin Roosevelt's appointees, told Frankfurter that Vinson is "just like me, except that he is less well-educated."

Frankfurter described Vinson as "confident and easy-going and sure and shallow...he seems to me to have the confident air of a man who does not see the complexities of problems and blithely hits the obvious points."[25]

Vinson was not inclined to overrule *Plessy v. Ferguson*,[26] the Court's separate-but-equal decision, when *Brown v. Board of Education*[27] first came before the Court. Frankfurter worked strenuously and effectively in getting the case held over for re-argument the following term. When Frankfurter learned that Vinson had died before the case could be heard again, he uncharitably said, "This is the first indication that I have ever had that there is a God."[28]

The Associate Justices

Hugo Black
Born February 27, 1886, in Harlan, Alabama; died September 25, 1971; associate justice, 1937–1971. Black was a crusading U.S. Senator before being rewarded for his support of President Franklin D. Roosevelt's ill-fated "court packing" plan with the first opening on the Supreme Court. He was an uncompromising advocate of First Amendment absolutism and the incorporation of the Bill of Rights by virtue of the passage of the Fourteenth Amendment.

As a successful plaintiff's lawyer, Hugo Black gained a reputation of being able to sway any Alabama jury. Birmingham's lawyers so feared his tactics before a jury that they joked, "If you don't watch out, Hugo will get in the jury box with you every time."[29]

Once, after he had won a verdict for $20,000, his co-counsel, who had seen Black use this tactic successfully, asked, "How come you didn't cry [to win the jury's sympathy]?"

He answered, "Hugo Black doesn't cry for less than $25,000."[30]

Campaigning for the Democratic nomination for Senate, Black got lost on the way to Andalusia in southern Alabama. He stopped a young boy for directions, "Andalusia or Montgomery – which way is which?"

When the boy didn't know, Black said, "You don't know much, do you?"

"No," replied the boy. "But I ain't lost."[31]

Black was a partisan with a sharp wit. When he stood for reelection to the Senate, he was challenged in the primary by a "wet" who accused Black of softening his prohibitionist stand simply to get votes. Speaking in his opponent's hometown, Black simply responded, "I have no patience with a man who will ride into office on the dry issue and proceed to try to keep the state dry by drinking up all the liquor in existence."[32]

On another occasion, he almost soiled his shoes on a patch of manure.

"I almost stepped on the Republican platform," he informed his audience.[33]

Black was a controversial Supreme Court nominee, not the least because he had joined the Ku Klux Klan when he first sought office in Alabama. The joke in Washington was: "Hugo won't have to buy a robe; he can dye his white one black."[34]

Black believed justices should generally not speak to the press. When a reporter pressed him for comment once, Black responded that a friend had advised him to only talk to the press about Chinese art.

"Mr. Justice," the reporter inquired, "what do you know about Chinese art?"

Black responded, "Not a thing."[35]

After the Court ruled against President Harry Truman in the *Steel Seizure Case*,[36] Black planned a party for the president and the justices at his Alexandria home to help clear the air. Truman proved somewhat distant from his old friend Black at first, but warmed up after indulging in some of the food and drink.

"Hugo," he said, "I don't much care for your law, but, by golly, this bourbon is good."[37]

Frankfurter's orations in conference tried Black's patience. In March 1958, Black returned from conference early and prepared to leave for the weekend.

"Felix kept on talking and talking," Black told his secretary. "So, I told them that if he kept on, I'm just going to leave. It is still light outside, and I'm going to play tennis. See you on Monday."[38]

On one occasion Black attended the funeral of an important Washington mover and shaker that he had always detested. When a judge arrived in the middle of the service and asked Black what was happening, the wry justice reported, "They've just opened for the defense."[39]

Black remained a partisan Democrat all his life. He told one law clerk, "Those Republicans will ruin us all." He conceded that Justice John Harlan was "one of the smartest, nicest guys who ever lived; I love him." Still, Black noted, "He's a Republican. You know, that's [Justice] Potter [Stewart]'s problem, too."[40]

Black said his absolutist views on the First Amendment brought interesting mail: "Why, right after I really understood that 'no law' means no law and announced it, a certain critic of mine wrote me a letter and said that he had been wanting to express his opinion of me for a long time, but had been afraid of the libel laws. 'Now,' he said, 'I am at last free under your interpretation of the First Amendment to express my precise opinion of you. Mr. Justice, you are a son of a bitch.'"[41]

Black chose not to join his brethren in the Court's theater when the Court had taken it upon itself to determine whether the movies prosecuted as obscene had "redeeming social value." He said he doubted that men of the age of the justices knew much about sex. He added that if the justices wanted to watch dirty movies, they should go downtown and pay the price of admission just like everyone else.[42]

At the height of protests against the Vietnam War, the Supreme Court decided *Tinker v. Des Moines Independent Community School District*,[43] a major free-speech case that recognized the non-disruptive First Amendment rights of public school students who had worn black armbands to signify their opposition to that war. Justice Abe Fortas, who had a tense relationship with Black, wrote the Court's opinion. While Black was a free-speech absolutist, he disagreed with his brethren that conduct could be counted as protected speech. Black dissented in *Tinker*, arguing that wearing an armband was not speech.

Interestingly, shortly after oral argument in the case, Sterling Black, Jr., Hugo's grandson, was suspended from high school for circulating an underground newspaper. Black was angered by Sterling Jr.'s behavior and by his son, Sterling, who was then head of the New Mexico ACLU and planned to challenge the suspension in court. Black threatened, "If the case ever reaches the Court, I will disqualify myself not only in it but in every other case in which the ACLU takes any part, no matter how small."[44]

After Justice Abe Fortas was forced to resign because of a retainer he accepted from a foundation, it became known that Douglas accepted an expense account from the Parvin Foundation, which had ties to gambling interests. When an impeachment movement began against Douglas, some Southerners asked Hugo Black, Jr. to give a message to his father that they wanted Douglas off the Court.

The older Black responded with support for his old friend even though they had drifted apart over the last few years: "I have known Bill Douglas for thirty years. He's never knowingly done any improper, unethical, or corrupt thing. Tell his detractors that, in spite of my age, I think I have one trial left in me. Tell them that if they move against Bill Douglas, I'll resign from the Court and represent him. It will be the biggest, most important case I ever tried."[45]

Harold Burton
Born June 22, 1888, in Jamaica Plain, Massachusetts, died October 28, 1964; associate justice, 1945–1958. Burton's career took him from private practice to the Ohio legislature, to city law director and later mayor of Cleveland, and to the U.S. Senate. Burton's successful anti-corruption, anti-crime campaign for mayor of Cleveland earned him the nickname the "Boy Scout Mayor."

Today Harold Burton is probably best-known for his brief service in the Senate. He had been an early supporter of the United Nations and, with Senator Lister Hill, had sponsored the Hill-Burton Hospital Construction Act that provided millions of dollars in federal support for hospitals. Burton found the transition to the Court difficult, describing the move as going from "a circus to a monastery."[46]

Burton was deeply respectful of the Supreme Court. He would not enter the building without first doffing his hat. His manners were such that Chief Justice William Rehnquist, who served as a law clerk for Justice Robert Jackson during Burton's tenure, compared Burton to a "supremely cultured English butler one might see in a movie."[47]

In one of his frequent unkind moments, Justice Felix Frankfurter wrote of Burton that "one has an easy and inviting access to his mind. The difficulty is what one finds when one is welcomed to enter it."[48]

James F. Byrnes
Born May 2, 1882, in Charleston, South Carolina; died April 9, 1972; associate justice, 1941–1942. Byrnes served as a congressman and senator before being named to the Court by President Franklin D. Roosevelt. He served only one term, tapped by the president to run first the economic stabilization program

and then the War Mobilization Board. He served President Harry Truman as Secretary of State before quitting in a disagreement with the president to return home to South Carolina, where he was elected governor. In the FDR administration, Byrne's importance was such that he became known as the "assistant president."

James Byrnes was skeptical of the tradition of justices shaking hands before going on the bench but became convinced that it would be a salutary custom. Still, he said, "There were times when it reminded me of the usual instruction of the referee in the prize ring, 'Shake hands, go to your corner and come out fighting.'"[49]

In hosting a dinner at the Governor's Mansion, Byrnes announced to the guests that they would be enjoying the fare of a new cook. Because it was well-known that Byrnes brought inmates from a local prison to staff his kitchen, one guest inquired about the cook's crime. Byrnes could not resist the straight line and replied, "Poisoning his wife."[50]

Civil rights became the issue that caused Byrnes to turn his back on the Democratic party despite a lifelong allegiance. He conspired with fellow Southern governors to resist the *Brown* decision and provided the ballast to elect segregationist Strom Thurmond to the Senate as a write-in candidate after the Democrats rejected Thurmond as their standard bearer in 1954 in retaliation for his defection to the "Dixiecrats."

Byrnes endorsed Virginia Senator Harry Byrd as an independent candidate for president in 1956 after announcing that Democrat Adlai Stevenson was too committed to civil rights and President Dwight Eisenhower could not be forgiven for appointing Chief Justice Earl Warren, the author of *Brown*. When Thurmond later changed his party affiliation to Republican, he visited Byrnes to break the news to the then 82-year-old former justice and former governor.

Thurmond was unsure how Byrnes would react and feared the revelation went badly when Byrnes shouted out to his wife with a pained expression, "Maude! Maude! Bring me a drink!" Byrnes, however, was joking as he endorsed the party switch.[51]

Benjamin Cardozo
Born May 24, 1870, in New York, New York; died July 9, 1938; associate justice, 1932–1938. Cardozo achieved extraordinary fame as chief judge of the New York Court of Appeals, the state's highest court. For that reason, he was almost unanimously recommended to President Herbert Hoover for elevation to the U.S. Supreme Court. Solicitor General Charles Evans Hughes, Jr. said Cardozo was "a walking encyclopedia of the law." One reporter in Washington dubbed the justice "the Hermit Philosopher."

Benjamin Cardozo ran for the New York trial court, called the Supreme Court, on an anti-Tammany Hall ticket. He won by a narrow margin and credited his victory to the "support of Italian-Americans who voted for me on the supposition that since my last name ended with an 'o' I was one of their race."[52]

Cardozo had such a phenomenal memory that when he was on the New York Court of Appeals, his colleagues would pretend they were shocked if he could not remember the citation of a case that he or a colleague brought up during oral argument.[53] On one occasion, Cardozo recalled only the volume number of the case, causing one of his colleagues to exclaim, "By God, he's forgotten the page!"[54]

Cardozo never worried about his clothing not matching. His wardrobe consisted of 15 identical black suits.[55]

To take a break from the work of the Court, several justices went for an outing on a boat. When Cardozo became seasick, one of his brethren asked him if there was anything he could do. "Yes," Cardozo glibly answered, "overrule the motion."[56]

Cardozo never quite got used to the formalities of the Court. Often, the only opportunity for the justices to chat casually was in the communal toilets next to the Court's Capitol chamber. In the new building, Cardozo lamented: "Now that we have private washrooms, there is no pleasure even in urination anymore."[57]

Cardozo was famous for the breadth of his learning, but when it came to popular culture, he definitely had a gap. Overhearing the name mentioned in a conversation, he asked, "But who is Greta Garbo?"[58]

Hughes visited Cardozo when he was dying. Cardozo told him, "They tell me I am going to get well, but I file a dissenting opinion."[59]

Tom Clark

Born September 23, 1899, in Dallas, Texas; died June 13, 1977; associate justice, 1949–1967. Clark served in a variety of capacities in the Justice Department before President Harry Truman made him the attorney general. He was appointed to the Court, despite charges of cronyism, and confirmed by a 73-8 vote. He retired from the Court so that President Lyndon Johnson could appoint his son, Ramsey, attorney general.

President Harry Truman regretted appointing Tom Clark to the Supreme Court. The former president told biographer Merle Miller that his biggest mistake as President was putting that "damn fool from Texas" on the Court.[60]

Clark, in true Supreme Court tradition, disagreed with himself when he previously served in a presidential administration. In the *Steel Seizure Case*,[61] Clark asserted that the president had no authority to seize the steel industry in order to maintain war production in light of a workers' strike. As Truman's attorney general, however, Clark had prepared the memo that Truman had used to justify the seizure.[62]

Clark was never known for risqué behavior, but the Justice Department would have been surprised at Clark's behavior on the bench in one case. The department had sent the justices a stack of obscene material to bolster its argument in *Roth v. United States*.[63] Postmaster General Arthur Summerfield had urged the department to present the Court with the allegedly obscene material. What no one had expected is that Clark, along with Justice William Douglas, kept the material circulating among the brethren during the argument.[64]

William O. Douglas

Born October 16, 1898, in Maine, Minnesota; died January 19, 1980; associate justice, 1939–1975. Douglas taught at Columbia and Yale law schools before being tapped as a member and later chair of the Securities and Exchange Commission. Just as he was about to return to academe as dean of Yale Law School, President Franklin D. Roosevelt named Douglas to the seat of retiring Justice Louis D. Brandeis. Known for his extremely liberal views on the Court, Douglas surprised opponents to his nomination, who had labeled him an extreme conservative who danced to Wall Street's tune. As a child, Douglas was nicknamed "Treasure" by his mother. In later life, some of his friends called him "Spence" for his resemblance to actor Spencer Tracy, who was an acquaintance of Douglas's. His outlandish behavior and extreme views also earned him the nickname "Wild Bill."

The name of his birthplace caused Justice William O. Douglas some amusing moments from time to time. He once told of returning from overseas at four in the morning and being confronted by an immigration officer, who tested him by asking where he was born.

"Maine, Minnesota," Douglas answered.

"Make up your mind, buddy," the official replied. "Them are two different states."[65]

Douglas probably thought himself the luckiest boy in the world when he landed a job in an ice cream factory. Instead, it cured him of his love for ice cream. He reported that the men who mixed the ingredients at the plant chewed tobacco, the juice of which they would discharge into the vat of ice cream. Their constant refrain: "That should beef it up a bit."[66]

As a top graduate of an Ivy League law school, Douglas decided to try his luck with the large New York law firms on Wall Street rather than return to Washington. The rounds eventually brought him to John Foster Dulles, later Secretary of State. Dulles, Douglas reported, "made it appear that the greatest favor he could do a young lawyer was to hire him." Pompous and absolutist in his views, Dulles was not the kind of employer Douglas was seeking. When Dulles helped the young Douglas on with his coat at the end of the interview, Douglas decided to make a statement: he tipped his haughty interviewer a quarter.[67]

Douglas and fellow Yale law professor Thurman Arnold worked with the National Commission on Law Observance and Enforcement to produce a 14-volume report. They contributed the section of the report detailing crime statistics. Both contributors believed the report was significant and contained important empirical information. Each ordered 100 copies, expecting it to be in considerable demand. Thirty years later, Douglas told Arnold that he had counted his copies and still retained 99.

Arnold was amazed: "Ninety-nine? You must have given one away, I still have my original hundred."[68]

Douglas's mother was a committed Republican until a Democrat named her son to the Supreme Court. She traveled to Washington, DC to watch her son take the oath of office. At lunch that day, she said, "You know, I think this man Roosevelt has got something to him after all."[69]

Not everyone greeted the Douglas nomination as enthusiastically as his mother did. His hometown newspaper, the *Yakima Daily Republic*, headlined their editorial, "Yakima Not to Blame."[70]

Thurman Arnold used to like to describe the investiture ceremony of his good friend Douglas at the Supreme Court this way: "He no sooner reached the Bench than a man jumped up and shouted, 'God save the United States and this Honorable Court.'"[71]

One day, Douglas went to a Washington Senators baseball game with Jerome Frank, his successor as chair of the Securities and Exchange Commission (SEC). During the game, a runner was called out at first base. The player protested loudly, but the umpire merely folded his arms and turned his back on the runner. Douglas exclaimed, "That is what we call giving them a fair hearing at the SEC."[72]

After an initial period when Douglas looked upon Felix Frankfurter as a mentor, the two became estranged. As a result, Douglas made special efforts to get under Frankfurter's skin. Douglas said he once told Felix that Hugo [Black, who also feuded with Frankfurter] was the nutcracker and he, Felix, was the nut. "After Hugo got finished with him, I just picked up the pieces. Felix never thought this was very funny. Again, once after I read the story in the paper that Felix and I weren't speaking I came into conference and offered to shake his hand. Felix just stood there. I said, 'you'll have to hurry, Felix, I am a busy man.' He didn't think that was funny either."[73]

In one case, Frankfurter browbeat an advocate by asking over and over for "one case that stands for that proposition!" Douglas finally shortened the exchange by declaring, "Don't bother to send Justice Frankfurter the list he wants; I'll be happy to do it myself."[74]

In *Hazel-Atlas Co. v. Hartford-Empire Co.*,[75] the case turned on an affidavit. Douglas asked the lawyer before them, "Who prepared the affidavit?"
The lawyer immediately fainted, striking his head against the table as he sunk to the floor.
Court reconvened after the man regained consciousness. He finally replied, "I drafted the affidavit."[76]

In dinner remarks following a singing quartet, Douglas opined that if he could sing like the tenor that proceeded his speech, he would resign the Court in favor of a musical career. Over the following weeks, Douglas reported he received "several hundred letters" proffering free singing lessons.[77]

Joining an American Bar Association breakfast meeting, Douglas was unexpectedly asked to say grace. He froze for a moment, then recalled something his mother had said at breakfast to her sons and made that the prayer he gave the legal group: "Easy on the butter, boys, it's 10 cents a pound!"[78]

In the 1950s, the FBI, with the approval of J. Edgar Hoover and Attorney General Herbert Brownell, monitored the activities of Justice Hugo Black and Douglas, in part, because of their liberal First Amendment views. The FBI seriously entertained the view that Douglas was either a Communist dupe or a spy who controlled a communist ring of left-wing law clerks.[79]

Douglas, who harbored presidential ambitions and had been considered by President Franklin Roosevelt as a possible running mate instead of Harry Truman, was offered the vice-presidential nomination by President Truman. Douglas declined, stating that he would rather stay on the Court. He told his friends, however, that he did not want to be a number two man to a number two man.[80]

Douglas could be tough on his law clerks. He sent angry notes to those who were "wasting" their time by watching the argument in a case. He believed they should be at work instead. He "fired" law clerks with alacrity, even though he permitted them to resume their duties within days. Some have called a clerkship with Douglas the equivalent of a year-long boot camp.[81]

To get around Douglas's thinking that clerks should be working and not wasting time at oral argument, his clerks figured out that standing behind a certain pillar along the side of the courtroom would prevent their boss from seeing them. As a result of this use of that marble column, it became known as the "Douglas pillar."[82]

Douglas's one-time deep admiration for Felix Frankfurter turned into a rivalry that became pure animosity. When Frankfurter began to lecture an advocate before the Court at some length, Douglas could not resist passing a note to Justice Frank Murphy: "Why in hell don't you choke that torrent on your right? We shouldn't carry free speech too far."

At times, Douglas would attempt to short-circuit a Frankfurter performance by jumping in to answer a question his rival would pose for the lawyer in the case. After Douglas had done this several times on one occasion, Frankfurter said to the lawyer, "I thought you were arguing this case." The embattled lawyer replied, "I am, but I can use all the help I can get."

Finally, Douglas relished infuriating Frankfurter when someone ill-prepared and perhaps less-than-competent appeared before the Court to argue a case by sending Frankfurter a note that said, "I understand this chap led your class at Harvard Law School," or "Rumor has it that this lawyer got the highest grade at Harvard Law School you ever awarded a student."[83]

Douglas would, to use his words, "drive Felix Frankfurter crazy" in conference by following one of the former professor's lectures with a statement along the lines of: "When I came into this conference, I agreed with the conclusion that Felix has just announced, but he's just talked me out of it."[84]

Douglas was fond of an old hat, which he tended to wear on his frequent trips into the backwoods. The hat "had been sat on, slept on, and stepped on," according to Douglas. One friend had quipped, "If I should ever see this man's hat in a cow pasture, I'd step over it."

On one trip with a friend, Jim Bowmer, Douglas stopped into a coffee shop in the village of Frijole in westernmost Texas. Jim spotted a local justice of the peace, Noel Kincaid, and introduced the disheveled, hat-wearing figure beside him as "Justice Douglas."

"Justice Douglas?" Kincaid said questioningly. "I've been here thirty years, and I'd have sworn I knew every goldarn justice of the peace in these parts."[85]

Douglas valued his time away from the Court and hid away from it all at a telephone-free cabin he had in the Washington woods. In August 1970, two ACLU lawyers trekked into the woods to seek an injunction from the justice, only to discover that he had lit out to the mountains. With the help of a forest ranger airplane that located the justice's camp, the professionally attired lawyers hiked six miles to reach Douglas. They argued in favor of their injunction, but Douglas wanted time to consider their petition. He pointed to a tree stump, where he said they would find his decision if they returned at noon the following day. The attorneys left, with only one of them having the stamina to make the trip again the following day. Douglas had broken camp and moved on, but he left a piece of paper on the designated tree stump – turning down their request.[86]

Douglas liked to get under the collars of his ideological opponents. At conference, when Chief Justice Warren Burger spoke for some time on why he was voting to uphold the lower court's decision, Douglas replied, "Chief, for the reasons you have so well expressed, I vote to reverse."[87]

In spite of a debilitating stroke, Douglas was reluctant to resign from the Court. Burger said, "Bill [Douglas] is like an old firehouse dog, too old to run along with the trucks, but his ears prick up just the same."[88]

Felix Frankfurter

Born November 15, 1882, in Vienna, Austria; died February 21, 1965; associate justice, 1939–1962. Early in his legal career, Frankfurter was an assistant to the U.S. attorney in Manhattan and a lawyer in the William Howard Taft and Woodrow Wilson administrations. He was one of the founders of the New Republic *magazine. Described by Justice Louis Brandeis, with whom he worked on progressive causes, as the "most useful lawyer in America," Frankfurter went from being an activist Harvard law professor to an outspoken advocate of judicial restraint once he was named to the bench.*

Felix Frankfurter and his family emigrated to the United States when the future justice was 12 years old. Living on the Lower East Side of New York City, the Vienna-born Frankfurter began the process of learning English slowly. One day he came home and told his parents, "This man Laundry must be a very rich man because he has so many stores."[89]

Frankfurter later went to work in the War Department for Secretary Henry Stimson. Stimson's successor, Lindley Garrison, found Frankfurter less useful and complained about the assistance given him by the young lawyer: "Every time Mac [Attorney General and later Justice James McReynolds] or I ask this fellow a question of law ... instead of getting an answer of what the law is, we usually get about 65 pages of what the law ought to be."[90]

Frankfurter began his teaching career at Harvard Law School in 1914. He taught a class called "Public Utilities." Although intended to cover regulatory law, it was an entertaining romp through Frankfurter's personal opinions on all matters, trivial and important, as Justice Harry Blackmun, who had been one of Frankfurter's students, recalled.

Another of his students, Francis Plimpton, caught the flavor of the course in a bit of doggerel he composed:

> You learn no law in Public U
> That is its fascination

> But Felix gives a point of view
> And pleasant conversation.[91]

When Frankfurter was nominated to the Court, it was estimated that he had placed about 125 former students in key positions in government.[92] His acolytes were called Felix's "Happy Hot Dogs."[93]

In oral argument defending Oregon's ten-hour maximum workday law, Frankfurter was set upon by a hostile Justice McReynolds.

"Ten hours! Ten hours! Ten! Why not four?" McReynolds asked.

"Your honor," Frankfurter said after a pregnant pause, "if by chance I may make such a hypothesis: if your physician should find that you're eating too much meat, it isn't necessary for him to urge you to become a vegetarian."

"Good for you!" shouted Justice Oliver Wendell Holmes.

Frankfurter savored the exchange and the congratulatory remark by Holmes even more than the eventual narrow court ruling in his favor.[94]

Frankfurter's considerable verbal skills caused him to dominate most conversations. His wife, Marion, opined that Felix only had two faults. For one, "he always got off the subject." If that were not enough, "he always got back onto it."[95]

Frankfurter must have cut quite the image for his first Supreme Court conference, showing up in an alpaca coat and slacks. He was so embarrassed to discover his brethren in suits that he made a mad dash home at lunch so that he would be more appropriately attired for the afternoon. When he returned to the conference room, he found Chief Justice Charles Evans Hughes in an alpaca coat, having made a similar quick change to put the new justice at ease.[96]

In 1939, the Supreme Court heard argument in *Nurbo Co. v. Bethlehem Shipbuilding Corp.*,[97] Frankfurter was at his most professorial, peppering the respondent's counsel with complex questions that were largely beyond the ken of his brethren on the bench, let alone the attorney before him. McReynolds was so upset with his young colleague's questions that he left the bench muttering something under his breath. Upon his departure, Justice Hugo Black leaned over to Frankfurter and said, "now that you have driven McReynolds from the bench, you have finally justified the President's appointment of you."[98]

Brandeis donated his papers to the University of Louisville. Shortly after Brandeis died in 1941, Frankfurter is said to have shown up at the University, stormed into the library, obtained the file that had his correspondence with Brandeis, took almost everything out of his file, and walked out with the papers after telling the librarian, "These are my papers, and I'm taking them back."[99]

When importuned to preside at a friend's wedding, Frankfurter demurred. He explained that a U.S. Supreme Court justice had no jurisdiction over marriage because it was not considered a federal offense.[100]

In announcing the Court's decision in one case, Frankfurter elaborated at some length about the reasons for the decision, going much further than the opinion he wrote. As the justices left the courtroom, Chief Justice Harlan Fiske Stone took him aside and said, "By God, Felix, if you had put all that stuff in the opinion, never in my life would I have agreed to it."[101]

Frankfurter knew he was in a battle for philosophical primacy with some of his colleagues. Frankfurter had expected to be the Court's intellectual leader but came up against an unexpected rival in Hugo Black. He took the competition seriously and once warned a law clerk, "This is a war we're fighting! Don't you understand? A War!"[102]

He labeled his ideological foes, Black, along with William O. Douglas, Frank Murphy, and Wiley Rutledge, "the Axis," the worst designation he could muster during World War II.[103] Murphy, who had once greatly admired Frankfurter, began referring to his scholarship as "elegant bunk."[104]

Seeking allies on the Court, Frankfurter lobbied hard for Judge Learned Hand's appointment to the high bench when Justice James Byrnes resigned. Realizing that it was best to do it by indirection, he used various emissaries to approach President Roosevelt. The subterfuge did not work.

At a poker game, FDR teased Justice William Douglas, "Aren't you curious as to the appointee?"

"I'm bursting with curiosity, Mr. President," Douglas responded.

"Then ask me."

"No, I'll not ask you that question," said Douglas, believing it overstepped the bounds of propriety. "But I will ask you who is not going to be appointed."

"That's a good question," said the president, "and I'll answer it. Learned Hand is not going to be appointed."

"You are passing by a fine man, Mr. President."

"Perhaps so," said FDR. "But this time, Felix overplayed his hand. Do you know how many people asked me today to name Learned Hand? Twenty, and every one a messenger from Felix Frankfurter. And by golly, I won't do it."

Instead, Wiley Rutledge was appointed.[105]

Black dissented in *Adamson v. California*[106] and argued that the Fourteenth Amendment's due process clause made the first eight amendments to the Constitution apply to the states, a position that is nearly identical to the Court's current position. It was a viewpoint with which Frankfurter strongly disagreed. After Black finished his dissent, he asked one of his law clerks, Louis Oberdorfer, later a respected federal judge, to deliver it to Frankfurter. Oberdorfer handed the dissent to Frankfurter, who asked him to stay while he read it. After reading the dissent, Frankfurter threw the dissent across his desk at Oberdorfer and scattered the pages on the floor. He dismissed Oberdorfer, a Yale graduate, saying, "At Yale they call this scholarship?" Frankfurter, of course, had been a professor of law at Harvard.[107]

Although Frankfurter was the first justice to appoint an African American as his law clerk, he was unwilling to appoint a woman. In 1960, a woman applied for a clerkship with Frankfurter, and he rejected the application, saying that he was not ready to hire a woman. He also explained that she had a couple of children and an ill husband, which would have distracted her from the job. Besides, he said, the work was hard, and he sometimes cursed. The unsuccessful applicant was Ruth Bader Ginsburg, who was nominated to the Supreme Court thirty-three years later by President Bill Clinton.[108]

Law clerk Fred Fishman worked on a first draft of a separate opinion for Frankfurter, thinking he had done a rather good job, only to have it returned drowning in red ink. Bravely, he said to Frankfurter, "I'm glad to see that you used some of my words." Frankfurter, knowing the new draft was completely changed, inquired, "Oh, which ones?"

Fishman responded: "the" and "a."[109]

Frankfurter's advice to his colleagues could border on the unbearable. He once sent a two-page memorandum to Justice Stanley Reed on the correct usage of "cf." claiming that the abbreviation "has to be treated by the bench and bar as is the Koran by the faithful."[110]

Great tensions often characterized relations between the justices. On one occasion, Frankfurter missed a conference where judicial tempers flared. Jackson wrote Frankfurter, "Congratulations on your absence from today's session. Only if you had been caught playing the piano in a whore house can you appreciate today's level of my self-respect."[111]

On his deathbed in 1965, Frankfurter still retained his sharp wit. In correspondence, he made note of some of the decisions written by Warren and Brennan. He said, "They aren't doing much for my recovery."[112]

Robert H. Jackson
Born February 13, 1892, in Spring Creek, Pennsylvania; died October 9, 1954; associate justice, 1941–1954. Although he put in a year at Albany Law School, Jackson was the last member of the Court to enter membership in the bar by reading the law as an apprentice, rather than graduating from a law school. Jackson first came to Washington as general counsel to the Internal Revenue Service. He also served as U.S. Solicitor General and Attorney General. While on the Court, he went to Nuremberg as Chief Counsel for the U.S. in the Nazi war crimes trials.

As the federal government's representative before the Supreme Court, Robert H. Jackson was so effective and so skillful that Justice Louis Brandeis suggested that Jackson should be made solicitor general for life.[113]

Despite the evident skill Jackson displayed as an oral advocate before the Supreme Court, he wrote:
> I used to say that, as Solicitor General, I made three arguments in every case. First came the one I had planned – as I thought, logical, coherent, complete. Second was the one actually presented – interrupted, incoherent, disjointed, disappointing. The third was the utterly devastating argument that I thought of after going to bed that night.[114]

Chief Justice Harlan Fiske Stone did not approve of Jackson's decision to become chief prosecutor at the Nuremberg war crimes trial. Noting Jackson's leave of absence from the Court, Stone wrote, "Jackson is away conducting his high-grade lynching party in Nuremberg."[115]

Jackson is regarded as one of the most eloquent writers to grace the Supreme Court bench. And he was well aware of his skill. He once told a law clerk, "You know, I write so well that I have to be very careful, once I've written a first draft, that I'll find it so convincing I won't be adequately critical of my own stuff."[116]

Jackson had a fondness for early decisions of the Court. He explained: "When the Court moved to Washington in 1800, it was provided with no books, which probably accounts for the high quality of early opinions."[117]

Jackson and Justice Sherman Minton, as was Chief Justice Vinson, were offered the job of baseball commissioner. Jackson had no interest in the job or in baseball. He explained, "You know, I don't even know one field from another." In February 1951, he was nominated for the Nobel Peace Prize for his earlier work as prosecutor of the Nazi war criminals at Nuremberg. Jackson said, in reference to the Peace Prize, that he didn't "expect anything will come of it, but if nothing more than the nomination comes, it is a recognition of the work from a quarter that I think is particularly helpful. Anyway, it is better than Baseball Commissioner!"[118]

Playing off Justice Oliver Wendell Holmes's assertion that Franklin Roosevelt had a "first-rate temperament, second-rate mind," journalist Max Lerner described Jackson as a first-rate mind and second-rate temperament.[119]

Sherman Minton

Born October 20, 1890, in Georgetown, Indiana; died April 9, 1965; associate justice, 1949–1956. After law school, Minton was briefly in private practice, served in the army, obtaining the rank of captain, and returned to private practice. The political bug, though, hit him. After an unsuccessful run for the Democratic nomination for Congress, Minton became head of a state utility regulatory commission. He then successfully won the U.S. Senate election but failed to win reelection. He was appointed a judge on the U.S. Court of Appeals for the Seventh Circuit before his elevation to the Supreme Court. His nickname was "Shay."

Sherman Minton won election to the U.S. Senate as a New Dealer, decrying the Supreme Court's penchant for striking down legislation. His slogan was, "You can't offer a hungry man the Constitution!"[120]

As a close friend of Truman, Minton was always good for a laugh. Serving together on a senate committee investigating America's industrial preparedness, the two senators traveled together across the country. Upon arriving in a new city, Minton was fond of declaring loudly, "Should we check into the hotel and leave our bags or go direct to the whorehouse?"[121]

When a seat opened on the Supreme Court, Minton did not lobby for it through intermediaries. He simply flew to Washington, walked into the White House, and sought out Truman.

"What can I do for you, Shay?" the president asked.

"Harry," Minton answered, "I want you to put me on the Supreme Court to fill that new vacancy."

Simple as that, Truman agreed.[122]

Minton had been a college athlete, lettering in several sports, one of which was baseball. Like many players of the day, he got into the habit of chewing tobacco, a vice that remained with him as a justice. At the foot of each justice's chair, to this day, is a spittoon. Minton was probably the last justice to use it for its actual purpose.[123]

To honor their native son on the Supreme Court, Indiana lawyers decided to present Indiana University School of Law with a portrait of Minton. To mark the occasion and honor Minton, they invited the newly appointed chief justice, Earl Warren, to make the presentation. Just before the ceremony got underway, Minton, ever mindful of protocol, urged the emcee to "call on the Chief before you call on me."

Warren's remarks were enthusiastically received with a standing ovation. While standing, however, Minton's chair had been moved so that when he attempted to sit down again, he landed in a heap on the floor. From that position, loud enough for all assembled to hear, he said to the emcee, "Tom, I didn't know I was going to take the floor so soon!"[124]

Frank Murphy
Born April 13, 1890, in Sand Beach, Michigan; died July 19, 1949; associate justice, 1940–1949. Murphy served in the Philippines as governor-general and first high commissioner. He followed that post with the governorship of Michigan. When he lost his reelection bid, he was rewarded with the office of U.S. Attorney General until he succeeded Justice Pierce Butler for what was regarded as the "Catholic seat" on the Court. Because he considered Murphy to be impossibly sure of the moral superiority of his positions, Justice Owen Roberts nicknamed Murphy "The Saint."

Frank Murphy understood that he could not match the brilliance of his colleagues on the Court and chose not to try. He said, "There are eight good intellects" among the justices, "and they have my heart." He used his compassion to inform his views and, unlike his brethren, delegated opinion-writing to his law clerks. One, Eugene Gressman, who wrote the leading treatise on Supreme Court practice, served for five years and earned the title, bestowed by other law clerks, of "Mr. Justice."[125]

Murphy's conference notes indicate how lightly some of the justices took the case discussions, even in important cases. For *United States v. Darby*,[126] his notes indicate: "C.J. [Charles Evans Hughes] This is the most important case we have had by far in connection with the commerce power... ([Justice James] McReynolds is sound asleep mouth open – and [Justice Harlan Fiske] Stone snores [or stares] away."[127] Of course, that disinterest did not excuse one from work. Stone wrote the Court's *Darby* opinion after that conference.

Stone privately concurred with Murphy's self-assessment of inadequacy for the job. Moreover, he believed Murphy had no capacity for growth. "He can no more grow than that stone," he said.[128]

After Murphy wrote the Court's opinion in *Schneiderman v. United States*,[129] where the Court upheld the citizenship rights of a naturalized citizen who had been active politically in the American Communist Party, Justice Felix Frankfurter, who had dissented, began a small campaign of harassment against the decision's author. Mocking Murphy's opinion that Communist Party membership was not "absolutely incompatible" with fealty with the Constitution, Frankfurter added that "Uncle Joe Stalin was at least a spiritual co-author with Jefferson of the Virginia Statute for Religious Freedom." He later authored a possible headnote to the case that he signed "F.F. Knaebel":

> The American Constitution ain't got no principles. The Communist Party don't stand for nuthin', and the Hell with the U.S.A. so long as a guy is attached to the principles of the U.S.S.R.

Murphy replied:
My dear F.F.: Many thanks for your original and revised headnotes in the *Scheiderman* case. Not only do they reveal long and arduous preparation, but best of all, they are done with commendable English understatement and characteristic New England reserve.[130]

Murphy was considered quite the ladies' man. Perhaps Frankfurter was a little jealous when he imitated the speech of a showgirl and said, "Us girls call him Murph."[131]

Murphy's reputation with women, even though overstated, often preceded him. The Chevy Chase Country Club blackballed Murphy because it was said he chased "wild women."[132]

Murphy did have some exotic women friends. One, a nightclub performer, came to Washington in December 1947 and sent the justice a note inviting him to her opening. Murphy, tongue firmly planted in cheek, penned a card to Douglas: "I would be obliged if you would represent me at the lady's gala opening. If you can't make it, ask Wiley [Rutledge, who was extremely straitlaced] to do so in an academic way."[133]

In spite of his active social life, Murphy was a religious man. Therefore, he was shocked when attending mass at St. Patrick's Cathedral with Joseph Kennedy and Kennedy turned to him on the steps and asked, "By the way Frank, are you still sleeping with that Miss Kelly?"

"Can you imagine it?" Murphy said to Douglas when he related the story. "Here we are almost inside the holy place when Joe starts talking about fornication."[134]

In *Mortensen v. United States*,[135] the Court, in a 5-4 decision written by Murphy, found that a couple who ran a house of prostitution in Grand Island, Nebraska, did not violate the Mann Act, which prohibited transporting women across state lines for purposes of illicit sexual conduct when the couple gave their employees an out-of-state vacation and then returned them to Nebraska.

The following summer, Justice William O. Douglas and a friend had occasion to pass through Grand Island. Though they searched in vain for the establishment that had been the subject of the case, the best they could do was find the Grand Island Chamber of Commerce, where they borrowed some stationery and typed a letter to Murphy expressing the "Chamber's" appreciation for his solicitude toward the "local industry" of Grand Island.

When Douglas returned to the Court, Murphy proudly showed Douglas the letter he received from the "good people" of Grand Island. Something in Douglas's reaction, though, gave the joke away. Murphy immediately asked Douglas, "You didn't write that letter, did you?"[136]

Because Murphy had an innate sympathy for the underdog, Frankfurter once humorously listed "Frank Murphy's Clients" as "Reds, whores, crooks, Indians, and all other colored people, railroad workers, 'women, children, and most men.'"[137] Of Murphy's penchant to champion civil liberties, Frankfurter mocked him as "St. Francis" and "Dear God" in his letters.[138]

Toward the end of his life, Murphy's health problems made him dependent on painkillers. He began making illegal drug purchases, and though he relied heavily on his law clerks, he fell behind in his work. His close friend on the Court, Wiley Rutledge, began casting votes for him.[139]

Stanley F. Reed

Born December 31, 1884, in Minerva, Kentucky; died April 2, 1980; associate justice, 1938–1957. Reed served in Kentucky's General Assembly, as counsel to the Federal Farm Board, and as general counsel to the Reconstruction Finance Corporation. He then became special assistant to the attorney general, arguing the Gold Clause Cases,[140] before getting the solicitor general's job more permanently as the government's advocate before the Supreme Court. When Reed retired from the Court, he briefly served as chair of the Civil Rights Commission and continued to sit in lower federal courts by designation. For his unflappable nature, he earned the nickname "Unshaken Reed."

Attorney General Homer Cummings told newly appointed Solicitor General Stanley Reed, "Stanley, you are going to win some cases in the Supreme Court, and you are going to lose some. For your first case, pick out one that you can win."

Reed selected *Humphrey's Executor v. U.S.*,[141] which he later said "couldn't be lost." The case involved the President's power to remove a person as a commissioner of the Federal Trade Commission. Reed was confident that a recent Supreme Court ruling in a case involving a postmaster required the Court to rule in the administration's favor. Instead, Reed lost *Humphrey's Executor* by unanimous vote.[142]

Reed and Frankfurter disagreed about search and seizure cases. Reed explained their differences this way:

> Do you know why Felix and I decide these search and seizure cases differently? ... Well, when Felix was a young Jewish boy growing up in Vienna, there could be a knock at the door in the night. It could be a policeman coming to take him away. When

I was a young boy I had a white pony and I used to ride [him] down the main street...and as I passed the main intersection, there was a policeman there and he would stop traffic for me. And as I passed, he would pat me on my golden curls. And when Felix thinks of a policeman, he thinks of a knock on the door in the night, and when I think of a policeman, I think of the man stopping traffic for me and patting me on my curls.[143]

Although Frankfurter and Reed enjoyed a friendship, Frankfurter clearly saw Reed as his intellectual inferior. One of his law clerks said that Frankfurter described Reed as "a man who crawls from detail to detail." Reed, however, could tolerate Frankfurter's patronizing manner and did so better than most. One law clerk recalled an occasion when Frankfurter came into Reed's office to discuss a case, "Reed just sat there quietly, nodding his head very politely, and [when] Frankfurter was satisfied with himself, he wheeled out, going out like a little bird.... Reed turned to us and said, 'What a wonderful disquisition. What a marvelous analysis. What a brilliant mind. Don't you envy that capability? If only he had some common sense!'"

Still, another clerk described Reed's reaction to Frankfurter in this way, "Felix would be jumping around like a hummingbird [with] this great smiling...benign figure watching [and] listening with a kind of bemused tolerant smile. At the end of which, he would say, 'Thank you very much, Felix. I appreciate your spending time with me.'"[144]

In 1947, Reed vetoed a proposal made by some of the law clerks to have a Christmas party for the entire Court staff because that would mean the party would be racially integrated. The following year, the first African American law clerk was hired, but it was not until 1967 that the second African American law clerk was chosen.[145]

Reed was the last hold-out in the school desegregation decision, *Brown v. Board of Education*. He finally succumbed to Chief Justice Earl Warren's persuasiveness after twenty lunchtime discussions.[146]

Reed was "a tall, quiet person [who] never raised his voice or lost his temper." Black and Douglas liked Reed immensely, even though they often disagreed with his views. When Reed retired, Black and Douglas would gleefully inform him "whenever one of his reactionary opinions was overruled."[147]

Wiley Rutledge
Born July 20, 1894, in Cloverport, Kentucky; died September 10, 1949; associate justice, 1943–1949. Rutledge was a law professor at the University of Colorado, Washington University in St. Louis, and the University of Iowa. His outspoken support of the New Deal landed him a seat on the U.S. Court of Appeals for the District of Columbia and then the Supreme Court.

Teaching law as a young professor at Washington University, Wiley Rutledge was warned by the chancellor that the school had a "serious disciplinary problem." Sure enough, while teaching, a moan or long burp echoed across his classroom, apparently while Rutledge's back was turned. It was said that the disruptive student was Clark Clifford, who later became a distinguished advisor to presidents Harry Truman, John F. Kennedy, Lyndon B. Johnson, and Jimmy Carter.

In response to the unearthly moan, the five-foot-ten, stocky Rutledge removed his jacket and declared: "If there's a joker here big enough to acknowledge it, I'm ready to meet him outside." No one owned up to the moan, and that type of disruption never interrupted class again.

When Rutledge was a justice, he once spotted the now-distinguished Clifford in the courtroom and sent a note to him that read: "Don't you dare give a B___rrr__p in here ...Wiley."[148]

Though much beloved as a law school dean, Rutledge had a reputation as a slow grader. One year, during the "law revue," an annual series of skits put on by students that often made fun of faculty, Rutledge, referred to in one skit as "Mr. Wiley Asafox," was portrayed as a judge still grading papers while sitting in a courtroom. Besides the bench, an old man with a long white beard sat in a wheelchair and interrupted the "judge." "Did my pappy pass Business Organizations?" he asked.[149]

Rutledge came to President Franklin D. Roosevelt's attention as a critic of the initial Flag-Salute decision[150] of the Supreme Court, a decision he voted to overrule as a justice. He quickly began to gather support for a Supreme Court appointment, only to be passed over by several appointees prior to later joining the Court. Still, the process of grooming him for that appointment began with his nomination to the U.S. Court of Appeals for the District of Columbia Circuit.

The *Washington Star* newspaper announced the nomination by describing Rutledge of Iowa as an "authority on matters affecting the western section of the country, such as Indian problems, water rights, and land cases." They were also not the bread and butter of the court to which he was nominated. Perhaps even more importantly, they were not subjects on which Rutledge claimed any special expertise.[151]

Rutledge was born in Kentucky, attended college in Tennessee, and then transferred to Wisconsin. He then attended law school in Indiana, then went to North Carolina, taught in New Mexico, taught and went to law school in Colorado, and then went to Missouri. From there, he went to Iowa and then to the District of Columbia. When President Franklin D. Roosevelt nominated Rutledge to the Supreme Court, he told the nominee: "Wiley, we had a number of candidates for the Court who were highly qualified, but they didn't have geography – you have that." In fact, Roosevelt added, "Wiley, you have a lot of geography."[152]

Rutledge recused himself *in Shelley v. Kraemer*,[153] which found that racially restrictive covenants in deeds were unenforceable. The reason for the recusal was that the deed to his home contained a racially restrictive covenant.[154] That restriction applied to his entire neighborhood and prevented any property in the area from being used or owned by African Americans, Jews, Persians, Armenians, or Syrians.[155]

Justice John Paul Stevens, who clerked for Rutledge, recalled in one obscenity case that the justice did not, as was his habit, rely on the record, the petition for certiorari, the clerk's memorandum, or the briefs. Instead, "[h]e read the book."[156]

Rutledge admitted that he smoked "voracious[ly]" and enjoyed coffee "incessantly," particularly when working on cases. When told he should not smoke so much, he would say, like Mark Twain, he quit "every twenty minutes."[157]

7

The Warren Court

The Warren Court fomented a legal revolution in civil rights, the rights of the accused, freedom of speech, separation of church and state, and the application of many fundamental rights to the States, to name a few. Its landmark decision in *Brown v. Board of Education*,[1] overturning the "separate-but-equal" doctrine, is only rivaled by *Marbury v. Madison*[2] in the annals of constitutional law. At the time, though, *Brown* led to massive resistance in the Southern states. The Court's further rulings on criminal justice issues led to protesters putting up billboards that urged "Impeach Earl Warren." The Court's deep expansion of rights prompted University of Chicago law professor Philip Kurland to observe that "If, as has been suggested, the road to hell is paved with good intentions, the Warren Court has been among the great roadbuilders of all time."[3]

Earl Warren, Chief Justice (1953–1969)

Associate Justices:
William Brennan, Jr. (1956–1990)
Abe Fortas (1965–1969)
Arthur Goldberg (1962–1965)

John Marshall Harlan (II) (1955–1971)
Thurgood Marshall (1967–1991)
Potter Stewart (1958–1981)
Byron White (1962–1993)
Charles Whittaker (1957–1962)

The Chief Justice

Earl Warren

Born March 19, 1891, in Los Angeles, California; died July 9, 1974; chief justice, 1953–1969. Warren was a successful politician who capitalized on his reputation as a top-notch district attorney and later as California Attorney General. He served three terms as the state's governor and then secured the vice-presidential nomination on the Republican ticket in 1948. His political skills proved valuable in leading a divided Court, which withstood considerable criticism for its landmark decisions. His leadership skills earned him the affectionate designation from fellow justices of "Superchief."

Earl Warren was a born politician, even as a youth, and made friends with everyone he met. His sister said that when their mother wanted to find Earl, "she'd just look for a group of people, and he'd be in the middle of it."[4]

As district attorney, Warren was called upon to speak at various events. His wife, Nina, often joined him at these events. At one, she was invited to say a few words. Warren intervened. He said, "We have a strict rule in our family. I do all the speaking in public, and Mrs. Warren does it all at home."[5]

Warren said that when he was district attorney, he argued his first case before the Supreme Court in defense of Alameda County in a case brought by the Central Pacific Railroad. It was January 2, 1932, the last argument heard by Justice Oliver Wendell Holmes. After the case, Holmes announced, "I won't be here tomorrow," and he retired from the Court. Warren said that his friends used to tease him saying that he drove Holmes from the bench. His friends would say, "[O]ne look at you and he said, 'I quit.'"[6]

Warren was a reluctant nominee for vice president on the Republican ticket in 1948 because he did not want to leave California or take the cut in pay with his children's college tuitions soon wrecking his budget. He accepted the next day, and one of the staff explained the change of heart by saying, "They put a gun to his head."

He had no prepared acceptance speech, telling delegates, "For the first time in my life, I know what it feels like to be hit by a streetcar. I had no idea, I assure you, that there was any such shock as this awaiting me today, and before you change your mind, I want to say that I accept the nomination."

When he called home to break the news, 13-year-old Bobby answered the phone.

"Well, Bob, did you hear what happened today in Philadelphia?" Warren asked.

His son replied, "No, Dad. What happened?"

Warren answered, "Well, I was nominated for vice president."

His son then asked, "Is that good?"[7]

Warren's nomination as vice president on the Republican ticket with Thomas Dewey drew a chuckle from President Harry Truman, the Democratic nominee. Truman described Warren in this way: "He's a Democrat and doesn't know it." Warren responded, "Yes, but with a small 'd.'"[8]

The Democrats unexpectedly defeated the 1948 Republican presidential ticket with Warren as the vice-presidential nominee. Warren explained what happened: "Mr. Truman just got too many votes."[9]

Warren hated fellow Californian Richard Nixon with a passion. When Nixon ran for the Senate, Warren's son, James, asked what his father thought of Nixon. Warren replied, "Whenever he's dealing, be sure to cut the cards."[10]

When Dwight D. Eisenhower was primed to select Nixon as his running mate in the 1952 election, Warren went to Eisenhower to oppose the move. Warren carried considerable weight as the party's 1948 vice-presidential nominee and as governor of the nation's most populous state. Yet, Eisenhower was determined to pick Nixon.

Eisenhower made a deal with Warren. In return for Warren's silence on the Nixon nomination, Warren was promised the first vacancy on the Supreme Court by the Eisenhower administration. During Eisenhower's first year in office, Chief Justice Fred Vinson died unexpectedly. Herbert Brownell, the Attorney General, flew to California to talk to Warren.

Brownell asked Warren, "Surely, you don't believe the promise included the chief justiceship."

Warren's response was pointed: "The first opening."[11]

Warren did not have judicial robes for his swearing-in ceremony. He had brought along an old academic robe that he had used for academic ceremonies in California, but he was told that it was not appropriate. He then borrowed a spare robe he found in the Court's robing room. It was, however, so long that he tripped over it when he stepped up to the bench to take the chief justice's seat after being sworn in. Later, he wrote, "I suppose it could be said that I literally stumbled onto the bench."[12]

Although his comment has been recast since he made it, Eisenhower believed that: "I have made two mistakes [during my presidency], and they are both sitting on the Court." Those mistakes, in Eisenhower's view, were Warren and Justice William Brennan.[13] On one occasion, Eisenhower was asked who recommended Warren for the chief justiceship. Eisenhower replied, "I wish I could remember because I'd like to shoot him."[14]

The John Birch Society campaigned to impeach Earl Warren. Letters were mailed to Congress, and bumper stickers appeared urging impeachment, as did billboards. On Warren's library wall, he had a 1965 New Yorker cartoon that showed an angry Whistler's Mother embroidering a sampler saying, "Impeach Earl Warren." Warren told one of his Southern law clerks that if he got fired, he could go home to California and run unopposed for Governor based on the impeachment campaign.[15]

At one point, the John Birch Society ran an essay contest about all the things that were wrong with Warren. When the chief justice heard about it, he said, "I'll have to get Mrs. Warren to enter the contest. She knows more of my faults than anyone else."[16]

After reading a quotation from Justice Abe Fortas in the newspaper that "black robes were too awesome for the Members of the Supreme Court of the United States," Warren wrote his fashion-conscience colleague a joking letter in which he claimed to have consulted with the top designers about a new look for the robes. As to color, he himself favored the University of California colors of blue and gold. He suggested Justice Hugo Black would want to remain with the color that bears his name. Douglas, he thought, "might prefer a 'robe of many colors' as worn by Joseph in the Bible, to match the vivid neckties he formerly wore. However, he may have an open mind as he has recently been wearing more subdued and somber neckties."

Justice Tom Clark, the chief felt sure, would stay "loyal to the color of the 'yellow rose of Texas.'" Warren believed he could count on Justice John Marshall Harlan to "dissent regardless of the color." Stewart, Warren assumed, "might object to the crimson red as it might detract from his bronzed suntan. Royal purple might be a substitute but might raise the question of a number of 'reigning monarchs.'"

Warren speculated that Justice Byron White, unlike Black, would avoid the color of his name "because of the obscenity cases."

He said that animal furs might also be considered. This, he noted, would open the Court to criticism from opponents "who might shout 'dirty skunk,' and, Abe, that would be difficult to 'weasel' out of."

Warren ended his letter with a postscript: "For your information, appropriate and becoming wigs have been forwarded to you for your approval."

Fortas replied in good spirit that perhaps an international competition should be held with one writ of certiorari as the prize. He warned that some rules might be necessary, at least to ensure that some Californians did not "submit a proposal for a topless robe."

Fortas closed by stating: "I'm for the crimson robe, with leopard trim and coral – I think coral is correct – but maybe it's part of an automobile, like the exhaust pipe. I don't think I said anything as silly as the statement quoted in the papers – but maybe I did. If the robes are too awesome, maybe bathing suits would do. But the Court has always guarded its secrets, and this is no time for initiating disclosure."[17]

After Warren retired, he spoke at Notre Dame Law School. A student in the back began a question by stating, "Some people have suggested that you'll go down in history with Marshall as one of the two greatest chief justices." A pleased Warren smiled and said, "Could you say that again – a little louder, please? I'm having a little trouble hearing."[18]

The Associate Justices

William J. Brennan, Jr.
Born April 25, 1906, in Newark, New Jersey, died July 24, 1997; associate justice, 1956–1990. Generally considered one of the most influential justices of the 20th century, Brennan made a rapid rise from prominent lawyer to state trial judge to state supreme court justice, before being tapped by President Dwight Eisenhower for the Supreme Court. Because of a certain resemblance

to the small, wise, and wrinkled 900-year-old creature from the Star Wars movies, one law clerk nicknamed the justice "Yoda."

William Brennan's legal career did not begin auspiciously. He went to work for a Newark law firm, Pitney, Hardin & Skinner, whose tactics sometimes caused it to be called "Pluck 'em, Hook 'em & Skin 'em,"[19] Coincidentally, the Pitney in the firm's name was the last New Jerseyan on the Supreme Court, Mahlon Pitney.[20]

Early on at the firm, Brennan was dispatched to the city jail to represent a client accused of participating in a knifing. Upon his arrival, Brennan was mistaken for an escaped prisoner and cooled his heels in jail until another lawyer from his law firm could arrive and bail him out.[21]

In one of his earliest courtroom appearances, Brennan was caught off-guard. He was defending a man in a vehicular manslaughter case. His character witness, a retired policeman, seemed unresponsive when Brennan asked about the accused's reputation for "veracity." Each of the three times the question was asked, the witness merely replied, "he's a good automobile driver."

Just as his exasperation reached its limit, the judge intervened, "Is this boy in the habit of telling the truth?"

"Oh yes, your honor," the witness responded. "I've never known him to tell a lie."

"That's what Mr. Brennan was asking," the judge told the retired officer, "But he's a Harvard graduate and doesn't speak English."[22]

Brennan had no inkling of the impact that he would have on the Supreme Court. Upon his appointment, he told a friend, "I'm the mule that was entered in the Kentucky Derby. I don't expect to distinguish myself, but I do expect to benefit from the association."[23]

Upon his arrival as a new justice in 1956, Brennan was given a tour of the Supreme Court building by Chief Justice Earl Warren. When they reached the justices' lounge, Warren turned on the light to discover the rest of the Court watching the 1956 World Series between the Brooklyn Dodgers and the New York Yankees on television. Warren attempted introductions but instead discovered the justices' priorities as one judicial baseball fan shouted: "Shut out the lights."[24]

Frankfurter bridled at the independence shown by his former student, after Brennan joined his professor on the Supreme Court. According to Brennan, Frankfurter complained to some dinner companions one evening, "I always encouraged my students to think for themselves, but Brennan goes too far!"[25]

Being a Supreme Court justice does not spare one from parental criticism. One of Brennan's earliest written opinions was in *Jencks v. United States*,[26] which overturned the conviction of a New Mexico union member for falsely swearing he was not a member of the Communist party. The Court held that the government was obliged to turn over written documents from federal informants upon which the conviction rested and had been denied to Jencks.

The issue had seemed straightforward to Brennan and the majority, but it stirred up a storm. Even Brennan's mother questioned his opinion. She said to him in a phone call, "I don't understand, dear. I never had any difficulty being proud of your opinions on the New Jersey Supreme Court. But how could you do this?"[27]

Judge Richard Arnold, a Brennan law clerk during October Term 1960, reported: "Harlan was the soul of dignity. He deserved the title of 'august' if anyone ever did. And yet, when Justice Brennan saw him in the halls, he would say delightedly, 'Hiya Johnny.' I do not believe that anyone else, including his mother, ever called Justice Harlan 'Johnny.'"[28]

The February 1974 issue of *National Lampoon* magazine contained a cartoon centerfold of justices occupied with a variety of sexual behaviors. Justice William Rehnquist found the depiction sufficiently humorous and thought it unlikely that the other justices would otherwise see it, so he brought a copy to pass around the conference table.

Upon his return to chambers, Brennan told his law clerks about the cartoon, noting that while the other justices were portrayed as sex fiends, he was shown as a protector of children. After all, he said, he was holding open his judicial robes in front of a number of children, shielding their eyes from what the other justices were doing.

His law clerks, reluctantly, drew straws for the unpleasant duty of explaining to the justice just what "flashing" was.[29]

Three months after his wife Marjorie died in late 1982, Brennan emerged from depression to surprise his colleagues on the Court. At the beginning of a two-week recess in 1983, the justices found a note left by Brennan: "Mary Fowler [Brennan's secretary of 26 years] and I were married yesterday, and we have gone to Bermuda."[30]

Abe Fortas
Born June 9, 1910, in Memphis, Tennessee; died April 5, 1982; associate justice, 1965–1969. Fortas taught at Yale Law School, was in the Public Works Administration and Interior Department during the FDR administration, served as a United Nations advisor for the Truman administration, founded a prominent Washington, DC law firm, and became a lifelong friend of Lyndon Johnson's from his government service and later his representation of LBJ in the 1948 contested Texas Democratic Senate primary. His reward, years later, was nomination to the Supreme Court and a failed nomination for chief justice. For his passion for the violin, Fortas earned the nickname "Fiddlin' Abe."

When he was in high school and college, Fortas played the violin in the Colie Stolz band. Fortas was a capable player who also gave violin lessons to children. Stolz said Fortas "could read anything ever written" but could not play by ear. Much later, while serving as undersecretary at the Department of the Interior, Fortas threw a party at his home and told his guests that Stolz was the "only man in the world who had the brazen effrontery to fire Abe Fortas. He fired me for crass incompetence." The announcement won Stolz a standing ovation.[31]

Fortas considered himself a good writer and an even better editor. One colleague once commented that Fortas's "only regret is that he never had a chance to rewrite the Lord's Prayer before it was published."[32]

Fortas amazed his law professors with his natural ability. One said, "Fortas can talk law in terms that the farmer and businessman can understand. Why, that boy can pick peaches or irrigate a field with the Due Process clause of the Constitution."[33]

Fortas was proud of his work but had a sense of humor about it. After completing a major investigatory report at the SEC, Fortas penned a note to the secretary of SEC Chairman William O. Douglas, who had been one of Fortas's law professors: "Will you please send me ten or fifteen additional copies of the report? I received only two copies, and the result is that I have been unable to send a copy to my Mother, my Aunt Katherine, my Uncle Louis, and Miss Catt, my first-grade teacher. This is a hell of a situation."[34]

One of the crowning achievements of Fortas's career was his appointment as counsel in the landmark case of *Gideon v. Wainwright*,[35] which established an indigent defendant's right to appointed counsel when charged with a felony. Though he received great credit for his willingness to take on the case and his brilliance in arguing it, he had little use for his putative client, Clarence Gideon, the small-time thief who had been wrongfully accused of a crime. Asked if he wanted to meet Gideon, Fortas replied, "Why the hell would I want to meet a son of a bitch like that? He's no good."[36]

His success in *Gideon* brought Fortas a surfeit of letters from prisoners who also sought his help. Fortas did not appreciate attention from that quarter. He composed a mock reply that informed his correspondent that he would be unavailable because he was leaving town "perhaps forever." He also wrote, "There is no particular reason for this except I am damned tired of receiving and answering letters like yours." Then, in a dig at a prominent legal rival, he added that having "reviewed the list of attorneys available to practice in the Supreme Court and not yet disbarred...I can and do recommend that you retain the services of Clark M. Clifford, certainly one of the nation's foremost experts on the Presidency – its cause and cure." Fortas then sent a copy of his letter and the collection of prisoner letters to Clifford.[37]

Arthur Goldberg
Born August 8, 1908, in Chicago, Illinois; died January 19, 1990; associate justice, 1962–1965. Goldberg served during World War II in the Office of Strategic Services, a precursor of the CIA, became a prominent labor lawyer, served as Secretary of Labor in the Kennedy administration, and, after his tenure as a Supreme Court justice, as UN Ambassador during the Johnson administration. For his effective leadership advancing policies as labor secretary, he earned the title, "Galloping Goldberg."

In a 1963 speech to the American Bar Association, Arthur Goldberg opined on the difference between being Secretary of Labor and a justice on the Supreme Court: "The Secretary continually worries about what the President and an unpredictable Congress will do to his carefully formulated legislative proposals; the President, the Congress, and the Secretary wonder what the Justice will do to theirs."[38]

On his first day on the bench as a justice, Goldberg penned what he later described as a "mash note" to his wife, Dorothy. When the page mistakenly delivered the note to Justice John Harlan's wife, Goldberg's face "turned a deep and unnatural red."[39]

As U.S. ambassador to the United Nations, Goldberg brought the same self-assured and aggressive style that had served him so well in the law. He awoke one morning, however, to a newspaper article that labeled him arrogant.

"Dorothy," he asked his wife, "the *New York Times* says I am arrogant. Do you think I am arrogant?"

"Not at all, Mr. Justice," she answered.[40]

Goldberg delighted in being able to be the first to report news. In one instance, he was able to outdo the Central Intelligence Agency. He was lunching with CIA Director Alan Dulles, when Dulles received an envelope containing an urgent message. The CIA chief opened the first envelope, then a second one, and finally a third one before he got to his message. After reading it, Dulles asked Goldberg, "Do you know what this says?"

"Yes, I do," Goldberg replied to the CIA director's surprise. "It says that [French President Charles] de Gaulle has just died."

"How ever did you know?" Dulles asked.

"I heard it on the radio on the way over to lunch," the justice said.[41]

John Marshall Harlan (II)

Born May 20, 1899, in Chicago, Illinois; died December 29, 1971; associate justice, 1955–1971. John Marshall Harlan, whose grandfather of the same name also served on the Supreme Court, was an Assistant U.S. Attorney for the Southern District of New York, a Special Assistant New York Attorney General, and a judge on the United States Court of Appeals for the Second Circuit before his appointment to the Supreme Court. He was the Warren Court's conservative conscience. For his intellectual outlook being similar to that of Justice Felix Frankfurter but without the same off-putting attitude about others or their contrary views, Harlan was called "Frankfurter without the mustard."

While his grandfather was something of a good old boy from Kentucky, John Marshall Harlan was a creature of sophisticated New York. Felix Frankfurter said, "Harlan on the bench and in the conference is to the manner born." Tom Clark was not above referring to Harlan as "milord." Once, when Harlan was ill, Clark sent him a get-well note that said, "Your Lordship should be more careful of your whiskey and your habits."[42]

A souvenir of the earlier Justice John Marshall Harlan, Harlan's grandfather, graced the justice's chamber: a bench chair. When he pointed it out to a Japanese visitor, the visitor remarked, "I did not know that the post was hereditary."[43]

Harlan grew up in an era when gentlemen were taught never to curse but found, from time to time, discussions during the Court's conference *required* that ability. He relied upon his fellow justice, Thurgood Marshall, to supply the necessary phrases from his colorful and diverse vocabulary when needed.

Once, during conference, Harlan got into an argument with Chief Justice Earl Warren. During a break in the proceedings, Harlan asked Marshall for some strong language to use when the issue was rejoined, and Marshall accommodated with several alternatives. As the discussion restarted, Warren said that he just did not understand Harlan's point. Harlan replied, "Chief, it is as clear as a goat's ass going up a hill."

Warren immediately turned to Marshall and said, "Thurgood, I know that was you who gave him that."[44]

Under the Court's free-speech jurisprudence, sexual expression comprises protected speech, but obscenity is unprotected. After the Court held that, for sexual material to be obscene, it must appeal to prurient interests and be utterly without redeeming value, the justices were inundated with cases involving prosecutions for obscenity and were called upon to determine whether redeeming value could be discerned or not. Many of these cases involved films.

Black and William O. Douglas, having rejected the idea that any expression was without constitutional protection, did not attend the screenings. Others, including Justice Harlan, who by this time was nearly blind, felt an obligation to attend the screenings, which took place in the Court's basement studio.

Because Harlan could not really see what was happening on-screen, he would have Marshall sit next to him and explain the action. Marshall, who may have appointed himself for the task, claimed, "That was a fun assignment. Lots of fun. I really enjoyed it." As Marshall understood what he needed to do, he undertook describing what happened in the film with real attention to detail to enable Harlan to make a judgment on the obscenity question. As Justice Harry Blackmun reported, Harlan was frequently heard to declare, "Oh, you don't say," in response to Marshall's narrative.[45]

Marshall would also turn to Blackmun after a film, and ask, "Did you learn anything new from that one, Harry? I didn't."[46]

Chief Justice Warren Burger was not particularly pleased when the Court took up the issue of whether a protester could be arrested for wearing a jacket emblazoned with the words "Fuck the Draft" inside a courthouse. When the Court decided that the sentiment was protected free speech in *Cohen v. California*,[47] Burger was concerned that the Court's dignity would suffer a considerable blow.

"John," he said to Harlan who was set to announce the Court's decision, "You're not going to use 'that word' in delivering the opinion, are you?"

Harlan dodged the question, even though he did not plan to do so, largely because it would leave Burger in some suspense and a little discomfort.

"It would be the end of the Court if you use it, John," Burger admonished.

Harlan delivered the Court's decision in careful words, looking from time to time at the chief justice who sat stiffly in preparation for the worst. Harlan probably chuckled to himself as he left the Chief twisting in the wind until he had completed his announcement – without ever mentioning the word at issue.[48]

When Harlan found a case particularly challenging and unable to wrap up his task that evening, he would take it home and assure his clerks that it would "succumb to a little bourbon."[49]

Even the illness that ultimately took his life could not stop Harlan from discharging his duties while he still breathed. Despite his failing eyesight and other physical infirmities, Harlan insisted that his clerks bring to his hospital bed any work that needed his attention. One day, a clerk appeared with an emergency petition. Harlan discussed the matter with the clerk and concluded that he must deny the request. He took the necessary paperwork and a pen from the clerk, scribbled his signature, and returned the papers. The clerk discovered no signature on the paper.

"Justice Harlan, you just denied your sheet," the clerk reported. Sure enough, Harlan had missed the paper and signed his bedsheet.

Judicial work was not all that law clerks brought to Harlan's hospital room. They also sneaked in Lark cigarettes and Rebel Yell bourbon. The latter was put into hospital cups with straws to fool the nurses.[50]

Thurgood Marshall

Born July 2, 1908, in Baltimore, Maryland; died January 24, 1993; associate justice 1967–1991. A slave descendant, Marshall became the first African American to serve on the U.S. Supreme Court. As director of the NAACP Legal Defense and Educational Fund, Marshall launched a successful litigation strategy to attack racial segregation and discrimination, best exemplified by the historic decision in Brown v. Board of Education. *Marshall's work, which ranks him as one of the most important lawyers of the twentieth century, resulted in successive appointments to the U.S. Court of Appeals for the Second Circuit and U.S. Solicitor General before sitting on the Supreme Court. For his pioneering legal work, Marshall earned the nickname "Mr. Civil Rights."*

In the 1940s, Thurgood Marshall targeted travel agencies that violated New York's anti-discrimination law by calling and asking for a Miami Beach hotel booking known to reject black guests. When the agency was willing to book the reservation until it heard that his name was Thurgood Marshall, he would force the agency to leave the city for violating the law by being willing to book a reservation for a more typical customer at a discriminatory hotel.

Once, though, a woman took his reservation and wished him a good vacation. Startled, Marshall said, "Excuse me, isn't this a restricted hotel?" The woman replied, "Oh, Mr. Marshall, I didn't know you were Jewish." Marshall could only reply, "Ahh've got NEWWSS for you."[51]

Marshall was sent to Korea to investigate charges of discrimination against black soldiers. Returning to a military site after being in the field, he was stopped by a sentry who demanded the password. The tall, African American Marshall looked down at the soldier and asked, "Do you really think I'm North Korean?"[52]

After arguing the Central High School case[53] before the Supreme Court, Marshall and Wiley Branton flew back to New York. Although he was well-known within the civil rights community as "Mr. Civil Rights,"[54] he did not always get the credit he deserved. In the taxi from the airport, the driver, hearing legal talk, asked, "Isn't it great what Dr. King did today?" Marshall inquired about what King had done. The driver replied, "Oh, he got the Supreme Court to let those black kids stay in Central High School." Marshall told Branton, "Wiley, did you hear that? Did you hear what *Dr. King* did today?"[55]

During his work on the Kenyan Constitution, he met Prince Philip, who asked Marshall whether he wanted to hear the prince's opinion of lawyers. Marshall replied, "Only if you care to hear my opinion of princes."[56]

Early in his tenure as a judge on the Second Circuit, Marshall was invited to join the other judges for a group portrait. The photographer had blown a fuse, and the judges were awaiting the arrival of an electrician to make the necessary repairs. When Marshall arrived, a secretary said, "You must be the electrician." Marshall's response to his law clerk indicates how he often shrugged off such slights: "Boy, that woman must be crazy if she thinks I could become an electrician in New York City."[57]

Once, Marshall and a friend went for lunch at a popular New York restaurant and were in a waiting line. Marshall turned to his friend and said, "Watch how it works. Now that I'm a judge, they'll treat us nice."

Soon, the maître d' walked past others in line and told Marshall and his friend, "Sir, please come with me." After they were seated, the maître d' said, "And now, Congressman [Adam Clayton] Powell, what would you like to drink?"[58]

When Lyndon Johnson was about to name Thurgood Marshall to the Supreme Court, Marshall suspected that he was about to be informed of the nomination when he was called to the White House. He and his wife, Cissy, had discussed the possibility, but he wanted Johnson to believe that he was surprised by the nomination. When he was told, he exclaimed, "Oh, boy! Wait till Cissy hears this. Is she ever gonna be shocked!"

Johnson put Marshall on a speaker phone so that he could surprise his wife and, Mrs. Marshall answered the phone without knowing that she was on a speaker phone. Marshall said, "It's me, honey." Mrs. Marshall replied, "Yeah, honey. Did we get the Supreme Court appointment?"[59]

Marshall had great fun providing occasional commentary during the days when the Court would screen films to determine whether the movie had any redeeming value and, therefore, was not illegally obscene. Often, the films would contain some high-minded comment toward the end to try to escape the censor's label.

In one movie, the final scene portrayed a psychologist sadly concluding, "And so our nymphomaniac subject was never cured." Marshall quipped, "Yeah, but I am."

In another, the central female character was hijacked by a Communist, who lectured about the differences between communism and Western democracy. Marshall shouted out, "Ah, the redeeming social value."[60]

Marshall would play along with tourists who visited the Court and did not realize that they were in the presence of the first African

American justice. When the tourists boarded the justices' private elevator in error and found Marshall standing there, they seemed to assume that he was an elevator operator. Upon hearing a request for the "First floor, please," Marshall would answer, "Yowsa, yowsa" and ceremoniously hold open the door at the first floor for the departing and puzzled visitors.[61]

In 1970, Marshall was struck by pneumonia and was hospitalized at Bethesda Naval Hospital (now Walter Reed) for several weeks. Marshall's doctor told him that President Richard Nixon had called and wanted a full report on Marshall's illness. Marshall, understanding that the call was about whether there might soon be a vacancy on the Court to fill, told the doctor, "Well, Admiral, you have my permission to give it to him only on one condition. That you put at the bottom of it, 'Not yet.'" And, claimed Marshall, the doctor did just that.[62]

When the Warren Court era ended, Marshall frequently found he was in the minority on a conservative Court. He told his clerks about the votes in a judicial conference on one occasion, "Well, I was in the majority on one issue—breaking for lunch."[63]

Marshall reported, "Somebody [it was former Chief Justice Burger as part of the Constitution's 1987 bicentennial celebration] months ago made the suggestion that this present Court should sit in Philadelphia like it did two hundred years ago, and I made the point, 'Well if you're gonna do what you did two hundred years ago, somebody's going to give me short pants and a tray so I can serve coffee.'"[64]

Marshall enjoyed tweaking the formality that Chief Justice Warren Burger prized. He was famous for seeing Burger in the hall and asking, "What's shakin', Chiefy baby?"[65]

A 1991 television movie told the story of Marshall's most famous case, *Brown v. Board of Education*.[66] The film shows Marshall receiving a telephone call that tells him the decision will be announced the following morning and that he should be in attendance. The telephone call pierced the Court's ironclad veil of secrecy. After seeing the docudrama, Justice Anthony Kennedy asked Marshall whether it was true.

"I'll tell you half the story," Marshall replied. "Yes, it's true I got a call the night before."

"From whom did the call come?" Kennedy wanted to know.

"That's the half I'm not telling," Marshall said.[67]

Kennedy once expressed puzzlement about a case in which an attorney had dismissed all postal workers from a jury, even though the case had no connection to the postal service.

"Now, don't be too sure," Marshall cautioned his colleague. "I once excused all of the postal workers from a jury panel. Of course, that was because Life magazine was my client."

When Kennedy still seemed confused, Marshall added, "Don't you know? Mail carriers detested a magazine that put 10 or 15 pounds of weight in their bags and on their shoulders once a week, 52 weeks a year."[68]

In *Perry v. Louisiana*,[69] the Court faced the issue of whether a state might administer psychotropic drugs to a person in order to render him sane so they might then carry out the death penalty. Upon being told at oral argument that the drugs were injected into the convict, Marshall said, "Well, if all you say is true in the interest of Louisiana, while you're giving him the injection, why don't you give enough to kill him then? ... It would be cheaper for the state."

When the lawyer for the state responded that such a procedure might amount to cruel and unusual punishment as well as violate considerations of due process, Marshall had made his point.[70]

To remind the law clerks who worked for him of their place when they began to feel comfortable about telling the justice what position he should take in a case, Marshall was known to opine: "I'm the one who was nominated by President Lyndon B. Johnson and confirmed by the Senate of the United States...not you."[71]

By the late 1980s, Marshall had experienced two decades of chronic health problems, and with new appointees on the Court, he was increasingly marginalized in dissent. His goal was to try to ensure his successor shared his liberal ideology although, as time went by, that became increasingly unlikely. At one point, he told his law clerks that if he died on the bench they should "prop [him] up and keep on voting."[72]

Before his retirement press conference, Marshall gathered his current crop of law clerks and broke the news to them. To temper their obvious disappointment, he suggested that they were lucky to have survived the whole term with him. He said, "When I saw this group of clerks, I shoulda quit the first week!"[73]

Potter Stewart

Born January 23, 1915, in Jackson, Michigan; died December 7, 1985; associate justice, 1958–1981. Stewart served as a city council member and vice mayor of Cincinnati before his appointment to the U.S. Court of Appeals for the Sixth Circuit. After a mere four years on that court, President Dwight D. Eisenhower elevated him to the Supreme Court. He was known to a small circle of friends as "Potsy."

Potter Stewart was once asked if, when he was a law student at Yale, he would have thought he would become a Supreme Court justice. He replied:

> Never, never, never, never, No. But I have often thought that if somebody had stood in front of our class and said, one of you birds is going to be President of the United States, and it's up to each one of you to write down on a piece of paper who you think it's going to be, everyone would have gotten at least one vote except our classmate Jerry Ford. At least each of us would have voted for himself, but Jerry Ford and the rest of us knew that he was going to return to Grand Rapids and practice law....[74]

Stewart served in the Navy during World War II, but his unglamorous service caused him to refer to it as the "dungaree navy." He was assigned to an oil tanker in the Atlantic, where German submarines were known to roam. He described his service as "floating around on a sea of 100 octane gas, bored to death 99 percent of the time and scared to death 1 percent."[75]

Stewart's nomination to the Court engendered significant Southern opposition as a result of a Sixth Circuit opinion he had recently written in a civil rights case.[76] After some delay, he won approval by the Senate despite negative votes from 17 members from the South.

Stewart told then-Attorney General William Rogers, "At my first confirmation hearing, you warned me not to say too much. Why didn't you warn me not to write too much?"[77]

Stewart loved to sleep in and found getting up in the morning a most difficult chore. When he was first appointed to the Supreme Court, its sessions did not begin until noon. A friend congratulated him on landing a job that would actually let him get to work on time. When the Court changed its schedule to a ten o'clock start, he – as might be expected – was late the first day.[78] Nonetheless, he said appointment to the Court was "like dying and going to heaven."[79]

Stewart's wry wit was often displayed to his law clerks. Once, when he was surprised that Abe Fortas agreed with a Stewart draft opinion in a Fourth Amendment case, *Katz vs. United States*,[80] he wrote a note to law clerk Larry Tribe (who later became a distinguished Harvard law professor): "With such prompt and enthusiastic support from such an unexpected quarter, maybe we better *re-read* the memo carefully to see what we say (and what we don't)..."[81]

The 1973 National League playoffs of Major League Baseball featured the New York Mets against Stewart's beloved Cincinnati Reds. During the deciding game of that match-up, the Court was in session. Stewart told his clerks to send him notes about the game's progress, at first each inning, then each half inning, and, finally, batter by batter. When, during the game, news broke that Vice President Spiro Agnew had resigned, the clerks understood Stewart's priorities. Their note read, "[Mets player Ed] Kranepool flies to right. Agnew resigns."[82]

In *Jacobellis v. Ohio*,[83] Stewart opined that he couldn't define obscenity, but "I know it when I see it." The phrase became much quoted, to his regret, and he feared that those words would later be engraved on his tombstone.[84]

In fact, at his retirement announcement, he said that of "all the other thousands of words that I have written, and the late nights I have spent trying to write opinions for the Court or my separate opinions, I regret a little bit that if I am remembered at all, I will be remembered for that particular phrase, which, in my view, is far from deathless."[85]

Across the street from the Supreme Court stands the Methodist Building, which used to serve an inexpensive lunch in its cafeteria. In June 1972, Potter Stewart and William Brennan repaired to the cafeteria for lunch. Soon, because of the repeated use of the word "fuck," they were asked to leave. Only after they explained who they were and that they were discussing an obscenity case did the manager allow them to remain and finish their meal.[86]

Stewart retired at age 66 saying, "It's better to go too soon than to stay too long."[87] Some retired justices sit by designation on lower federal courts to keep their hand in judging. Stewart found such a prospect particularly unappetizing. He said it was "no fun to play in the minors after a career in the major leagues."[88]

Byron R. White
Born June 8, 1917, in Fort Collins, Colorado; died April 15, 2002; associate justice, 1962–1994. White was a sensation as a college and professional football player, leading the National Football League in rushing as a rookie. He also

chalked up impressive scholarly credentials, earning a Rhodes Scholarship. He clerked at the Supreme Court for Chief Justice Fred Vinson before returning to Colorado to practice law. Immediately prior to joining the Court, White served as deputy attorney general during the Kennedy Administration. Though he did not like the nickname, a sportswriter, referring to his speed on the college gridiron, dubbed him "Whizzer White," and the name stuck.

Justice Bryon White was a college football star almost from the beginning of his career as a freshman. The Boulder Daily Camera covered an intrasquad game and declared "the strong-legged young freshman from Wellington...the whole show on offense" after he scored on runs of 25 and 12 yards. In a game later in the season, he intercepted a pass and ran it back 85 yards for a touchdown, "zig-zagging[,] straight-arming, shaking tacklers off with his powerful legs for one of the prettiest runs" the same paper's reporter had ever seen. A reporter from the *Rocky Mountain News* said White "can go thru a broken field like measles in a crowd."[89]

In one of his first outings as a running back, Denver Post sports reporter Leonard Cahn observed that he was "a real whizzer." The name stuck, and the new collegian became known as "Whizzer" White.[90] The Tenth Circuit's website, whose courthouse is named after the justice, notes that even 65 years after he played for the University of Colorado, he still held 15 football records.[91]

For example, White set a record of 246.3 all-purpose yards in 1937, which was not eclipsed until Barry Sanders of Oklahoma State won the Heisman Trophy with 295.5 all-purpose yards in 1988.[92]

As with his athletic prowess, White took the same competitive spirit to the academic field. Once, his football coach spotted White reading a textbook and commented that the young player should be studying his playbook instead. White retorted, "You take care of the football. I'll take care of the books."[93]

As a law clerk to Vinson, White continued his vigorous exercise regimen, even while working at the Court. There is a basketball court on the top floor of the Supreme Court building, known affectionately as the "highest court in the land." It is situated directly above the courtroom. During an unusually raucous badminton match on the court's basketball court, the competition reached such volume that the justices sent up a note requesting that such activity cease and desist during oral argument.[94] To this day, possibly because White would retreat to the basketball court while the court was in session, the court sports a sign at the entrance that states: "PLAYING BASKETBALL AND WEIGHTLIFTING ARE PROHIBITED WHILE THE COURT IS IN SESSION."[95]

In 1961, as White joined the Justice Department under newly inaugurated President John F. Kennedy, a waitress serving him in a Washington restaurant thought she recognized the former football star.

"Say, aren't you Whizzer White?" she asked.

"I was," White replied.[96]

White had an unusual reaction to the telephone call from President John F. Kennedy, who told White he was being appointed to the Supreme Court. White told the president that Kennedy was "putting him out to pasture mighty early."[97]

White's physical strength impressed even the hardiest of his law clerks. Pierce O'Donnell, a law clerk during the October Term 1973 and a former college football player himself, said the "good morning" handshake he received his first day on the job was so powerful and "vise-like" that he does not remember anything else about that day but how his hand hurt.[98]

One day when he was in private practice, former law clerk Pierce O'Donnell got a call from the justice.

"How are you today?" the former clerk asked.

"I'm fine, but one of my new law clerks, John Spiegal, has a little problem," White replied.

"What's that, sir?"

"His glasses got in the way of my elbow up on the basketball court. What's the name of that optician on Capitol Hill you used a lot?"[99]

When the new clerk brought his glasses to that repair shop, the optician said, "You work for that man, White? He is an animal. You have to get contacts."[100]

In 1982, White spoke at a meeting of the Utah Bar Association. After being introduced, a large man stormed the stage and took a swing at the then 65-year-old justice. White ducked the blow, but the man continued to swing, landing a couple of punches. White merely scowled as others subdued the attacker, though White gave every impression that he had been prepared to deck his assailant. The attacker apparently wanted to protest the Court's recent obscenity decisions, unaware that White wrote the majority opinion three weeks earlier in *New York v. Ferber*,[101] which upheld a state statute criminalizing child pornography. He was also apparently unaware that White was the justice most likely to take a punch without worry. In fact, White began his speech by remarking that he had been "hit harder than that when I came to Utah to play football."[102]

Chief Justice William Rehnquist has written that White's "gruff voice and penetrating questions still strike terror into the hearts of unprepared attorneys arguing orally before the Court the way he used to terrify his football opponents."[103]

In a 1988 public television documentary on the Supreme Court, journalist Paul Duke interviewed White and Justice Lewis Powell. He read the Rehnquist description to Powell and asked about its accuracy. Powell replied, "Sometimes he strikes terror in some of us."

White immediately growled a low and elongated, "Lewis Powell."[104]

Another witness to White's gruffness was former Harvard law school dean and U.S. Solicitor General Erwin Griswold, who was among the top advocates before the Court in the 20th century. Griswold liked White but noted that "he can give the appearance of brusqueness."[105]

Even White's high school English teacher, Evelyn Schmidt Ely, recalls that the future justice "was always somewhat gruff, even in 8th grade." She recalled an instance when White saw her "greasing" her car, came over, and commanded her without much grace to "[g]et outta the way; I'll do it."[106]

White always made sure his law clerks understood the hierarchy at the Court, even though he introduced them as the "Great (name)" and referred to their "big brains." He would explain that law clerks were "rarely in doubt and often in error," while the justices themselves "were often in doubt and rarely in error." One clerk, having written a memo about a case that called attention to a prior decision by stating "we have previously held," received a response from White: "I didn't know you were on the Court then, Bill."[107]

White believed that there was a five-year adjustment period after joining the Court. When Clarence Thomas joined the bench, White advised, "Well, Clarence, in your first five years you wonder how you got here. After that, you wonder how your colleagues got here."[108]

White asked advocates particularly sharp questions. Former Solicitor General Charles Fried described the questions as a "skewer," given how piercing they could be. Still, White could take heart when an advocate was on the receiving end of another justice's consternation. In one case, a woman who was probably making a first-time appearance was so nervous that she literally read a prepared written statement. She was admonished that the Court had a "rule which frowned on reading oral arguments." Before the reprimand could further unsettle her, White jumped in and told her not to worry. He pointed out that the "Solicitor General does it all the time." [109]

Future Justice Neil Gorsuch clerked for White after he had retired. Gorsuch recalled walking with him down a hallway at the Court that was lined with portraits of past justices. White asked him how many of the justices he recognized, and Gorsuch responded that he could only recognize about half. White replied, "Me too. We'll all be forgotten soon enough."[110]

Charles E. Whittaker
Born February 22, 1901, near Troy, Kansas; died November 26, 1973; associate justice, 1957–1962. Whittaker climbed the ladder of the federal judiciary courtesy of President Dwight D. Eisenhower, serving in rapid succession on a federal district court in Missouri, the U.S. Court of Appeals for the Eighth Circuit, and then the Supreme Court. He left the Court to become chief counsel to General Motors.

Charles Whittaker was born and raised on his father's farm and attended a one-room public school. As a recreation and to make money, he trapped skunks and sold their pelts for $3 each. "They [the skunks] didn't make me very popular at school," he later recalled. "I used to sit near the stove. When it became hot, the skunk odor would grow more and more noticeable, so I would have to move to the corner of the room. Many times, the teacher sent me home."[111]

Whittaker made a rapid ascent from the federal district court to the Court of Appeals to the Supreme Court in the space of three years. The rapidity of that rise caused Justice Felix Frankfurter to say, "We can get a judge from the District Court quicker than we can get a case from that court."[112]

It is not common for a Supreme Court justice to compare himself to a monkey, but Whittaker once did just that. After he had retired from the Court, Whittaker was invited to address the Nebraska Bar at its annual meeting. He noted in his remarks that he suspected that he was invited as:

> a curio, someone who would "pack 'em in," one that the folks might turn out not so much to hear as to see. And it seems that a Justice, even a retired one, very well meets those specifications,

as there are fewer of them in existence than there are monkeys in the local zoo.

I must say that I feel a keener sympathy than before for the old chimpanzee who had been longer in captivity than any other. His keeper, seeking to stimulate interest in the zoo, awakened to this fact and thought it would be good for the zoo to tell the people about it, and so he got an audience. There was the old chimpanzee, whose name was Hokum, and there was a ladder. All things needed being on hand, he started the show. He said, "Hokum, climb the ladder." Well, the old chimpanzee managed cumbersomely in one way or another to climb up the ladder. Then the keeper said, "Hokum, make a noise like a chimpanzee. And Hokum made a noise that most of the people thought sounded like a chimpanzee. Now, that concluded the show, ladies and gentlemen. That is all there was to it – and that's about all there'll be to this. But it did help to advertise the zoo, which thenceforth was on its way."[113]

Before Whittaker gave his Nebraska Bar speech, he was approached by a woman who asked for a copy of his remarks.

"Well, I have only the one," the retired justice said, "and I will need it here this evening."

"Will it be published?" she asked.

"Maybe it will be some day," Whittaker answered. "Perhaps posthumously."

"Well, I hope it won't be long," she said enthusiastically.[114]

Whittaker was assigned the majority opinion in a closely divided case,[115] where Douglas took the dissent. Because he was a very quick writer, having completed his task, Douglas went to visit Whittaker in his chambers and found Whittaker stymied in trying to write his part.

"That's because you are on the wrong side," Douglas suggested, obviously hoping to make his dissent into a majority opinion by winning over Whittaker.

"Not at all. Not at all," Whittaker insisted. "I am right, but I can't get started."

Douglas offered, "Would you like me to send you a draft of the majority opinion?"

"Would you, please?" Whittaker asked.

In an hour's time, Douglas sent him a draft, which ended up being the majority opinion, giving him a chance to say later that he wrote both the majority and minority opinions.[116]

8

The Burger-Rehnquist Courts

Richard Nixon campaigned successfully for president in 1968 on a law-and-order theme, blaming the liberal Warren Court for going overboard in securing criminal defendants' rights and handcuffing the police in the discharge of their duties. DC Circuit Court Judge Warren Burger had long cultivated a law-and-order reputation, was known to Nixon from Republican politics, and stood out as a conservative voice on an otherwise liberal circuit court. Nixon replaced Earl Warren with Warren Earl Burger, believing it would herald in a period of counterrevolution to the liberal decisions that had made the Warren Court controversial. Nixon added other justices, including Harry Blackmun, Lewis Powell, and William Rehnquist, but the counterrevolution did not take place; rather, there was only some retrenchment in certain areas of law. Moreover, the Burger Court issued a number of controversial decisions of its own, including the abortion decision *Roe v. Wade*,[1] and extended the right to counsel for criminal defendants. The Burger Court also issued decisions advancing women's equality. Yet, its most far-reaching decision came in *U.S. v. Nixon*,[2] which ended the presidency of the man who appointed Burger.

When Burger retired to run the Commission on the Bicentennial of the U.S. Constitution, President Ronald Reagan elevated Associate Justice William H. Rehnquist to the center seat. Rehnquist, who had been the most conservative member of the Burger Court, often dissenting alone from its decisions, was expected to accomplish the conservative revolution that Burger did not. Although the Court became more conservative, adopted a strong stance on federalism, and struck down a record number of significant federal and state laws, it did not go as far as many expected. For example, despite being a long-time critic of *Miranda v. Arizona*,[3] the case that gave rise to the famous Miranda Warning, Rehnquist surprisingly wrote the decision that upheld, rather than overturned it, calling the rule a function of the Constitution and not susceptible to congressional abridgement.[4]

Warren Burger, Chief Justice (1969–1986)
William Rehnquist, Chief Justice (1986–2005), Associate Justice (1972–1986)

Associate Justices:
Harry Blackmun (1971–1994)
Stephen Breyer (1994–2022)
Ruth Bader Ginsburg (1993–2020)
Anthony Kennedy (1988–2018)
Sandra Day O'Connor (1981–2006)
Lewis Powell, Jr. (1972–1987)
Antonin Scalia (1986–2016)
David Souter (1990–2009)
John Paul Stevens (1975–2010)
Clarence Thomas (1991–present)

The Chief Justices

Warren E. Burger

Born September 17, 1907, in St. Paul, Minnesota; died June 25, 1995; chief justice, 1969–1986. Burger brought experience as an assistant attorney general during the Eisenhower administration and a judge on the U.S. Court of Appeals for the District of Columbia Circuit to the Supreme Court. In addition to his judicial duties, Burger gave considerable attention to the administration of the Supreme Court building. Before retirement and into the first years of retirement, Burger chaired the Commission on the Bicentennial of the U.S. Constitution. For his ability to master maritime law as an assistant attorney general, Burger was called "Admiral." His shock of white hair also earned him the nickname "The Chief Justice from Central Casting."

The other justices found Chief Justice Warren Burger to be formal, given to unnecessary ceremony, and somewhat imperious. His lifelong friend Harry Blackmun, who joined him on the Supreme Court, reported to Justice Potter Stewart that none of this was new; Burger had "been doing that since he was four."[5]

Another time Blackmun said, "[The chief justice] is a very domineering person, and he gets away with it much of the time, but we all love him just the same. It's part of his personality. One doesn't change from fourth grade on, I guess."[6]

Burger's strong sense of justice and his role in it was evident when, as a young lawyer in St. Paul, he effected a citizens' arrest on the street. He also was vocal in his opposition to the internment of Japanese Americans during World War II and took one family into his home for a period of months. Even after taking office as chief justice, he found it necessary to intervene in a street fight during a visit to London.[7] Reportedly, Burger stopped five stick-wielding hooligans who were attacking a single individual.[8]

Burger had a long-running feud on the U.S. Court of Appeals for the District of Columbia Circuit with fellow Judge David Bazelon. When Burger was elevated to the chief justiceship, Bazelon denied making disparaging remarks about his former bench mate in the press after the appointment was announced. "I couldn't have," Bazelon exclaimed, "I was speechless and sick for a week."

Burger, for his part, blamed Bazelon for letting a horde of reporters into the court building against the newly nominated chief justice's express wishes. "The only way they could have gotten in is Bazelon," Burger said. "If I can prove it's true, I'll punch him in the nose."[9]

Burger was called the "Chief Justice from Central Casting" because he looked and sounded like a chief justice should. Much of this description was due to his mane of white hair. Once, when asked if the luxurious mane of hair was due to washing it in champagne, Burger replied, "No, I just use beer."[10]

Burger was an energetic chief justice, constantly in motion. Mrs. Burger once urged him to slow down. "You're only human," she said. His driver, however, interjected, "If he were only human, he'd have been dead years ago."[11]

Taking advantage of Burger's predilection for dignity, then Associate Justice William Rehnquist played an April Fool's joke on the chief justice in 1985. As a neighbor of Burger's, Rehnquist asked for a lift to the Court one morning. When the limousine passed the front of the court building as Burger always asked the driver to do, there was a photographer offering to take tourist pictures with a life-size cardboard cut-out of the chief justice for one dollar. Burger was visibly upset. What he didn't know is that Rehnquist had set up the whole thing and asked for the ride to court so he could see Burger's reaction.[12]

Early on in their joint tenure, before a falling out changed their relations, Burger and Blackmun joined the same opinion in 89.9 percent of the Court's decisions. The two men had long been close personal friends: Blackmun, in fact, was best man at Burger's wedding, and Burger recommended Blackmun's appointment to the Court to President Nixon. The two justices were both Minnesotans and sports-oriented newsmen covering the Court dubbed them "the Minnesota Twins."[13]

Justices have long had strong views, even harsh opinions, about their colleagues. Lewis Powell, who was noted for his civility, told a law clerk that, back when he was practicing law, he would have fired an associate who wrote opinions as badly as Burger.[14]

Justices are remembered by court employees often by their kindnesses or their officiousness. At least some court employees remembered Burger for the latter. As people were saddened by the retirement of Justice Lewis Powell, a gentle soul, in 1987, Marshall's ancient messenger commiserated with the funeral-like atmosphere that enveloped the Court and added: "And I remember when Burger retired; it was just like Christmas morning."[15]

During his final years as chief justice and for a continuing period afterward, as chairman of the Commission on the Bicentennial of the U.S. Constitution, Burger brought an evangelical fervor to this work. He believed that teaching the American people about the Constitution was both an appropriate capstone to his career and fated from the beginning. His birthday was the same as the Constitution's – September 17. He turned 80 on the day the Constitution turned 200.

In January 1986, while still on the Court, Burger called ABA President William Falsgraf with a request that he come to Washington to discuss an urgent bicentennial matter. At Burger's request, Falsgraf brought the ABA staffer, Robert Peck, a co-author of this book, who was heading the group's bicentennial projects. Burger sent a car to pick up the two from Falsgraf's hotel. At the Supreme Court building, Falsgraf and Peck were introduced to Gannett newspapers executive Charles Overby, who had been similarly summoned. Overby, who had flown up to Washington on the corporate jet from the pre-Super Bowl festivities in New Orleans, was also in the dark about the subject of the meeting.

Burger arrived, exchanged some small talk, and invited his visitors to sit down to lunch in the justices' conference room. He soon complained that Congress had appropriated very little money for his commission's work. The bicentennial of the Declaration of Independence received a $276 million appropriation, he said, "We have only been approved for about $12 million."

An aide then interrupted Burger: "We won't be getting the full amount."

"Why not?" Burger asked.

"Because of Gramm-Rudman [a statute passed to cut appropriations in order to balance the budget]," the aide replied.

"Oh, don't worry about that," Burger said. "We're declaring that unconstitutional."

In fact, Burger authored the opinion, published just a few months later, that indeed declared the Gramm-Rudman law unconstitutional on separation-of-powers grounds,[16] but to his audience, it was unclear whether that was a joke or a scoop.

Burger then told his guests that he had decided his commission was going to sponsor a high-school essay contest on the Constitution. He wanted Gannett to pay for it and the ABA to judge it. Demurrers on any commitment were swept aside, and the lunch came to a close.

Overby headed back to New Orleans for the Super Bowl, while Falsgraf and Peck were invited to join Burger in chambers. While the two expected some other shoe to drop that would explain the urgency of the original invitation, the talk quickly turned to football. In the end, Burger obtained both the Gannett funding and the ABA assistance for the essay contest.[17]

William H. Rehnquist
Born October 1, 1924, in Milwaukee, Wisconsin; died September 3, 2005; associate justice, 1972–1986; chief justice, 1986–2005. Rehnquist had previously served at the Court as a law clerk to Justice Robert H. Jackson. He was assistant

attorney general in the Office of Legal Counsel at the Justice Department when he was named to the Supreme Court. Upon Chief Justice Warren Burger's retirement, Rehnquist was elevated to chief justice. During the long period he served as an associate justice, he often found himself in lonely dissent for which he became known as the "Lone Ranger."

The release of FBI files on Rehnquist in 2007 revealed that he was arrested once when he was a college student for what the chief justice believed was a charge of vagrancy. He was a freshman at Kenyon College who had gone to visit a friend at Kent State University, some 100 miles away. A mix-up occurred so that the friend was out of town when Rehnquist arrived. Without money to get a room for the night, Rehnquist tried to spend the night sleeping on the lawn at the Ravenna courthouse. A police officer discovered him, told him it violated the law, and took him to jail. He was released the next morning with no further consequences.[18]

When Rehnquist enlisted in the army, he changed his middle name as he signed up. He was born "William Donald Rehnquist." He jettisoned Donald in favor of his maternal grandmother's last name, Hubbs. According to his former law clerk, now Chief Justice John Roberts, Rehnquist's mother was told by a numerologist around that time that her son would have a successful career if his middle initial were "H."[19]

During World War II, Rehnquist served as an Army Air Corps weather observer, which sparked a life-long interest in weather. When, in 2001, the chief justice was honored by the Washington, DC chapter of the American Meteorological Society, Rehnquist quipped that he likes to think his decision to leave meteorology in favor of the law improved both professions.[20]

At the end of his clerkship with Justice Robert Jackson, Rehnquist asked the Library of Congress to provide a listing of the U.S. cities with the most sun during the year. Tampa was number one on the list, but

Rehnquist thought it was too humid. Albuquerque was second, but Rehnquist decided there was too much "old money" in the city and that it would be hard to enter the community. Phoenix was third on the list and became Rehnquist's choice to establish a home.[21]

Rehnquist's interest in history led to a fascination with Judge Isaac Parker who was the famous 19th century Hanging Judge depicted in the novel and the movie, "True Grit." In 1953, Rehnquist was driving from his clerkship in Washington, DC to his new home in Phoenix and made a detour to Fort Smith, Arkansas, where Parker had held court. Rehnquist did further research on Parker and considered writing a biography about him.

Years later, Rehnquist wrote an opinion in *Oliphant v. Suquamish Indian Tribe*,[22] which held that non-Indians could not be tried by tribes if they committed crimes on reservations. He wrote a three-paragraph mini-biography of Parker in footnote 10 of the opinion. It turned out that Parker had been the only federal judge who had addressed this question in a written opinion[23] prior to *Oliphant*.[24]

In September 1971, Rehnquist was asked whether he had any chance of being named to the Court. He replied, "None at all because I'm not from the South, I'm not a woman, and I'm not mediocre."[25]

The first time Rehnquist met Richard Nixon, he made an impression, though not the type he might have preferred. Rehnquist came to talk about a Justice Department declassification project. He had mutton-chop sideburns and heavy black eyeglasses, wore a "pink shirt that clashed with an awful psychedelic necktie, and Hush-Puppies." When Nixon left the meeting, he turned to his aide, John Ehrlichman, and asked, "John, who the hell is that clown?"

Erlichman did not know who Nixon was referring to.

Nixon specified, "The guy dressed like a clown, who's running the meeting."

"Oh, you mean Bill Rehnquist," Erlichman answered.

As the president went into his office, he added, "That's a hell of a costume he's wearing, just like a clown."[26]

As an associate justice, Rehnquist had become "by popular acclaim," the "architect, engineer and general contractor" for the Court's annual Christmas party, in Burger's words. He penned some lyrics to popular Christmas songs that reflected his conservatism, though no offense was taken by his brethren. Among the ditties:
Pack the Court with hacks and cronies, fa la la la la...
Weed out all those liberal phonies, fa la la la la...[27]

Rehnquist started taking the anti-insomnia drug Placidyl in 1971 to address constant back pain, the year before he joined the Court as an associate justice. His drug use continued through 1991, when he was hospitalized for back pain and drug dependency. In 1981, the drug caused him to slur occasionally when talking. He checked himself into George Washington University Hospital to address his back pain and his addiction. A 1986 FBI investigation reported he suffered paranoid delusions when he tried to stop taking drugs. While hospitalized, he believed there was a CIA plot against him and went into the "lobby in his pajamas in order to try to escape."[28]

Once, when future Justice Ruth Bader Ginsburg was arguing a sex discrimination case, Rehnquist quipped at the end of the case, "You won't settle for putting Susan B. Anthony on the new dollar, then?"[29]

The February 1974 issue of the *National Lampoon* contained a cartoon centerfold of the nine justices occupied with a variety of deviant sex acts. Rehnquist found the depiction sufficiently humorous and thought it unlikely that the other justices would otherwise see it, so he brought a copy to pass around the conference table. Most of the justices laughed goodheartedly at the fun being poked at their expense, but Burger apparently found the caricature offensive and its presence in the conference room inappropriate. Thurgood Marshall's reaction was quite the opposite. He sent a clerk to purchase copies that he could send to his sons away at college.[30]

Rehnquist clearly had his priorities. When he took up painting, he took classes at the local adult education center. Reluctant to miss a class, one year he skipped President Reagan's annual State of the Union address, the only justice absent, to follow his muse. He explained to his clerks, "I've paid $25 for five classes. I can't miss it."[31]

Rehnquist loved to make small wagers about every topic under the sun, from historical facts to weather conditions. Once, the *Washington Post* captured a picture of Rehnquist and his law clerks standing in deep snow outside the Supreme Court building one January as anti-abortion protesters went by. But Rehnquist was not there to see the protest; he was measuring the snowfall so he could collect on a bet on its depth with other justices.[32]

Rehnquist liked to talk about cases with his law clerks while walking outside. The weather never deterred him, but one year a clerk from Miami balked, calling the cold day "Florida school closing weather." Rehnquist liked the phrase so much that he adopted it to describe the perfect weather for one of these walks.[33]

Sometimes, on these walks around the building, Rehnquist would be stopped by tourists who had no idea who he was and who would ask him to take their picture as they posed on the steps of the Court. He always obliged.[34]

Rehnquist prized brevity in opinions. When future Chief Justice John Roberts, then a Rehnquist law clerk, drafted one opinion for Rehnquist, Rehnquist explained that he liked the first sentence of each paragraph in Roberts's draft. Roberts disagreed and argued that more than the first sentences should be included. Rehnquist offered a compromise that the rest of the material be put in footnotes.

Roberts followed Rehnquist's instructions and provided a draft with the first sentences of each paragraph in the body of the opinion and the rest in the footnotes. Rehnquist reviewed the draft and then told Roberts, "Well, all right. Now take out the footnotes."[35]

Rehnquist loved playing tennis and was very competitive as a doubles player. He frequently played with his clerks, and even though there was an agreement to rotate players every week to ensure the fair distribution of talent, Rehnquist somehow wound up on the side of the best player week after week.[36]

Rehnquist came to the Supreme Court bench without trial or judicial experience and had always wanted to try a case. After he expressed that interest in a speech as an associate justice, he received an invitation to preside over a federal jury trial and accepted. After the experience, it might be said he received a taste of his own medicine. The judgment he entered on the jury verdict was reversed, per curiam, by the Fourth Circuit. It proved to be his only experience with trial court judging.[37]

Although the *New York Times* reported that Rehnquist had "accepted a bribe last week in the full view of several hundred witnesses, no prosecution seems likely to result." The bribe took place during a cameo Rehnquist made in a production of Gilbert and Sullivan's *Patience*. Rehnquist played the role of solicitor, wearing a flowing white wig and robes, and was presiding over a raffle. His palms were greased to intervene in the raffle's result so that the heroine would take the first prize. Rehnquist, a fan of Gilbert and Sullivan, found the experience a delight, especially because his character did not utter a word so there was nothing for him to memorize.[38]

A reporter asked Rehnquist what his spouse said when it was announced that President Reagan would nominate the associate justice to be chief justice. Rehnquist unhesitatingly responded, "She said, unload the dishwasher."[39]

One benefit of becoming chief justice, Rehnquist said, is that "whenever I say something now people say, 'how interesting' and 'how profound.' Six months ago, they either ignored what I said or said I was crazy."[40]

Rehnquist had a vacation home in Greensboro, Vermont, where he spent summers over a period of almost 30 years. In Greensboro, he was a member of the "Romeos"—Retired Old Men Eating Out in Style.[41]

Rehnquist used to travel incognito. He would often wear a trench coat, a baseball cap, and sunglasses to hide his identity. On one occasion, he traveled to the Midwest, where he was to be met by a law student who was to take him to a moot court competition. He approached the student and tried to start a conversation, but the student did not recognize him and rebuffed him, saying he was there to meet the chief justice and needed to be left alone. Rehnquist told the student, "Well, what a remarkable coincidence. I happen to be the Chief Justice."[42]

When Anthony Kennedy first joined the Court, he attended a luncheon that the justices had on days when they heard oral arguments. Rehnquist, always inquisitive about where people were from, asked Kennedy, who was from Sacramento, what that city's annual rainfall was, and Kennedy replied, "Just over twenty inches."

Rehnquist, a stickler for precision, told him that amount was too high, and in about an hour, Kennedy received a memo from Rehnquist saying the annual rainfall in Sacramento was 18.9 inches.[43]

Some advocates before the Supreme Court were surprised and confused when Rehnquist suddenly stood up during their argument and disappeared behind the curtain that is a backdrop to the bench. Experienced argument-watchers could almost read the expression on the oralist's face: "Oh, no, the chief justice has just walked out on my argument." Rehnquist, however, was doing no such thing. He had a persistent back problem and stood and stretched to relieve pressure on his back. He used to take medication for it until he began to slur his words on the bench and developed a dependency on the drugs. His new regimen replaced the reliance on drugs.[44]

At least Rehnquist did not follow the practice of the first Justice John Marshall Harlan, who used to indicate his boredom with the argument by getting up and pacing back and forth behind his brethren.[45]

Rehnquist's need for speed in producing opinions was not just felt by his law clerks. He pushed his colleagues on the Court to get opinions out with memos and deadlines. One year, his memo contained this advice from an old Andrews Sisters song, "Ac-Cent-Tchu-Ate The Positive":

> Accentuate the positive
> Eliminate the negative
> Latch on to the affirmative
> Don't mess with Mr. In Between.[46]

Rehnquist's sense of humor was occasionally put to use while sitting on the bench. During the argument in *Forsyth County vs. Nationalist Movement*,[47] the attorney, Richard Barrett, who both represented a white supremacist group in a challenge to a user's fee to cover law enforcement costs for a planned demonstration and served as the group's first officer, was given to flights of rhetoric that had little to do with legal argumentation. Making references to kingdoms and drawbridges and "the shiny sword of reason that ousts tyranny," Barrett was reminded more than once to explain his legal theory. Barrett believed he was on an historic mission that was more important than the justices and whatever vote they might have in his case. He ended his peroration with the epitaph he wished for his tombstone: "The road not taken, but not the speech not given."

"How about the argument not made?" the exasperated Rehnquist observed. (Barrett's group won, nevertheless.)[48]

Rehnquist had wide-ranging musical tastes. He enjoyed singing just about anything, including "church hymns, Christmas carols, old standards, cowboy songs," and led sing-alongs at judicial conferences and meetings.[49] While light opera was a favorite musical form, particularly the works of Gilbert and Sullivan, he also made it a point to listen to Handel's *Messiah* every December for 50 straight years. Bored during one oral argument, he sent his law clerks a message from the bench, listing the opening lines of five college fight songs and asking them to identify the matching college. When they collectively answered only two correctly, he gave them a grade of 40. And, in a precedential ruling in *Fogerty v. Fantasy, Inc.*,[50] Rehnquist declared that Credence Clearwater Revival is "one of the greatest American rock and roll groups of all time."[51]

In January 1995, Rehnquist surprised traditionalists at the Court by altering his plain black robe with four gold "racing" stripes on each upper arm. Rehnquist designed the addition himself after admiring a similar robe worn by the lord chancellor in a local production of Gilbert and Sullivan's light opera, "Iolanthe." With this individualistic attire, Rehnquist joined two other members of his Court that added to their judicial garb: Sandra Day O'Connor and Ruth Bader Ginsburg had previously started to wear white jabots of different designs.[52]

Iolanthe also figured in Rehnquist's description of his role, presiding over the impeachment trial of President Bill Clinton. When asked about it in an interview, he quoted a line from the light opera: "I did nothing in particular, and I did it very well."[53] When pressed further by one of his law clerks, he said, "Those Senators just talk too much. I couldn't live in that world very long."[54]

Rehnquist donated the judicial robe he wore during the impeachment trial to the Smithsonian and received a tax deduction for the contribution. He had it appraised by Sotheby's for $30,000.[55]

The donation did not leave him without a souvenir he could wear that commemorated his role in impeachment. His law clerks gave him a T-shirt adorned with the gold stripes he wore on his robe and printing that said, "I presided over a presidential impeachment and all I got was this lousy T-Shirt."[56]

During the final public session of the Court and his last appearance on the bench, Rehnquist could not resist a humorous observation. He announced the decision in *Van Orden v. Perry*, concerning a Ten Commandments monument on the Texas State Capitol grounds, noting that it generated seven separate opinions by the justices. He quipped, "I didn't know we had so many Justices."

Even in his final week of life, while in the emergency room, when the doctor attending to him asked him who his primary doctor was, he could not resist a joke despite the struggle it took to utter it, answering, "My dentist."[57]

The Associate Justices

Harry Blackmun

Born November 12, 1908, in Nashville, Illinois; died March 4, 1999; associate justice, 1971–1994. Prior to his U.S. Supreme Court service, Blackmun served on the U.S. Court of Appeals for the Eighth Circuit. After two prior nominees were rejected by the Senate, Blackmun was easily confirmed as uncontroversial and came to refer to himself as "Old No. 3." His law clerks, playing off the slow pace with which Blackmun wrote his own opinions, dubbed him, "Fast Harry."

Having an unusual spelling for what otherwise seems like a straightforward name has been a source of some confusion for Harry Blackmun, who was often written up as "Blackman." At Harvard Law School as a student, Blackmun was once called upon by Professor Bart Leach as "Mr. Blackhorse." The name stuck, and fellow students began to refer to the future justice as "good ol' Blackhorse Harry."[58]

Blackmun's early penchant for voting like his boyhood friend, Chief Justice Warren Burger, and for their shared hometown baseball team earned the two of them the title "The Minnesota Twins." In fact, the two voted together in 113 of the first 115 votes after Blackmun joined the Court.[59] Yet, Blackmun's lonely and modest ways also caused radio personality Garrison Keillor to call Blackmun "the shy person's justice."[60]

Blackmun was overwhelmed when he first entered the Court's robing room and saw Hugo Black, William O. Douglas, William Brennan, and John Harlan. He said to himself, "What am I doing here?"[61]

Blackmun was apparently surprised that a seat on the Supreme Court came with gifts. After sitting at the bench, he realized there was a drawer there, in which he found some cough drops and a copy of the Constitution stamped with "O.W. Holmes" and signed by Felix Frankfurter and other predecessors in that seat. The court's marshal asked him to sign a Bible that originally belonged to the first Justice John Marshall Harlan and was signed by every member of the Court afterward.

Just as Blackmun thought that this was the end of it, Justice Byron White caught Blackmun's attention, whispering, "Harry! Harry, where's your spittoon?"

White then snapped a finger to get a page's attention and said, "Get the Justice his spittoon!"[62]

Each justice has a spittoon at the foot of his chair by tradition, used largely for trash.

Blackmun wrote his own opinions rather than have his law clerks handle some of the drafts or sections. As a result, he was often the slowest of the justices to produce his opinions. The subject was much discussed at the Court, but his clerks nonetheless gave him the sobriquet of "Fast Harry."[63]

Inevitably, his most important decisions would be issued at the end of the term. Potter Stewart noted this tendency when he quipped, "Circulations from Harry are like returns in an election from rural counties – late."[64]

After the Court's conference during which the justices vote on the cases, Blackmun would brief his law clerks on the discussions by impersonating his colleagues. He reportedly did a terrific imitation of Sandra Day O'Connor.[65]

Blackmun discovered that his hearing aid made a squealing noise when his hand went near it. If this happened in conference, Justice Sandra Day O'Connor would look around. Perhaps she thought the room was bugged, he speculated. As a prank, from time to time, he would comb his hand through his hair to watch O'Connor's reaction to the sound.[66]

Blackmun allowed the justices to speculate about being wiretapped for days before revealing that the sound was caused by his hearing aid.[67]

Once, when the four justices who were more senior than him were out of town, the mischievous Blackmun authored a memorandum as "Acting Chief Justice" and stating that he was planning a Court square dance and would also acquire a Court cat to rid the building of mice.[68]

Blackmun was not one to pull rank or think himself important because he was a U.S. Supreme Court justice. People he met away from the Court often did not know who he was. When asked what he did for a living, he would invariably answer, "I'm a lawyer in Washington."[69]

Blackmun once surprised his law clerks by telling them that when he had difficulty sleeping, he was a fan of the television show called, "The Love Connection," where couples discussed their dating experiences. Blackmun told the clerks, "It's really fascinating."[70]

Each year, Blackmun would take his law clerks to the Washington Marine Corps barracks for a public parade. One year, shortly before the event, a bullet pierced the window of his Virginia apartment. Security was tightened on the chance that it was not merely a stray bullet. Blackmun was forced to abandon his tired-looking VW bug for a vehicle driven by security people. When Blackmun and his clerks entered the barracks through a new metal detector, the justice told his clerks that obviously someone important would be there that day. Mark Schneider, a law clerk, suggested that Blackmun himself might be the famous person requiring heightened security, an idea that had never occurred to the justice.[71]

When speaking before a law student audience, Blackmun was often asked about his favorite opinion. Most expected him to respond with *Roe v. Wade*,[72] the controversial abortion decision for which he is best known. Instead, Blackmun told audiences his favorite is *Flood v. Kuhn*,[73] a case involving baseball's reserve clause. Blackmun, a tremendous baseball fan, devoted Part I of the decision to a list of baseball's all-time greats, listing 89 players. He always feigned some mystery as to why Burger and White joined the decision, except for Part I.[74]

The laundry list of baseball stars became a collective effort at the Court as Blackmun wrote the opinion. At one point, a Rehnquist clerk suggested that former Washington Senators pitcher Camilo Pascual be included.

The next day, Blackmun's clerk replied, "The Justice recalls seeing Pascual pitch and remembers his fantastic curve ball ... But he ... decided Pascual's [lifetime] 174 wins were not enough ... Justice Blackmun felt that Pascual is just not in the same category as Christy Matthewson's 373 wins. I hope you will understand."[75]

Potter Stewart searched for a gentle way to suggest that a hall-of-fame section did not belong in a Supreme Court opinion. At one point, he joked that he could only join the opinion if one of his beloved Cincinnati Reds were added to the list. Blackmun simply obliged.[76]

Blackmun's only regret about the decision was the inadvertent omission of former New York Giants great Mell Ott.[77]

Near the end of his life, to his great pleasure, Blackmun played the role of Justice Joseph Story in the Stephen Spielberg movie, "Amistad," about enslaved people who took over a Spanish ship and their legal battles for freedom.[78]

At Blackmun's memorial service, Justice Stephen Breyer explained that Blackmun received thousands of letters demanding his resignation in the aftermath of *Roe v. Wade*, the abortion decision where he authored the majority opinion. To one of those letters calling for his resignation, Breyer recalled that Blackmun wrote, "Dear Sir, No. Sincerely, Harry A. Blackmun."[79]

Stephen Breyer

Born August 15, 1938, in San Francisco, California; associate justice, 1994–2022. Breyer had taught at Harvard Law School, served as an assistant special prosecutor in the Watergate investigation, and as a special counsel to the Senate Judiciary Committee. He also served as a judge on the U.S. Court of Appeals for the First Circuit. News reports had Breyer being selected a year earlier for the seat that went to Ruth Bader Ginsburg. Pundits thought it unlikely that Breyer would get a second chance – but he did. Breyer had achieved the highest rank in the Boy Scouts, Eagle Scout, but apparently, he did not take to hiking because he was called the "Blister King."

As an undergraduate at Stanford, Breyer was arrested for underage drinking. However, he did not ignore academics: He received only one B as an undergraduate, a grade that frustrated him immensely. Breyer earned a Marshall scholarship to study at Oxford, but he failed to receive a Rhodes scholarship because it had an athletic requirement.[80]

In a speech to dedicate a new library at the University of Connecticut's law school, Breyer, known for his loquaciousness and his unusually long questions at oral argument, promised he would be brief. He recalled that a student of his at Harvard had finished a final examination and appended a note that started out as quite a compliment.

"Professor Breyer," it read, "if I had only one hour to live, I should like to spend it in your class."

Breyer then noticed what was written on the reverse side: "That's because only in your class does one hour seem an eternity."[81]

A few weeks after Jimmy Carter was defeated by Ronald Reagan in 1980, Senator Edward Kennedy pushed Carter to nominate Breyer for a vacancy on the U.S. Court of Appeals for the First Circuit. Kennedy wanted to reward Breyer, who had worked with Kennedy on airline deregulation. One potential barrier to Breyer's appointment was, of course, Republican opposition. However, Republican Senator Strom Thurmond of South Carolina liked Breyer, and while Breyer was working for Kennedy, he and another Kennedy aide would have breakfast with a Thurmond aide and try to work out differences. Thurmond became so supportive of Breyer for both his appellate court appointment and his Supreme Court nomination that he almost sounded like Kennedy in his praise for Breyer, notwithstanding different accents.[82]

Breyer had been considered for the seat on the Court to which Ruth Bader Ginsberg was appointed. While he was awaiting word from the Clinton White House about whether he had been selected, he told his fellow judges on the First Circuit, "I know all of you are curious about how I'm holding up. It's not affecting me at all except in one small way: I'm hysterical 100 percent of the time."

He added, "There's only two people who aren't convinced I'm going to be on the Supreme Court. One is me, and the other is Clinton."[83]

When Breyer joined the Court, many thought that the former Senate Judiciary counsel and Harvard law professor would be a good foil for the acerbic conservative, Antonin Scalia. During the October Term 1995, Breyer lived up to his advanced billing.

The case presented the issue of whether, consistent with the First Amendment, the Florida Bar could prevent lawyers from sending solicitation letters to accident victims within 30 days of an accident. The rule was passed, in part, to improve the practices and image of lawyers. The lawyer who was challenging the rule asserted that accident victims need the information to decide on whether they have legal recourse and that lawyers serve "important purposes righting wrongs."

Chief Justice William Rehnquist could not resist asking to laughter: "Well, what if the Florida State Bar tries that and it just doesn't work – people still think lawyers are greedy?"

The lawyer replied that the First Amendment prevents Florida from pursuing this image-improving remedy.

Justice John Paul Stevens then said: "We should probably pass a statute saying you can't say un-nice things about lawyers."

His response inspired the rest of the Court to pile on with similar solutions.

Justice Ruth Bader Ginsburg: "And not read Dickens or Shakespeare [who have written some unflattering things about lawyers]."

Justice David H. Souter: "And not admit greedy people to practice law."

Justice Scalia then, tongue firmly planted in cheek, said: "I'm certainly glad I never passed through the stage of being a lawyer."

Breyer then told Scalia: "It might have helped you, actually."[84]

When Breyer announced his first opinion for the Court, he became so taken with the opportunity to explain the intricacies of the arbitration issue before the Court that he sounded like the law professor he once was. He was so carried away that he neglected to announce whether anyone dissented in the case and had to be reminded by both Rehnquist and Justice Clarence Thomas.

"Oh," he said, "there was a dissent as well." In reality, there were two dissents and one concurrence.[85]

Breyer ended up serving as the junior justice for eleven years. One task he got used to was answering the door mid-conference to accept and deliver a cup of coffee to Justice Scalia, who had arranged for that to happen each conference. Breyer once quipped to Scalia, "I've been doing this for ten years. I've gotten pretty good at it, haven't I?" Scalia replied, "No, you haven't."[86]

Breyer became so used to being the junior justice that at the first conference in which he had yielded the position to Justice Samuel

Alito, he reacted to a knock at the door during conference by getting up immediately to answer it, even as Alito was processing the fact that he was responsible for that chore. Before Breyer made it to the door, however, Chief Justice John Roberts stopped him. "Steve, sit down, that's not your job anymore."[87]

Breyer is something of a Francophile. In 2004, he had an opportunity to meet French actress Jeanne Moreau at a luncheon in the Senate dining room. For the occasion, Breyer brought along a copy of a rare book, "Fallen Oaks: Conversations with de Gaulle," by Andre Malraux. He had purchased the book in a Boston bookstore. The reason for bringing the book was to ask Moreau to autograph it because it had been inscribed to her by the author.

Moreau reacted by saying, "I've been looking for this book for years. It was stolen from me."

Breyer responded that "I can't be a Supreme Court justice and the receiver of stolen goods." He immediately made a gift of the book to Moreau.[88]

Whether it is nerves or thinking about a case a justice has authored while answering another justice's question, attorneys, even experienced ones, misidentify the justices with amazing frequency. But Breyer was nonplussed the time he was invited with clerks from Sandra Day O'Connor's chambers, only to have one clerk ask, "Are you and Justice Breyer often confused?"[89]

During the Obama administration, there was some thought to encourage Breyer to retire so that a new and younger justice could be appointed. Walter Dellinger, a former acting solicitor general, suggested that Obama invite Breyer for lunch and say, "I believe historians will someday say the three greatest American ambassadors to France were Benjamin Franklin, Thomas Jefferson, and Stephen G. Breyer." Dellinger's proposal got back to Breyer, who ran into Dellinger at a party and said, "So Walter, do you still want to ship me off to France?" Dellinger sensed that Breyer was joking and responded, "Mr. Justice, I hear Paris isn't what it used to be."[90]

Ruth Bader Ginsburg

Born March 15, 1933, in Brooklyn, New York; died September 18, 2020; associate justice, 1993–2020. Ginsburg taught at Rutgers and Columbia law schools. She also headed the Women's Rights Project of the American Civil Liberties Union, where she brought a number of landmark cases, six of which she argued before the Supreme Court, dismantling official discrimination against women. She served as a judge on the District of Columbia Circuit before being elevated to the Supreme Court. Late in life, she acquired rock star status, becoming known as the "Notorious RBG."

As a student at Cornell University, Ruth Bader Ginsburg discovered that "[t]he most important degree for [a woman] to get was Mrs., and it didn't do to be seen reading and studying." Although she did not abandon her studious ways, she cultivated an image as a happy-go-lucky co-ed. She said, "the thing to do was to be a party girl." Some of her classmates were amazed that the live-wire they knew as Kiki Bader could become the prim and learned justice she became.[91]

Cornell was also the site of Ginsburg's first exposure to sexual harassment. She responded to an amorous professor by telling him, "How dare you, how dare you!"[92]

Although Ginsburg graduated from Columbia Law School, she initially attended Harvard Law School. At Harvard, she had been one of only nine women in her class and the dean of Harvard had asked her to justify taking up the place where a man could be.[93]

Ginsburg had been on the law review at both Harvard and Columbia, and she was first in her class at Columbia. However, when she first went on the job market, no firm in New York City offered her a job.[94] Years later, as a justice, reflecting back on that, she said she did not resent the cold shoulder she received, "Suppose there had been a Wall Street firm interested in me? What would I be today? A retired partner."[95]

When her husband, Marty, one year ahead of her in school, took a job in New York, Ginsburg requested that Harvard allow her to finish her degree at Columbia, but was turned down. She then transferred to Columbia, earned her law degree there, and tied for top grades in her class. She later returned to Columbia, where she became the first woman to receive tenure on its law faculty.

Some years later, when Ginsburg was serving as a judge on the DC Circuit, Harvard adopted a new policy that granted Harvard degrees to students in similar predicaments. Mr. Ginsburg wrote the Harvard Law Record an ironic letter recalling that the incident had left his wife's "career blighted at an early age." "I asked Ruth if she planned to trade in her Columbia degree for a Harvard degree," Mr. Ginsburg wrote. "She just smiled."

Harvard enticed her back with an honorary degree in 2011 at a ceremony during which Plácido Domingo, another honorary degree recipient that year, addressed her in song. Ginsburg, an opera devotee, called it one of the greatest experiences of her life.[96]

Despite her high grades and the enthusiastic support of her professors, she was turned down for coveted clerkships with Judge Learned Hand and Justice Felix Frankfurter. Hand was not prepared to hire a woman clerk, claiming that he cursed too much. Frankfurter claimed that a woman clerk would be out of the question, let alone one with small children.[97] Ginsburg did snag a two-year clerkship with federal district judge Edmund L. Palmieri, but only after Prof. Gerald Gunther threatened to boycott the judge for future clerks if he turned Ginsburg down.[98]

Ginsburg's husband, Marty, was a whiz in the kitchen, but it was a skill she never mastered. Her children banished her from the kitchen well before she joined the Supreme Court bench, and she no longer cooked. The only recipe she really developed any skill in producing, a tuna fish casserole, was no one's favorite.[99]

Explaining the genesis of the term "gender discrimination" in place of "sex discrimination," Ginsburg, the pioneer advocate in that field, explained, "I owe it all to my secretary at Columbia Law School, who said, 'I'm typing all these briefs and articles for you, and the word sex, sex, sex is on every page.'"[100]

Arguing as an advocate before the Supreme Court the first time, Ginsburg skipped lunch "because I didn't know whether I could keep it down." While she experienced the nervousness of a first-time advocate, it disappeared after two minutes when "I looked up at these guys and said, 'I have a captive audience. They have no place to go for the next half hour. They must listen to me.'"[101]

While a judge on the District of Columbia Circuit, she served on a panel that included judges Patricia Wald and Roger Robb. The lawyer before them was so undone by appearing before two women judges that he kept referring to both as Judge Wald.

"Here's the sign in front of me that says 'Ginsburg' and here's the sign in front of Pat that says 'Wald,'" said Ginsburg, "but the lawyer couldn't comprehend the idea that there were two women on the three-judge panel. It was just too unfamiliar. So, [he simply labeled both] women with Wald, even though we really don't look alike. But that's the way it was in September 1980."[102]

NPR Supreme Court reporter Nina Totenberg had a close friendship with Ginsburg that preceded the justice's appointment to the high court. In 1988, the prestigious Cosmos Club opened its membership to women but turned Totenberg down. Ginsburg was later invited to visit the club as part of the membership recruitment ritual. She made the visit but rebuffed the invitation to membership, saying, "You know, I think that a club that is too good for Nina Totenberg is too good for me, too."[103]

A great friend of Justice Antonin Scalia, with whom she frequently disagreed on legal issues, Ginsburg said sparring with him helped her sharpen her opinions in response to his dissents. She took his advice seriously, but it appeared often to be a one-way street. Occasionally, she would advise him that "his opinion was so strident he would be more persuasive if he toned it down." But "he never took that advice."[104]

Ginsburg loved opera. She once said, "If I could have asked God to give me any talent in the world, I would never have been a lawyer. I'd be a great diva."[105]

It may have been over opera that she bonded with her ideological adversary, Scalia. They often attended the opera together. In 1994, she and Scalia donned appropriate costumes as extras in the Washington National Opera's production of "Ariadne auf Naxos." Later, composer Derrick Wang assembled lines from their opinions to compose an opera called "Scalia/Ginsburg."

When asked why Scalia got top billing when, if alphabetical, she would have, she replied that Scalia had reached the Court first and that Supreme Court traditions value seniority.[106]

Ginsburg and Scalia would take trips together. Once, on a trip to India, the two were photographed riding an elephant. Scalia, who was overweight, was in front, and the very slight Ginsburg behind him. When asked why she was in the back, her simple answer was weight distribution.[107]

Another time, they were teaching together on the French Riviera. Scalia reported, "She went off parasailing!"

He added, "This little skinny thing, you'd think she'd never come down. She was sailing off a motorboat in the Mediterranean, way up in the sky, my God. I would never do that."[108]

Late in life, Ginsburg became a cultural icon known as the Notorious RBG. As a result, this otherwise unassuming person would occasionally be recognized on the street by a gushing fan. Her response: "so many people have told me that I look just like her."[109]

Ginsburg's notoriety also spread to the scientific community. At the Cleveland Museum of Natural History, entomologists noticed that one insect they were studying had a neck plate that reminded them of a jabot that Ginsburg wore with her robe. To honor the justice's "commitment to women's rights and gender equality," they dubbed the bug "Ilomantis ginsburgae."[110]

Years later, when her husband, Marty, was dying, her friend and NPR Supreme Court reporter Nina Totenberg came with her husband to see how the Ginsburgs were doing. Knowing the justice had little skill in the kitchen, they brought food in an aluminum tin that only needed to be heated. To be sure, they asked Ginsburg whether she knew what to do. She replied that she would just put it in the microwave. Totenberg's husband stopped suddenly, explaining that aluminum does not go into a microwave because it would create an electrical shortage. He suggested she put it in the oven.
When she looked at them puzzlingly, they realized Ginsburg did not know how to use the oven.[111]

At Justice Elena Kagan's White House swearing-in ceremony, President Barack Obama asked Ginsburg her thoughts on his appointment of another woman justice.
Ginsburg, true to form, responded, "I love them, but I'll be happier when you give me six more."[112]
Her answer to Obama was a variation on the response she traditionally gave when asked when there would be enough women on the Court: "When there are nine."[113]

Ginsburg nodded off more than once during State of the Union addresses. She joked that retired Justice David Souter had been her designated nudger.[114] In 2015, her explanation was, "I was not 100 percent sober." She said she had vowed to just drink sparkling water at the justices' dinner before the event, "but the dinner was so delicious it needed wine," and Anthony Kennedy brought some "very fine California wine."[115]

In 2018, Ginsburg had plans to visit Israel and Jordan. When she told her clerks and added that the trip included a visit by horseback to Petra, they expressed concern. After all, she was 85 years old. They asked whether it was a good idea.

She responded, "Oh yes, I know. They're all very worried. They're sending one of the Supreme Court police officers to walk alongside my horse the whole time."

After a brief pause, she added, with a smile, "Of course, he doesn't know which side I'm going to fall off."[116]

When the United States and the world faced the COVID-19 pandemic, medical officials urged people to wear facemasks. Ginsburg complied with the advice, donning a facemask featuring her own face.[117]

Anthony Kennedy

Born July 23, 1936, in Sacramento, California; associate justice, 1988–2018. Kennedy served as a legal advisor to California Governor Ronald Reagan, who later appointed Kennedy to the Supreme Court. He also served as a judge on the U.S. Court of Appeals for the Ninth Circuit. He received the nomination after Judge Robert Bork was rejected by the U.S. Senate and Judge Douglas Ginsburg withdrew his nomination. His influence as the swing vote in many cases caused some court watchers to call the Court of that era the "Kennedy Court" rather than one named after the chief justice.

Anthony Kennedy had a straight-arrow reputation among his classmates, leading many to wonder if he had ever been bad. As a kid, if any of his friends were doing something improper, he would simply go home so he would not be a part of it.[118] His wheeler-dealer father had once offered to pay young Kennedy $100 if he got into sufficient trouble to cause the father to go to the police station to bail the youth out. The money was never collected. When a college friend and Kennedy visited Europe between academic years, the friend expressed delight that Kennedy had brought along a bottle of whiskey, a sign, he was sure, that Kennedy might not be such a Boy Scout after all. Kennedy, however, insisted that the whiskey was only for medicinal purposes and that was how it was used.[119]

Apparently, Kennedy was not above a little mischief. After he was chosen high school valedictorian, the school newspaper commented, "Tony's big moment came when he dropped his gum off the Washington Monument on his trip to the East."[120]

As a law student, Kennedy attended a Red Sox game the day before his tax exam. He explained that it was one of the last times he would have been able to see Ted Williams play. He and a friend took their books to the game and behind them he heard Dean Erwin Griswold, "You don't bring the revenue code to the baseball game." Kennedy said that he did not know if Griswold thought that doing so "was a profanation of the code or of the game."[121]

Whether cameras should be allowed in the courtroom has been a long-standing issue for the Supreme Court. Most of the justices have opposed cameras, although Kennedy spoke about his experience as a Ninth Circuit judge during his confirmation hearing. He indicated that cameras were not necessarily as disruptive as the practice of allowing artists to sketch oral arguments. Kennedy explained that in a high-profile case before a packed courtroom, a man came in "... with all kinds of equipment and began setting it up. He disturbed me. He disturbed the attorneys. He disturbed everybody in the room. He was setting up an easel to paint our picture, which was permitted. If he had a little Minox camera, we would have held him in contempt."[122]

As a swing vote who often made the critical difference, Kennedy has upset more doctrinaire court watchers, who have variously dubbed him "Hamlet," "Flipper," or "Nini" ("Ninny"), a derivation of Antonin Scalia's nickname, "Nino."[123]

Kennedy seemed to try to promote the image of carrying the weight of the world. On the morning he was to announce his vote and unusual joint opinion upholding the right to abortion in *Planned Parenthood v. Casey*,[124] Kennedy was interviewed by a reporter for *California Lawyer* magazine. He closed the interview by saying, "Sometimes you don't know if you're Caesar about to cross the Rubicon or Captain Queeg cutting your own towline. I need to brood.... It's a moment of quiet around here to search your soul and your conscience."[125]

It was claimed that Kennedy was often influenced by "colleagues, the media and his affection for all things foreign." He was open-minded and often a swing vote, which led lawyers to focus on him during oral arguments. Other justices tried to woo him as well by generously quoting him in their opinions.[126]

It is said that Kennedy's strong support for free speech and freedom of the press may have been influenced by a desire to cultivate the press. Judge Lawrence Silberman of the DC Circuit also suggested that Kennedy suffered from the "Greenhouse Effect." In this instance, the effect was a reference, not to environmental concerns, but to the *New York Times* Pulitzer Prize-winning Supreme Court reporter Linda Greenhouse and meant that opinions were written to get a good write-up in the newspaper of record.[127]

Kennedy made a list of readings on liberty for his grandchildren that he later made available in connection with his civics education initiatives. It was, by any measure, an eclectic list. The readings include selections from such authors as Sophocles, Pericles, Plato, Martin Luther King, Jr., Abraham Lincoln, and Robert Frost. The readings also included Don McLean's hit song, "American Pie." Chief Justice John Roberts called the inclusion of the song "inscrutable." He noted that the composer was asked what the song meant, McLean answered, "It means I don't ever have to work again." Roberts said, "I'm fairly certain that is not the kind of freedom Justice Kennedy had in mind when he included the song on his list."[128]

Sandra Day O'Connor

Born March 26, 1930, in El Paso, Texas; died December 1, 2023; associate justice, 1981–2006. O'Connor served in various public capacities in Arizona, including deputy county attorney, assistant attorney general, state senator, senate majority leader, trial judge, and appellate judge. She had been a law school classmate of Chief Justice William Rehnquist. She made history as the first woman appointed to the Supreme Court.

Sandra Day O'Connor grew up on an isolated ranch in southeastern Arizona, where she said her only friends were her parents, various ranch hands, a bobcat, and several javelina hogs.[129]

O'Connor graduated third in her class at Stanford Law School and was a member of the law review; first was future Chief Justice William H. Rehnquist. The two dated for a short time in law school. She even brought him home one time for dinner at her parents' 260-sq. mile ranch, the Lazy B. That was the end of the romance. O'Connor's parents vetoed the relationship because of Rehnquist's bad table manners.[130]

Rehnquist apparently remained smitten with O'Connor. From his clerkship with Justice Robert Jackson, he wrote O'Connor proposing marriage. O'Connor, however, had started dating John O'Connor, whom she married. Nonetheless, she and Rehnquist remained friends, both raising their separate families in Phoenix.[131]

Despite her top grades at Stanford Law School, O'Connor was unable to find a job with any of the major California law firms. She later recalled being asked on job interviews, "Miss. Day, do you type?"[132]

Gibson, Dunn and Crutcher, a prominent Los Angeles law firm, offered her a job as a legal secretary. Years later, as a member of the Court, William French Smith of the firm, who had been U.S. Attorney General when O'Connor was placed on the Supreme Court, invited her to join a celebration of the firm.

O'Connor's remarks remembered her less-than-fabulous job offer:

I have calculated from looking at Martindale-Hubbell that had this firm offered me a job in 1952 as a lawyer, and had I accepted it, remained in the firm and progressed at the usual rate, I would now be at least the tenth ranking lawyer in the firm, which today numbers 709 attorneys...I want to thank Bill Smith. I can remember as if it were yesterday when he telephoned me on June 26, 1981, to ask if I could go to Washington, DC to talk about a position there. Knowing his former association with your firm, I immediately guessed he was planning to offer me a secretarial position—but would it be as Secretary of Labor or Secretary of Commerce? Of course, it was not. He had something else in mind...[133]

Shut out of law firms, O'Connor took a job as a deputy county attorney in San Mateo County, California, though she remained in the post only for a year to join her new husband, John, in Germany, where he served in the Judge Advocate General Corps for the army. There, she took a job as a civilian lawyer for the quartermaster.

In 1996, the county's historical society asked her permission to put her letter of application for the job on display. The request gave O'Connor an opportunity to read it 44 years after writing it. She said, "I was simply amazed. If I received that letter from a young law clerk, I'd have thrown it out. I'd say she is obviously a nut. I poured out my whole life story. I really wanted the job."[134]

As senate majority leader, O'Connor earned a reputation as exceptionally tough. In 1974, she delayed adjournment to complete legislative business. One committee chair was so upset with being stuck in session, he bellowed at O'Connor, "If you were a man, I'd punch you in the mouth." Unfazed, she replied, "if you were a man, you could."[135]

Thurgood Marshall later testified to O'Connor's toughness: "She's very nice, but if you cross her, she'll kick you in the [deleted] as hard as anybody."[136]

When O'Connor met with President Ronald Reagan to be interviewed for the Supreme Court, the two hit it off immediately. Raised on a real ranch and participating in the chores and issues of no running water, the two talked about horseback riding and mending fences. Afterwards, Reagan conducted no more interviews; he had found his nominee.[137]

O'Connor had little understanding of the Court's byzantine procedures. Justice Lewis Powell offered one of his secretaries to help her find her footing. At a party for O'Connor as a new justice, Powell danced with her, causing the *Washington Post* to note the historic first of two Supreme Court justices hitting the dance floor together.[138]

Surprising for the widespread publicity that accompanied the appointment of the first woman justice of the Supreme Court, not long after O'Connor was confirmed to the Court, she and her husband John attended a formal State Department dinner. John introduced himself to a man already seated, saying, "Hello, I'm John O'Connor." The man replied, "Oh, Justice O'Connor, I'm so happy to meet you. I've heard so many wonderful things about you."[139]

After reading in a 1983 *New York Times* article that SCOTUS, an abbreviation for "Supreme Court of the United States," was used by the "nine men" of the Court, O'Connor immediately fired off a chiding letter to the editor:
> According to the information available to me, and which I had assumed was generally available, for over two years now SCOTUS has not consisted of nine men. If you have any contradictory information, I would be grateful if you would forward it as I am sure...the SCOTUS and the undersigned (the FWOTSC) would be most interested in seeing it.[140]

O'Connor could be very kind and sometimes downright goofy. For Halloween in 1984, she went to the judicial conference in a Groucho

Marx-type of glasses that had a big nose with a mustache and bushy eyebrows.[141]

Advocates before the Supreme Court mix up the justices' names with surprising frequency, no matter how experienced they are. The problem became more acute once there were two women on the Court. This tendency caused O'Connor to order a special T-shirt that read, "I'M SANDRA, NOT RUTH."[142]

She may not have needed to order her own T-shirt. In 1993, the National Association of Women Judges made T-shirts for the two women justices. O'Connor's again said, "I'm Sandra, not Ruth." Ginsburg's said, "I'm Ruth, not Sandra."[143]

Justice Antonin Scalia was blunt in his criticism of O'Connor's refusal to supply the final vote needed to overturn *Roe v. Wade*,[144] the Court's controversial abortion decision, when the issue came up in *Webster v. Reproductive Health Services*,[145] where he called O'Connor's assertion of judicial restraint an argument that "cannot be taken seriously."[146]

When asked about the increasingly personal nature of this kind of criticism in 1994, O'Connor merely said, "Sticks and stones will break my bones, but words will never hurt me." However, after a moment's pause, she reconsidered: "That probably isn't true."[147]

Like some of her fellow justices, she has appeared on stage in a small role in a play. For her, the cameo was in Shakespeare's "Henry V" as Isabel, Queen of France. In what was both typecasting and highly appropriate, her line was, "Haply a woman's voice may do some good."[148]

After O'Connor notified Justice Anthony Kennedy of her retirement, O'Connor said, "You could hear corks popping in his office," by Kennedy's conservative clerks who believed O'Connor was an impediment to Federalist Society goals.[149]

Once O'Connor retired from the Court, she longed for another woman appointee. It did not come immediately. She reminded people that it took ten years after her own appointment for the next woman, Ginsburg, to be added. She quipped, "I've often said it's wonderful to be the first to do something, but I didn't want to be the last."[150]

O'Connor retired from the Court to care for her husband John who had Alzheimer's Disease. However, within six months of her retirement, John could no longer recognize her, and the disease had progressed so far that she could no longer help him.

John moved into a facility for those with the disease and acquired a girlfriend with whom he would sit contentedly, holding hands. As O'Connor would typically do, she saw the bright side of this development, pleased that he was comfortable and happy.

Still, she looked back on her retirement to help John as "the biggest mistake, the dumbest thing I ever did." If she had known that her plan to care for John would fall apart, she would have happily remained on the Court longer.[151]

O'Connor is the only Supreme Court justice ever inducted into the Cowgirl Hall of Fame.[152]

In 2007, after retiring from the Court, O'Connor accepted a nomination to run for President of the United States. It was for the Alfalfa Party, the party of the Alfalfa Club, one of those elite Washington institutions where officeholders and the politically connected gather once a year to make fun of one another. O'Connor said her platform would be "Quitus whinus over spiltus milkus." She told the audience that she obviously has "great resolve." After all, "[a]ny woman who can sit in chambers for 25 years listening to seven men talk about their prostates has total resolve."[153]

Lewis Powell Jr.
Born November 19, 1907, in Suffolk, Virginia; died August 25, 1998; associate justice, 1972–1987. Powell had served as president of the American Bar

Association and the Richmond School Board prior to his Supreme Court nomination. He was a reluctant nominee but was ultimately convinced to accept the nomination despite his seemingly advanced age. In announcing his nomination, President Richard Nixon said that "ten years of him is worth thirty years of most." Powell ended up serving 15 years. During his World War II service, because he studiously avoided salty language, the future justice was known as "Great Heaven Above Powell."

To teach his son some discipline, Powell's father bought a cow named Mollie that young Lewis had to care for and milk. The chore was draining and required attention both before and after school. "One of the happiest days of my life," Powell recalled, "was when I went out there and found the damn cow dead."[154]

Lewis and Josephine Powell were married in 1936 and honeymooned in Sea Island, Georgia. However, when they arrived at their hotel, they were initially denied access. Lewis's best friend, Harvie Wilkinson, the father of the highly regarded federal circuit judge, J. Harvie Wilkinson III, sent a telegram to the hotel care of Lewis to "Miss Josephine Rucker." The desk clerk insisted on seeing their marriage certificate, something they were not carrying. Lewis managed the crisis, although it was an awkward beginning to their six decades of marriage.[155]

During the war, Powell spent some time in Paris, where he bunked in a small mansion near Allied headquarters with several free spirits. One of these, Lowell Weicker, later became a U.S. Senator from Connecticut. Weicker entertained frequently and somehow knew all the celebrities. At one soiree, Powell met Gertrude Stein and Alice B. Toklas. Powell later wrote Weicker his appreciation for "the honor you did me ... when the charming Alice (mustache and all) was assigned as my dinner companion." The evening, however, had been "rough," he reported since he was taxed beyond his capabilities "trying to sustain my end of a conversation with Gertrude Stein on the subject of Pablo Picasso."[156]

After Powell joined the Philip Morris Board of Directors in 1963, he pretended to smoke at board events. He simply did not inhale. Photographs were frequently taken to show the board members enjoying the same cigarettes that anyone could buy. One Powell acquaintance heard about this practice of showing off the use of the goods and commented that "it's a good thing they don't sell condoms."[157]

Even as a college student, Powell confessed to a girlfriend that his dream was to sit on the U.S. Supreme Court. In 1969, that dream was in reach, as President Richard Nixon considered Powell to be his choice for the seat vacated by Abe Fortas after Clement Haynsworth's nomination was turned down by the Senate. Powell, however, demurred, telling Attorney General John Mitchell that "the nomination of a younger man less subject to controversy would best serve the public interest." After the Senate also rejected G. Harrold Carswell for the seat, Harry A. Blackmun was confirmed.

Three years later, Nixon again turned to Powell. This time, he played the role of Hamlet to the hilt, turning down the nomination, accepting it, calling in with second thoughts, and eventually accepting it."

At his investiture ceremony, Powell confided to his sister Eleanor that another 24 hours to consider the nomination would have resulted in his turning it down *again*.[158]

Upon nomination, Powell paid a courtesy call on Senate Judiciary Committee chair James Eastland. Eastland looked over the Supreme Court nominee, who had been drafted reluctantly because of his advanced age for such a nomination.

"You're going to be confirmed," Eastland told Powell.

A grateful nominee thanked him for that assessment.

Eastland then interrupted, "Do you know why you're going to be confirmed?"

"No," Powell admitted.

"Because they think you're going to die," Eastland announced.[159]

Powell's confirmation hearing for his Supreme Court appointment was a lovefest. The entire Virginia congressional delegation, the state's Governor and Attorney General, nine former American Bar Association presidents, the deans of Virginia's law schools, the state's most prominent civil rights lawyer, and a host of others had asked for time to sing Powell's praises. Powell's friend Harvie Wilkinson opined: "It is not recorded whether a choir of angels actually made an appearance on Powell's behalf, but one seasoned Senator was heard to mumble under his breath, 'Hell, he don't want to be confirmed. He wants to be canonized.'"[160]

When he became a justice, Powell resigned his membership from New York's University Club because he expected to be in that city infrequently. Nevertheless, club officials told him he would remain an honorary member and be entitled to use the club. An occasion arose several years later when he decided to stay overnight at the club. A desk clerk, however, interrupted the Powells' sleep that night to ask that they vacate their room – there was no record of any honorary membership, and the clerk did not care if his detainee was a Supreme Court justice. Powell had to call the lawyer who, as a member of the club's board, had offered the honorary membership, and the matter was straightened out.[161]

For the first few opinions, a new justice is often assigned something that will not touch off public controversy. For Powell, it was a tax case. Powell said, "It had been years since I had looked into the Internal Revenue Code, and I hoped never to see it again." Unlike when he was in private practice and could ask a tax partner to take care of it in three days, he said, "[i]t took me and a Clerk three weeks."

"Fortunately," he added, "the case has never been cited since I handed it down."[162]

When the Court decided *Brewer v. Williams*,[163] which involved the constitutionality of a police ploy about the need for a victim to receive a proper Christian burial to get the accused to give up the location of his murder victim, Powell wrote the majority opinion for a 5-4 Court that held the assertion of the right to have a lawyer present during questioning meant that police interrogation of all kinds must stop. Chief Justice Warren Burger dissented and expressed his disappointment with Powell privately, in a way that Powell described as "unshirted hell." Burger then read his dissent from the bench, fixing Powell with an icy stare the whole time. Powell's clerks expressed their sympathy by having a note delivered to their boss on the bench, indicating that they had "sent out for a bushel of rotten tomatoes."[164]

While *Bowers v. Hardwick*[165] was pending, Powell told his colleagues on the Court that he had never met a homosexual. However, one of his clerks at the time was gay. A book on gay rights cases at the Court found that Powell had hired gay clerks during six consecutive terms in the 1980s without realizing it. Apparently, Blackmun responded to Powell's remark about never having met a gay person by saying, "Look around your chambers."

A gay clerk for Powell during that term believed the justice must have known about him. "He had met my boyfriend," C. Cabell Chinnis told the *New York Times*. He believes Powell sought his advice because he knew his sexual orientation and wanted to understand gay sex. Chinnis found the conversation awkward: "This 78-year-old man is asking me about erections at the Supreme Court."

Interestingly, it was an earlier Powell law clerk, Paul M. Smith, who is gay, who won *Lawrence v. Texas*,[166] the case that overruled *Bowers* seven years later.[167]

Powell's retirement won him praise from some unexpected quarters. The American Civil Liberties Union, noting his influence as a swing vote, called Powell "the most powerful man in America." Powell reacted to this tribute by noting that this was true only when he was at home and, even then, only when his wife was out shopping.[168]

Antonin Scalia

Born March 11, 1936, in Trenton, N.J.; died February 13, 2016; associate justice, 1986–2016. Scalia, in addition to private practice and teaching law, served as general counsel to the Office of Telecommunications Policy, chairman of the Administrative Conference of the United States, assistant attorney general for the Office of Legal Counsel, and judge on the DC Circuit before his Supreme Court appointment. He was known to friends as "Nino."

Antonin Scalia insisted that when he had pizza it had to be from AV Ristorante, a small out-of-the-way joint that was no one else's idea of a gourmet pizza place. His favorite was pizza with anchovies.[169]

As former Ninth Circuit Judge Alex Kozinski recalled, Scalia approached a slice of AV Ristorante pizza "the way a wine connoisseur would approach a bottle of 1961 Lafite." He would sniff the aroma in a swoon before taking a bite and declaring, "*this* is what *I* call pizza." To Kozinski, though, the cheese was thin, tomato sauce too tart, and the crust soggy. He was not impressed.

When Kozinski had the opportunity to introduce Scalia to NPR journalist Nina Totenberg, Kozinski, then sitting on the U.S. Claims Court in Washington, DC, invited the two of them to his office for pizza. He thought he would impress his friend with a truly great pizza, ordering from the top-rated spot in town. He recalled, "a side-by-side comparison of an AV Ristorante pizza and a Vesuvio's pizza would be like putting Peewee Herman into the ring with Muhammad Ali."

When Scalia spotted the pizza, he said with disappointment, "It's not from AV Ristorante. I won't eat it." And he didn't.[170]

During Scalia's Judiciary Committee hearing on his Supreme Court nomination, Senator Howard Metzenbaum commented that he had played tennis with Scalia and lost. Scalia quickly responded, "[I]t was a case of my integrity overcoming my judgment."[171]

All justices have strong opinions about the cases they are assigned to write, and Scalia was no exception. He said that Chief Justice William

Rehnquist loved writing Fourth Amendment search-and-seizure cases, but they were not very interesting to Scalia. In fact, he hated them because they invariably were about whether a particular variation on the process in the case was or was not a constitutional violation. He would write them when assigned, "but I don't consider it a plum." Even worse, because Rehnquist thought these were great cases to write, it also meant, after giving a Fourth Amendment case, "he thought he was entitled to give you a dog. I didn't much like that," Scalia said.[172]

Chief Justice Charles Evans Hughes wrote that a Supreme Court dissent is "an appeal to the brooding spirit of the law, to the intelligence of a future day, when a later decision may possibly correct the error into which the dissenting judge believes the court to have been betrayed."[173] However high-minded that description is, Scalia's dissents sometimes adopted terminology that expressed quotable frustration and his derision.

In *Atkins v. Virginia*,[174] the Court held that the Eighth Amendment ban on cruel and unusual punishment prohibited the execution of mentally retarded criminals. Scalia dissented and wrote, "[s]eldom has an opinion of this Court rested so obviously upon nothing but the personal views of its members."[175] He added that "the Prize for the Court's Most Feeble Effort to fabricate 'national consensus' must go to its appeal (deservedly relegated to a footnote) to the views of assorted professional and religious organizations, members of the so-called 'world community,' and respondents to opinion polls."[176]

In *King v. Burwell*,[177] which upheld the constitutionality of the Affordable Care Act, Scalia labeled the reasoning adopted as "Pure applesauce." However, it was not the first time the description was used. Justice Stephen Breyer used "sheer applesauce" to describe a strange leap of logic eight years earlier. Still, Scalia was not done, calling another aspect of King "interpretive jiggery-pokery."

The Act at issue had established a health care program popularly known as "Obamacare," named after President Barrack Obama. Scalia's dissent considered the decision upholding the Act such a substantial rewrite of the statute to reach a constitutionally valid result that he suggested, "[w]e start calling this law SCOTUScare."

In *Glossip v. Gross*,[178] a death penalty case, he said there was nothing new being argued either by the parties challenging the three-drug protocol or by the dissenters, describing the case as similar to the movie, "Groundhog Day."[179] He called the dissenting justices a "vocal minority of the Court, waving over their heads a ream of the most recent abolitionist studies (a superabundant genre) as though they have discovered the lost folios of Shakespeare, [who] insist that now, at long last, the death penalty must be abolished for good."[180] He characterized Justice Stephen Breyer's dissent "gobbledy-gook"[181] that brandished "a let-them-eat-cake obliviousness to the needs of others."[182]

As for Breyer's assertion that one reason the death penalty is cruel and unusual is the lengthy delay between sentence and execution, Scalia pointed the finger for those delays at Breyer for supporting various procedural roadblocks to execution and compared the complaint to "the man sentenced to death for killing his parents, who pleads for mercy on the ground that he is an orphan."[183] If that were not enough, Scalia made plain his contempt for putting a constitutional gloss on the death penalty, rather than letting democratic decision-making prevail, by declaring, "Justice Breyer does not just reject the death penalty, he rejects the Enlightenment."[184]

Just like his rapid-fire questions from the bench, Scalia tended to drive fast. *Maryland v. Wilson*[185] held that police were entitled to order a passenger out of a car while making a traffic stop. During oral argument, Justice David Souter asked if the passenger would be free to leave the scene. Scalia chimed in with a plausible reason the passenger might leave: the passenger was disgusted with the driver's tendency to speed. Souter then added, "You can see what Justice Scalia's passengers tend to feel like."

Souter's description of Scalia's tendency to lay a heavy foot on the gas pedal proved very accurate some 15 years later. On his way to Court in 2011, Scalia slammed into the car ahead of him and created a four-car pile-up. Scalia's vehicle had to be towed away. Afterward, observers found Scalia uncharacteristically quiet that morning, at least early in the argument in *Wal-Mart Stores, Inc. v. Dukes*,[186] but, having gotten over it, the justice soon became the inquisitor everyone expected.[187]

Scalia was also passionate about classical music. He said that Bach, which he listened to along with other classical pieces, "sets our mind in order," so he often listened to it while drafting opinions.[188] However, the justice had little good to say about modern rock and roll. On a classical music station, he once requested "Sh-Boom (Life Could Be a Dream)," a doo-wop song first recorded in 1954 by The Chords, which he recalled fondly from his college days. He said, it was the last piece of popular music "I really remember liking before rock descended into noise and ugliness."[189] He added, "they claim that one of the tortures inflicted upon captured combatants was playing horrible rock music to them while they were in their cells. That would cause me to confess in no time at all."[190]

Another time, Scalia's turned to a takeoff of Cole Porter's "You're the Top" to poke fun at an opinion by Souter ("the *ne plus ultra*, the Napoleon Brandy, the Mahatma Gandhi, the Cellophane of subjectivity, th' ol' 'shocks-the-conscience' test.").[191]

Scalia took an originalist approach to interpreting the Constitution, looking back on what the Constitution meant when written. He felt it was illegitimate to consider the Constitution's meaning in modern terms, which is sometimes described as a "living Constitution" approach.

He explained his position simply in a speech at Southern Methodist University. "It's not a living document," Scalia said. "It's dead, dead, dead."[192]

Scalia said people frequently ask him, "'When did you first become an originalist?' like it's a weird affliction that seizes people, like 'When did you start eating human flesh?'"

He added that his "most important function on the Supreme Court is to tell the majority to take a walk."[193]

In a book he wrote with Bryan A. Garner, *Making Your Case: The Art of Persuading Judges*, Scalia titled one chapter, "Don't chew your fingernails,"[194] He regretted the title – not because it was too glib, but because he changed it when people thought his original title for the chapter was "too gross." The "more colorful title" the justice preferred was "Don't pick your nose."[195]

Scalia strongly believed that judges too often equate idiotic laws with being unconstitutional laws. He once gave the example that flogging, while "immensely stupid…is not unconstitutional." He reported that he once gave a speech in which he said federal judges should be equipped with an ink stamp that reads "STUPID BUT CONSTITUTIONAL." Afterwards, he reported, someone sent him one.[196]

David Souter

Born September 17, 1939, in Melrose, Massachusetts; associate justice, 1990–2009. David Souter served as New Hampshire Assistant Attorney General, Criminal Division before becoming state attorney general. He then embarked on a judicial career that included service on the state court of appeals and state supreme court. He joined the U.S. Court of Appeals for the First Circuit before becoming an associate justice on the U.S. Supreme Court. Because he had such a small paper trail on the issues that animated political fights, some took to referring to him at the time of his confirmation as the "Stealth Nominee."

There is an old-fashioned quality about David Souter, so much so that when he was appointed Attorney General of New Hampshire in 1976, friends celebrated with a cake that was inscribed, "Forward into the 19th century."[197]

When Souter was nominated for the Supreme Court, he had so rarely used a credit card that he feared he would not have enough credit to fund trips to DC to prepare for his Senate hearings.[198]

When President George H.W. Bush nominated David Souter to replace Justice William Brennan, Justice Thurgood Marshall said, "When his name came down, I listened to television. And the first thing I called my wife. Have I ever heard of this man?" His wife responded, "No. I haven't either." Marshall said, "So I promptly called Brennan because it's his circuit. And his wife answered the phone, and ... she said, 'He's never heard of him either.'"[199]

Souter was never a sparkling writer who might be quotable for centuries. Supreme Court reporter Dahlia Lithwick once described Souter's writing style this way: "Whatever the opposite of flair is, David Souter has it in spades."[200] When one of his clerks drafted an effervescent opinion that did not sound like the justice, he joked, "time for me to put some lead in it."[201]

Souter has long been considered something of a Luddite. He made no use of computers or even a typewriter, preferring to draft his opinions in longhand. His New England roots caused him never to spend unnecessarily so he preferred reading in his chambers by the window to the sunlight streaming through the window rather than turning on the electric lights until absolutely necessary. Rather than waste a piece of paper, he would leave a note on an unused napkin.[202]

Souter often found himself at odds with Justice Antonin Scalia. In one majority opinion, feeling the need to respond to Scalia's criticism in dissent, Souter wrote: "Justice Cardozo once cast the dissenter as 'the gladiator making a last stand against the lions.' Justice Scalia's dissent is certainly the work of a gladiator, but he thrusts at lions of his own imagining."[203]

Despite a warning about it from the Clerk of Court before argument, advocates sometimes call a justice by the wrong name. Once, referring to Souter, a government lawyer called him Justice Scalia. The lawyer, who realized his mistake immediately, apologized to Souter, but the modest Souter responded, "Thank you, but apologize to him."[204]

Souter retired in 2009. He rarely attended public events and kept a low profile on the Court. His introverted personality, however, was not without a sense of humor. Souter and Justice Stephen Breyer were frequently confused for one another. On one occasion when he was mistaken for Justice Breyer, he was asked what was best about serving on the Court. Souter replied, "The chance to serve with Justice Souter."[205]

Shortly after announcing his plans to retire from the Court in 2010, Souter attended the Third Circuit's annual conference. For Souter, it was something of a bookend to his tenure. As a Supreme Court justice, he served as the circuit justice for the Third Circuit, succeeding his predecessor, William Brennan, in that role as well. At that conference as a freshman justice in 1990, Souter says he was greeted by the judges with some reading material that included a copy of the Constitution, a gift he assumed reflected some questions about his familiarity with the document. At his final conference at the Third Circuit, Souter thanked the judges for not including another copy in the material he was given this time, though one explanation he offered himself is that the judges of the circuit "may have assumed that it's too late now," to do any good.[206]

Souter once described his role as a supreme court justice as the world's best job in the world's worst city.[207]

Souter was a bachelor, and both Justice O'Connor and Barbara Bush decided to try out their matchmaking skills on Souter. O'Connor arranged a couple of dates for Souter, but they came to naught. After one date, Souter told the woman, "That was fun. Let's do it again next year."[208]

Souter never considered Washington, DC to be his home during his 19-year tenure as a justice. He returned home to his native New Hampshire every chance he got. He never settled in and never fully unpacked. He mused, just several years before he decided to retire, that he considered unpacking some pictures he had brought down in a U-Haul when he first arrived in DC but thought again, "in a few years I'd be coming back to New Hampshire and I'd have to pack them back up, so I might as well leave them in the boxes."[209]

John Paul Stevens
Born April 20, 1920, Chicago, Illinois; died July 16, 2019; associate justice, 1975–2010. Stevens served in the U.S. Navy from 1942–1945. Once admitted to the bar, he served as a law clerk to Justice Wiley Rutledge, 1947–1948, and an associate counsel for the Subcommittee on the Study of Monopoly Power of the House Judiciary Committee. In 1970, President Richard Nixon named Stevens to the U.S. Court of Appeals for the Seventh Circuit. When President Gerald Ford elevated Stevens to the Supreme Court, the new justice was difficult to place on the ideological scale because of his frequently unique take on key issues. For that reason, he acquired the nicknames "Wild Card" and "Maverick."

John Paul Stevens enlisted in the Navy on Dec. 6, 1941, as an intelligence officer. One day later, the Japanese launched a sneak attack on Pearl Harbor. Stevens suggested that his enlistment encouraged the attack because the Japanese saw it as a sign of American desperation.[210]

The Northwestern Law School faculty could not decide between Stevens and his friend, Arthur Seder, on who would get to clerk for Justice Wiley Rutledge. Stevens won a coin toss. The consolation prize for Seder was that, after waiting a year, he would get to clerk for Chief Justice Fred Vinson.[211]

During Stevens' Senate confirmation hearings, Attorney General Edward Levi commented that Stevens's opinions were a "joy to read." Senator Phillip Hart asked Stevens if litigants before him would agree. Stevens quickly shot back that Levi "... might be half right."[212]

Stevens was known for his humility and unerring politeness. He did not just pepper oral advocates with questions, as some of his colleagues did, but asked whether he might pose a question. Clerks report that he waited to interrupt their work until he was noticed and then ask if they were busy, rather than disrupt their train of thought.[213]

Though his questions were incisive, he worked to put people at ease. In one instance, a first-time, evidently nervous advocate used the term "judge" instead of "justice" and was quickly rebuked by Justice Sandra Day O'Connor. She then made the same error again, referring to Justice Stevens, and immediately apologized. Stevens responded in a way that put the erring lawyer at ease by saying, "Your mistake in calling me 'judge' is also made in Article III of the Constitution."[214]

Stevens demonstrated the same cordiality and concern for law clerks as he did for lawyers arguing to the Court. One year, at the annual reception to welcome new law clerks, one justice approached a new female law clerk, not realizing her position, and said, "How nice that you're here. You can take the coffee around."

Concerned about getting her clerkship off to a bad start, even with a different justice, the clerk started to take the coffee service around. Stevens arrived at the reception and immediately surmised what had happened.

He retrieved the coffee pot from the clerk, saying, "Thank you for taking your turn with the coffee. I think it's my turn now," and was soon offering coffee to the new law clerks.[215]

In 1991, Stevens shocked the world with a letter he apparently sent to humor columnist Dave Barry, who was known to write more than a few pieces on cows exploding due to flatulence. Stevens wrote that he and his wife were longtime fans of Barry and shared the columnist's concern about exploding cows. For that reason, Stevens enclosed a copy of an advertisement with his letter, "the importance of which I am sure will be immediately apparent to you."

The enclosed advertisement was for Beano, a product that boasted to be a "scientific and social breakthrough" that "prevents the gas from beans."

While some questioned the letter's authenticity, the Supreme Court's spokesperson responded to inquiries with an ambiguous statement that suggested it was real.[216]

Stevens was a Chicago Cubs fan, and to his delight, near the end of his tenure, he was asked to throw the first pitch in Wrigley Field at a Cubs game. It was the same stadium where Stevens had watched Babe Ruth hit his famous "called" home run 73 years earlier. Stevens decided to practice his throw, and in the final days of his clerkship, Michael Gottlieb found himself playing catch with Justice Stevens in the Supreme Court gymnasium.[217]

At the end of the term, with Stevens stepping down in retirement, members of the audience at the Court showed up in bow ties, to honor the justice who made the bow tie his signature piece of fashion.[218]

Clarence Thomas
Born June 23, 1948, in Pin Point, Georgia; associate justice, 1991–present. Thomas had served as Chairman of the U.S. Equal Employment Opportunity Commission and a judge on the U.S. Court of Appeals for the District of Columbia Circuit before his nomination to the Supreme Court. President George H. W. Bush called him the "best-qualified" person for the nomination. Charges of sexual harassment engulfed Thomas' hearings in controversy after he had gone through an initial set of hearings rather smoothly. Like David Souter, Thomas lacked much of a paper trial of his views. Thomas's wife dubbed Thomas "Bigfoot."

The most influential person in Clarence Thomas's life was his grandfather, Myers Anderson. A bust of his grandfather sits in Thomas's chambers, inscribed with one of Anderson's favorite sayings: "Old Man Can't is dead. I helped bury him." Thomas and his brother moved in with their grandfather as boys. To prevent the boys from feigning sickness to get out of going to school, Anderson told the boys: "If you die, I'll take you to school for two days to make sure you're not faking." Thomas says that he "often wondered if the other students would object to a dead person being in the classroom."[219]

Thomas also proved a superb athlete, quarterbacking the football team and starring in both basketball and track. The school newspaper described him as "faster than a speedy spitball" and "more powerful than home brew."[220]

One April, after much effort, Thomas was enticed by his law clerks onto the Supreme Court's basketball court, dubbed "The Highest Court in the Land" because it is situated above the courtroom on the court's top floor. The clerks were surprised that the justice obviously knew what he was doing and showed himself to be a good player. The effort, though, only lasted a half hour before Thomas hit the ground, clutching his left leg in pain. The justice suffered a torn Achilles tendon that required surgery and the use of crutches. As the term ended for the law clerk who egged Thomas onto the basketball court, Thomas took the traditional photograph with his clerk but told the photographer to do a shot that included the walking cast he still sported.

He told the still-embarrassed clerk, "I want you to remember for the rest of your life what you did to me." The clerk, a former Canadian college player who was drafted into the NBA and played in the Pan American games and two Olympics, where he had faced NBA GOAT Michael Jordan and done well, has the photo with the justice hanging in his law office, right next to one where he is being guarded by Jordan.[221]

When Thomas returned to the Court for conference with his leg in a cast, Justice Kennedy immediately turned to Justice White, whose aggressive basketball play had often sent clerks to the infirmary. "Did you do that?" Kennedy asked White. White responded, "If I'd done it, it would have been both legs!"[222]

Thomas went to Yale Law School and said that he "learned the hard way that a law degree from Yale meant one thing for white graduates and another for blacks...." He wrote that he was so disillusioned that "I peeled a fifteen-cent price sticker off a package of cigars and stuck it on the frame of my law degree to remind myself of the mistake I'd made by going to Yale."[223]

Nearly all justices have expressed some concern about how the press covers them or the Court. In 1999, Thomas was a featured presence at the Media Research Center's ceremony, identifying the decade's most outrageous examples of liberal media bias. Of NPR's Nina Totenberg, he said, "I have finally had the opportunity to have my surgeon remove her many stilettos from my back, and I would like to return them."[224]

Thomas was fond of the late Justice Antonin Scalia, who was a great lover of opera. Thomas also liked opera, but he would not go to operas at the Kennedy Center with Scalia because, Thomas explained to Scalia, "Nino, I like opera. I just don't want to be around people who like opera."[225]

Scalia enjoyed hunting and could not understand why a Georgian like Thomas would not go hunting. When Scalia would try to talk Thomas into going on a hunting trip, Thomas' stock reply was, "No good comes from being in the woods."[226]

Thomas said that he thought choosing law clerks was like "selecting mates in a foxhole." He also noted, "I won't hire clerks who have profound disagreements with me. It's like trying to train a pig. It wastes your time, and it aggravates the pig."[227]

9

The Roberts Court

The story of the Roberts Court is yet to be written. During much of its first decade, Justice Anthony Kennedy served as the ideological center of an otherwise evenly divided Court. The Court issued some very conservative decisions during that period, which were controversial in some quarters, such as limiting the discretion of school districts to adopt voluntary desegregation plans, giving unlimited independent political spending by corporations First Amendment protection, and striking down part of the Voting Rights Act. At the same time, it issued some surprisingly liberal decisions, disappointing other quarters, upholding most of the provisions of the Patient Protection and Affordable Care Act three separate times, finding that the Constitution provides a right for same-sex couples to marry, and holding that transsexuals were protected from employment discrimination.

With Justice Kennedy's retirement and replacement by his former law clerk, Brett Kavanaugh, it appeared that Chief Justice Roberts would occupy not just the center seat at the Court but the ideological center, providing an opportunity to put his stamp on the Court's decisions. During that first year, the Chief Justice appeared to control the decisions.

However, after Justice Ruth Bader Ginsberg passed away, Justice Amy Coney Barrett joined the Court, causing observers to comment that the Court had shifted further to the right than at any time in recent memory, with five justices considered more conservative than Roberts.

John Roberts, Chief Justice (2005–present)

Associate Justices:
Samuel Alito, Jr. (2006–present)
Neil Gorsuch (2017–present)
Elena Kagan (2010–present)
Brett Kavanaugh (2018–present)
Sonia Sotomayor (2009–present)
Amy Coney Barrett (2020–present)
Ketanji Brown Jackson (2022–present)

John Roberts
Born January 27, 1955, in Buffalo, New York; chief justice, 2005–present. Roberts clerked for Judge Henry Friendly of the U.S. Court of Appeals for the Second Circuit and then-Justice William H. Rehnquist. He joined the Reagan Justice Department as a special assistant to the U.S. Attorney General, moved from there to the White House Counsel's Office, and then to private practice. He returned to government as principal deputy solicitor general during the administration of President George H.W. Bush. After returning to private practice, Roberts was successively nominated by President George W. Bush to the U.S. Court of Appeals for the District of Columbia and Chief Justice of the United States.

John Roberts saw some absurdity in the memorialization of work while at the Department of Justice during the Reagan Administration. As a cover to his files, as he ended his Justice Department tenure, he wrote:

> How fascinating and edifying it must have been for you to review the files I compiled during my service to the attorney general.

I assume that the archivist will deposit my files in one of those hermetically sealed display cases that drop into a concrete vault in the event of nuclear attack, similar to the cases housing the Constitution and the Declaration of Independence. Once this is done, I will consider donating my personal papers, at a time to be determined by my tax advisers.

Just in case you're thinking of it, if you plant compromising material in my files I will "amend" your FBI file with a large bottle of "Wite-Out."[1]

As a judge on the U.S. Court of Appeals for the DC Circuit, Roberts had difficulty choosing among the well-qualified recent law school graduates who applied to spend a year with him as a law clerk. His criteria – nice people who were self-confident and whose oral skills were as good as their writing talent – did not always separate the applicants.

One year, he hit on an idea he hoped would make a difference. On a day when he was interviewing no fewer than 13 law clerks, he bought a dozen Krispy Kreme doughnuts, both glazed and powdered. He told his secretary to offer the applicants a doughnut prior to the interview. Roberts reasoned that anyone confident enough to chance a doughnut disaster of glaze or powdered sugar on their interview suit had the self-confidence he sought. Those candidates would be automatic hires. Alas, no one accepted a doughnut. Roberts lamented, "I had to go back and look at their resumes."[2]

Roberts was regarded as a formidable advocate before the Court when he was in private practice and in the Solicitor General's office. Once, however, he was on the short end of a unanimous decision. When his client asked him how he could have lost by that 9-0 margin, Roberts responded, "Well, because there are only nine justices."[3]

As is often the case with modern nominees, President George W. Bush introduced Roberts and his family at a White House press conference.

Roberts's young son, Jack, made a big impression on the television audience. Rather than demurely standing by his dad, Jack seemed to careen about. As Roberts later explained, Jack "was not dancing. He was being Spiderman. He was shooting the webs off."[4]

While Chief Justice Rehnquist once cited a comic opera from Gilbert & Sullivan in a dissent, *Richmond Newspapers, Inc. v. Virginia*,[5] Roberts, a former law clerk to Rehnquist, similarly called upon lyrics to frame a dissent, making history by becoming the first justice to cite a rock lyric in a Supreme Court opinion. In *Sprint Commc'ns Co., L.P. v. APCC Servs., Inc.*,[6] Roberts dissented from a decision according standing – the right to bring a lawsuit – to a plaintiff, a collection company, slightly quoting the Bob Dylan song, *Like a Rolling Stone*, to hit home his point: "When you got nothing, you got nothing to lose."[7]

Music aficionados were quick to point out, though, that Roberts had improved Dylan's grammar in his citation. Dylan wrote: "When you ain't got nothing, you got nothing to lose."[8] It is unclear, though, whether the correction reflected an aversion to the word "ain't" or double negatives or, perhaps, reliance on a website that posted the more properly grammatical version of the lyrics.

In *FCC v. AT&T Inc.*,[9] the Court considered and ultimately rejected the media company's attempt to stop the Federal Communications Commission from divulging information from an investigation that AT&T overcharged for administering FCC programs in response to a Freedom of Information Act request. Specifically, it tried to shoehorn itself into the exemption for information that might constitute an unwarranted invasion of personal privacy. AT&T argued that, as a corporation, it was a person under the law with privacy rights.

This argument went a bit too far for Roberts, who made clear his view that the adjective "personal" did not simply mean something belonging to a person. He told counsel for AT&T that he had come up with a number of examples "where the adjective was very different from the root noun. And it turns out it's not hard at all."[10]

Roberts started with "craft" and "crafty," which he said is "Totally different." He added that "'[c]rafty' doesn't have much to do with 'craft.' 'Squirrel,' 'squirrelly.' Right?"[11] Roberts continued, "you have a 'pastor' and 'pastoral.' Same root, totally different. So I don't understand – I don't think there's much to the argument that because 'person' means one thing, 'personal' has to be the same relation."[12]

As the author of the Court's unanimous opinion in the case, he continued this riff:

> The noun "crab" refers variously to a crustacean and a type of apple, while the related adjective "crabbed" can refer to handwriting that is "difficult to read;" "corny" can mean "using familiar and stereotyped formulas believed to appeal to the unsophisticated," which has little to do with "corn," ("the seeds of any of the cereal grasses used for food"); and while "crank" is "a part of an axis bent at right angles," "cranky" can mean "given to fretful fussiness."[13]

He found it irresistible to end the opinion by writing that, although the company had no personal privacy rights under the statute, "[w]e trust that AT&T will not take it personally."[14]

During arguments in *Nichols v. United States*,[15] the courtroom lights went out. Without missing a beat, Roberts quipped, "I knew we should have paid that bill."[16] Five minutes later, the lights were restored. It wasn't the first time Roberts experienced an incident with the lights in the courtroom. Early in his tenure, a light bulb exploded during oral argument. Roberts was also quick to say: "It's a trick they play on new chief justices all the time. We're even more in the dark now than before."[17]

Among the most celebrated of justices are those who burnished their reputations as wordsmiths, employing words that are deeply memorable or turns of phrases that are eminently quotable. Sometimes, it is an advocate who employs a word that causes the justices to sit up and take notice. University of Michigan law professor Richard Friedman, arguing

Briscoe v. Virginia,[18] attempted to move past a question he was asked by asserting that the "issue is entirely orthogonal to the issue here."

Roberts interrupted him, saying, "I'm sorry. Entirely what?"

"Orthogonal," Friedman responded nonchalantly, defining the math term as meaning "[r]ight angle. Unrelated. Irrelevant."

Justice Scalia then interrupted to say that he liked the word and suggested "we should use that in the opinion."

Roberts, however, rejoined, suggesting some disagreement with his brethren: "Or the dissent."[19]

One reason the traditionalist Roberts chose Harvard Law School over Stanford Law School was that the Stanford interviewer wore sandals and also had no tie.[20]

Roberts fouled up the administration of the presidential oath to President Barack Obama, which caused him to administer a second oath to Obama after the official inauguration. Choosing to say it from memory for ceremonial reasons, he said, and Obama repeated, "I will execute the office of president of the United States faithfully." He should have said, "I will faithfully execute the office of president of the United States."[21]

Roberts has two degrees from Harvard. He was asked if he thought it was desirable only to have justices with degrees from elite institutions. Roberts replied, "First of all, I disagree with your premise. Not all of the justices went to elite institutions. Some went to Yale."[22]

Roberts told a group of Harvard law students that he thought that, of all the former justices, Chief Justice William Howard Taft, who sometimes weighed over 300 pounds, would be the ideal dinner companion. Roberts said, "You know you'd get a lot of food, and it would be good."[23]

Samuel Alito Jr.

Born April 1, 1950, in Trenton, N.J.; associate justice, 2006–present. Alito clerked for the U.S. Court of Appeals for the Third Circuit Judge Leonard I. Garth. He then joined the United States Attorney's office for the District of New Jersey; later in his career, he returned as the U.S. Attorney. He also served in successive positions in the Justice Department during the administration of President Ronald Reagan, first as a lawyer in the Solicitor General's office and then as Deputy Assistant Attorney General in the Office of Legal Counsel. President George H. W. Bush appointed Alito in 1990 to the appellate court upon which he had previously clerked, which proved to be a stepping stone to the Supreme Court.

Samuel Alito's legal preferences were set by the time he attended Yale Law School. He told an audience at a Federalist Society dinner that he recalled that he was assigned to a constitutional law class taught by liberal Charles Reich rather than conservative Robert Bork. He was not allowed to switch classes, and, as a result, said Alito, "I was forced to teach myself."[24]

When Reich taught Alito, the professor was more interested in American counterculture than he was in law and had written a widely read book, "The Greening of America," which pictured a disintegrating society. Speaking to a group that was dismayed over the re-election of Barack Obama, Alito said that the book pictured an era in a "moment of utmost sterility, darkest night, most extreme peril." He then added, "So our current situation is nothing new."[25]

When Alito was U.S. Attorney in Newark, he was rankled by criticism of a failed mob prosecution by his office. It was a two-year trial of 20 defendants, then the longest criminal trial in history, and was at times circuslike. The indictment and trial began before Alito was U.S. Attorney and defense lawyers even said that he was not at fault for the acquittals. However, when the National Law Journal mentioned the failed prosecutions in an article, Alito fired off a complaint to the

Journal. While he wrote that he took responsibility for the work of his office, he also wrote that he had inherited the case. His complaint was twice the length of the article.[26]

When his nomination was pending and had raised some controversy, Alito overhead a conversation while traveling by train back to Washington. The two women seated in front of him, not knowing that he was behind them, had noted that a piece of the Supreme Court's building had fallen off the day before and wondered out loud whether that was a sign that Alito's nomination should be rejected. In a speech to the Palm Beach County (Fla.) Bar Association after his confirmation, Alito admitted that he had wondered the same thing.[27]

The rough treatment Alito felt he received from the Senate while his nomination was pending had a continuing effect on him. He told the Federalist Society that when he is walking and is about to pass the Hart Senate Office Building, "invariably without thinking ... I cross to the other side of the street. He also told the Federalist Society that he had long been a member but was not pushed on that fact during his visits with Senators or during his confirmation hearing. He explained, "Now, I think the reason for that probably was that some senators found so many other objectionable features about my record that they could attack that they had no need."[28]

Alito is a fanatic Philadelphia Phillies fan, something he has said has been true since he may have been 4 or 5 years old. By tradition, a new justice is welcomed to the Court with a dinner. As the pleasant affair ended, Justice Stephen Breyer, who had taken responsibility for arranging the dinner, announced a surprise guest. He opened the door to the room, and in stepped the team mascot, the "Phillie Phanatic."

Alito had met the mascot once before when he had been invited to throw out the first pitch at a Phillies game. He reported that the mascot's costume was a bit "fragrant" from the on-field antics on a hot day and was probably prepared for the worst when the Phanatic greeted Alito at the Court with a hug. Instead, Alito reported that it was "great." Apparently, the Phanatic had either gotten the outfit "dry-cleaned or he has his traveling suit," Alito said.[29]

Typically, the new justice receives a first assigned opinion, in which the Court is unanimous and the issue is relatively uncontroversial. That was true of Alito's first assignment as well, although none of that made the assignment any less nerve-wracking. As Alito reported, he had been an appellate judge for 15 years and had written hundreds of opinions. Still, he "had never revised an opinion as many times as I did before I sent that one out."

After he finally circulated it, he received the much-wanted "joins" with few suggestions for changes – and one note that warned him: "Don't think it's going to be this easy all the time in the future."[30]

Moving from the U.S. Court of Appeals for the Third Circuit to the Supreme Court was also something of a cultural shock for Alito. His old court would politely wait until the advocate finished a paragraph of the presentation before interrupting with a question. Alito said, "I learned here that if you wait, you'll never get a chance to ask one."[31] Another difference, he noted, is that it takes longer for a lower court judge to figure out what the Supreme Court means in any particular case; as a justice, he worries less about that.[32]

In *Brown v. Entertainment Merchants Association*,[33] Alito could not resist giving Scalia a hard time about his "originalist" approach to interpreting the Constitution according to the constitutional Framers' understandings of its meaning. After Scalia posed a question to counsel, Alito "helpfully" said, "What Justice Scalia is asking is what did James Madison think about video games." He then added, "Did he enjoy them?"[34]

At a conference at Yale Law School attended by fellow alumni Justices Clarence Thomas, Sonia Sotomayor, and Alito, Justice Sotomayor commented that while she was a poor dancer, she liked salsa and, "I have a facility that some of my colleagues will find very strange, I can follow." To that Alito quickly responded, "It's a revelation to me that Sonia likes to follow. I think we're going to start dancing at conference."[35]

At Yale with Justices Thomas and Sotomayor, Justice Alito was asked what he had been reading. Alito answered, "I have two books that are inspirational. I keep them on a table by my bed, and I try to read a little bit of them every night. It's 'My Grandfather's Son' (by Justice Thomas) and 'My Beloved World' (by Justice Sotomayor)." [36]

Amy Coney Barrett

Born January 28, 1972, in New Orleans, Louisiana; associate justice, 2020–present. Barrett clerked for Judge Laurence Silberman of the U.S. Court of Appeals for the DC Circuit and then for Justice Antonin Scalia. After practicing law and teaching at Notre Dame Law School, she was appointed to the U.S. Court of Appeals for the Seventh Circuit in 2017. She was confirmed to the Supreme Court in nearly record time after the death of Justice Ruth Bader Ginsburg and before the 2020 presidential election.

Amy Coney Barrett was on the shortlist for the seat vacated by Justice Kennedy and filled by Justice Kavanaugh. The possibility of nomination at that time was enough to bring out the media. Knowing that if she had stepped out of a church service one morning, she would be mobbed by photographers and reporters, she decided to leave by a back door. She discovered it led to the yard behind the private residence. However, there was no exit from there. "I decided in my high heels to climb the fence so gracefully," she reported. Once she was over the fence, she landed in the church's vegetable garden, where an associate pastor "helped me make my escape."[37]

Unfortunately, when Amy Coney Barrett was introduced by President Trump in a Rose Garden ceremony, it was during the COVID pandemic, and the ceremony became a superspreader event.[38]

Like all other recent new justices, Barrett was expected to introduce some new innovations into the Supreme Court cafeteria. The COVID-19 pandemic, however, had closed the cafeteria, so she never had to undertake the task. Even so, Barrett shares the uniformly low regard for the cafeteria. She said, "[It] would not be a date night destination or it would be a very brief relationship if it were."[39]

Being interviewed at a public event at the Ronald Reagan Presidential Library, Barrett proved unfazed when her answer to a question was interrupted by a shouting protester, even though it might have thrown off another person. "I'm the mother of seven," she explained. "I'm used to distractions and sometimes even outbursts."[40]

Barrett was the only justice in the current court who had not gone to Harvard or Yale Law School. She had gone to Notre Dame. When asked about that, she responded, "I love all my colleagues and would never criticize their alma maters."[41]

Neil M. Gorsuch
Born August 29, 1967, in Denver, Colorado; associate justice, 2017–present. Gorsuch clerked on the U.S. Court of Appeals for the District of Columbia for Judge David B. Sentelle and then for Justices Byron White and Anthony Kennedy on the Supreme Court. After a period in private practice, Gorsuch served as principal deputy to the associate attorney general in the Civil Division of the Bush (2) Justice Department. From there, he became a judge on the U.S. Court of Appeals for the Tenth Circuit where he served until he took his Supreme Court seat.

As a law clerk to Justice Byron White the year the justice retired, it fell to Neil Gorsuch to hand White's successor, Ruth Bader Ginsburg, the law clerk manual that White had kept over the years that provided his clerks with instructions on how things were done in that chamber and the Court more generally. On the day that Gorsuch took office as a justice, Ginsburg returned the favor, handing the new justice the same manual he had given her 25 years earlier.[42]

Neil Gorsuch replaced Antonin Scalia on the Court. During his confirmation hearings, he was dubbed "Scalia without the scowl."[43]

Gorsuch was the first justice to serve at the same time as the justice for whom he had clerked. Gorsuch clerked for Justice Anthony Kennedy during the 1993–94 Term and had Kennedy swear him in as an associate justice. When it came time for Gorsuch to write his first opinion for the Court, Kennedy was determined to be the first justice to join the opinion. The draft was completed one evening after Kennedy had headed home. Anticipating the opinion, Kennedy had one of his current clerks fax the draft to him. Somehow, that didn't work, so Kennedy had a hard copy driven to him at home.

First thing in the morning, Gorsuch was greeted with a handwritten "join memo" from Kennedy. Gorsuch reported that he kept that first "join" in the top drawer of his desk.[44]

In *Masterpiece Cakeshop, Ltd. v. Colorado Civil Rights Commission*,[45] the Supreme Court was asked to find that a state-law requirement that businesses do not discriminate on the basis of sexual orientation violated a bakery's First Amendment rights. The baker had turned down an order for a same-sex wedding cake because of personal religious objections to same-sex marriages. The U.S. Justice Department filed an amicus brief and argued in support of the baker.

During the course of oral argument, U.S. Solicitor General Noel Francisco argued that making a baker use his artistic talents on behalf of a same-sex wedding violated free-speech rights in compelling him to convey a message with which he disagreed. Francisco said, "People pay very high prices for these highly sculpted cakes, not because they taste good, but because of their artistic qualities."

Indicating his apparent agreement, Gorsuch chimed in: "In fact, I have yet to have a … wedding cake that I would say tastes great."[46]

Asked why he would want to go through the workload of the Court every day, Gorsuch responded, "Somebody's got to run the zoo."[47]

Ketanji Brown Jackson

Born September 14, 1970, in Washington, DC; associate justice, 2022–present. Jackson clerked for Supreme Court Justice Stephen Breyer, whose seat on the Court she now occupies. She was vice chairwoman of the U.S. Sentencing Commission, a federal district court judge in Washington, DC, and a judge on the U.S. Court of Appeals for the District of Columbia Circuit. Justice Jackson's parents chose to name her Ketanji Onyika, meaning "Lovely One," after receiving a list of strong African names from an aunt then serving in the Peace Corps.

When Jackson was a federal public defender, she was contacted by an uncle who was serving a life sentence in Florida for a nonviolent drug crime. The uncle was her father's older brother, whom Jackson had not seen or heard from in years. Jackson referred the case to a law firm that took such cases on a pro bono basis, and years later, President Obama commuted the sentence. Jackson's uncle was released from prison at the age of 78 and died a year later.[48]

In 2012, Jackson was nominated by Barack Obama to serve on the U.S. District Court in Washington, DC. She was introduced to the Senate Judiciary by Representative Paul Ryan, to whom she was related by marriage. In 2012, Ryan was the Republican Vice-Presidential nominee and would become the Speaker of the House in 2015. Ryan said of Jackson, "Our politics may differ, but my praise for Ketanji's intellect, for her character, for her integrity, it is unequivocal. She is an amazing person."[49]

In 2016, President Obama interviewed Jackson to fill the late Justice Scalia's seat on the Supreme Court. Prior to the interview, Jackson's young daughter told her that her middle school friends had decided that Jackson should apply for the position on the Supreme Court. Jackson explained that one did not apply for such a position, and so her daughter wrote to President Obama asking him to consider her mother for the Court. Her handwritten note read, "[S]he is determined, honest, and never breaks a promise to anyone, even if there are other things she'd rather do. She can demonstrate commitment and is loyal and never brags."[50]

Supreme Court justices have had many pastimes that have served to give them time away from the law and the tough cases that demand so much of their time. Justice William Douglas, for example, was an outdoorsman who escaped Washington, DC for the backcountry of his beloved State of Washington. Justices Antonin Scalia and Ruth Bader Ginsberg loved to attend the opera. Justice Clarence Thomas has expressed fondness for RV cross-country traveling, with Walmart parking lots providing a favored camping spot. Justice Sonia Sotomayor has a renowned love of salsa dancing. What is Justice Ketanji Brown Jackson's guilty pleasure? The television show *Survivor*. She told graduates at American University's law school at commencement that:

> I am a *Survivor* superfan. I have seen every episode since the second season, and I watch it with my husband and my daughters even now, which I will admit, it's not easy to do with the demands of my day job, but you have to set priorities, people.

She advised the graduates that busy people have to find different things to do that they love. She added, "And I love that show."[51]

Jackson is not just a fan of *Survivor*, but also musicals, which she contends can teach important life lessons. At a commencement at Boston University School of Law, Jackson cited three musicals that helped her see life more broadly: *Little Shop of Horrors*, *Hamilton*, and *American Prophet*.

The lesson she drew for the students about *Little Shop*, a musical comedy about a sentient bloodthirsty plant that brings its owner celebrity but is bent on world domination, was not about how "the legal profession is like a dangerous plant; if you aren't careful, it will eat you up." Instead, "the lesson...I want you to remember as you practice, is to always start by asking why when you confront a new situation." It will help you reach an appropriate solution, she said.

Taking a cue from one of the songs in *Hamilton*, "The Room Where It Happens," Brown told graduates to be like Aaron Burr – and the justice herself as she pursued her career – and "Find something you care about and get yourself into the room where it happens."

Finally, Jackson referenced *American Prophet*, a musical about abolitionist Frederick Douglass, for its repeated use of quotations from Douglass's writings in different contexts to appreciate "words matter, and the framing does, too," so that "how you say it" makes a difference.[52]

Elena Kagan

Born April 28, 1960, in New York, NY; associate justice, 2010–present. Kagan served as a law clerk to Judge Abner Mikva of the U.S. Court of Appeals for the DC Circuit and then Justice Thurgood Marshall of the U.S. Supreme Court. She was a member of the White House Counsel's office and later a policy advisor for President Bill Clinton, who nominated her to the DC Circuit, but her nomination never received a hearing. President Barack Obama made Kagan Solicitor General, even though she had never argued a case before a court, and then successfully nominated her to the Supreme Court. Because of her diminutive height, particularly when compared to him, Justice Marshall dubbed her "Shorty."

Marshall was fond of his law clerks but could not resist teasing them. Even in offering a clerkship, Marshall could have a little fun with the candidate. He called future Justice Elena Kagan in 1986 to offer her a clerkship and she said she would "love a job." Marshall feigned that he heard her wrong. "What's that?" he asked. "You already have a job." Kagan insisted she did not as emphatically as she could.

"Well, I don't know," Marshall said, "if you already have a job…"

He then let her off the hook and revealed that he had been joking. He ended the conversation with his traditional question: "Do you enjoy working on dissents?"[53]

As a law clerk, Kagan occasionally participated in the games on the Supreme Court's own basketball court located above the courtroom. At 5'3", which earned her the nickname "Shorty" from her boss, Justice Thurgood Marshall, she had low expectations in the games. When a very good player who clerked for Justice Byron White tried to help her score, he would set a pick to give Kagan an open shot. As she reports it, she felt the pressure to "try to hit a jump shot." She further reports, "And very occasionally, I would do that."[54]

When she was a law clerk, Elena Kagan was voted by her fellow law clerks as "the most likely to serve on the Supreme Court." She said that while it was somewhat embarrassing to reveal that vote, "It was definitely better than being voted 'the first person to be indicted.'"[55]

In defending the constitutionality of the Antiterrorism and Effective Death Penalty Act of 1996 in *Holder v. Humanitarian Law Project*,[56] then-Solicitor General Kagan attempted to draw a defensible line between the types of activities that illegally give material support or expert advice to a designated terrorism group and that which is constitutionally protected. She posited that a lawyer writing an amicus brief in support of the terrorist group steps over the line of illegality because it is a specialized activity.

Justice Sonia Sotomayor apparently thought that went too far. Under your definition, she told Kagan, "Teaching these members [of the terrorist group] to play the harmonica would be unlawful."

Kagan responded that "maybe training a – playing a harmonica is a specialized activity. I think the first thing I would say is there are not a whole lot of people going around trying to teach Al-Qaeda how to play harmonicas."

Scalia then jumped into the conversation: "Well, Mohammed Atta [one of the leaders of the 9/11 terrorist attack] and his harmonica quartet might tour the country and make a lot of money. Right?"

Kagan tried to steer the conversation back to the issue at hand. "I don't mean to make fun of the hypothetical at all, Justice Sotomayor, because I think you're raising an important point, but it's really a point that goes to how to sensibly read a statute."[57]

Kagan's argument succeeded in winning a favorable decision but did not win Sotomayor's vote.

As Solicitor General, Kagan once responded to a question by Justice Scalia, saying, "Mr. Chief – excuse me, Justice Scalia – I didn't mean to promote you quite so quickly."

Chief Justice Roberts then chimed in, "Thanks for thinking it was a promotion."

Scalia added, "And I'm sure you didn't."[58]

During her confirmation hearing, Senator Lindsey Graham seemed to be beginning a line of questioning about terrorism. He referred to the "Christmas Day bomber" who had attempted to blow up a Northwest Airlines flight on Christmas and then asked, "Where were you at on Christmas Day?" Thinking he was asking about terrorism cases, Kagan indicated she could not answer questions about pending cases, but Graham said that all he was asking was where she was on Christmas Day. Kagan responded, "Like all Jews, I was probably at a Chinese restaurant." That led the entire room to erupt in laughter.[59]

In an effort to explore her views on gun rights, during her confirmation hearing Kagan was asked if she had ever gone hunting. She had not but said that if she were confirmed, she would ask Justice Scalia, a well-known hunter, to take her with him on a hunting trip. After she got on the Court, she explained her promise to go hunting with him and, after lengthy laughter, Scalia agreed to take her. They went hunting together several times afterward.[60]

When Joe Biden was chair of the Judiciary Committee, he would have an academic help develop questions for confirmation hearings. Elena Kagan helped design questions for Ruth Bader Ginsburg's hearings, but Kagan found the hearings very frustrating because Ginsburg was so good at not answering questions. As a result, she wrote a University of Chicago Law Review article criticizing the confirmation process.

Years later, when Kagan was nominated to the Court, she said that every time she said, "... Senator, I really can't answer that," the senators would say, "... you wrote this article calling the nomination process a vapid and hollow charade." Kagan noted, "... that was inconvenient."[61]

Traditionally, the junior justice is placed on the Court's cafeteria committee. Kagan commented that this was a way for the Court to tell a new justice, "You think you're hot stuff, you're a member of the Supreme Court, you just got confirmed? No. You're going to be on the cafeteria committee, where you are going to meet once a month with a bunch of people to discuss what happened to the good chocolate chip cookies."

Kagan noted that the justices ate together a lot, and someone would say, "There's too much salt in the soup, Elena." Then another justice would say, "I don't know. There's not enough salt in the soup."[62]

As an innovation, Kagan got the cafeteria to add a frozen yogurt machine, which was welcomed by her colleagues. Chief Justice John Roberts commented, "No one at the court can remember any of the prior justices on the committee doing anything."[63] Still, Kagan worried that her good deed would be rewarded by becoming known as the "frozen yogurt justice."[64]

The first assignments for a new justice tend to be unanimous and non-controversial cases that may not hold much public interest. One of Kagan's first opinions fit that bill. *Smith v. Bayer Corp.*[65] dealt with class action certification. Kagan opened her announcement of the opinion in Court, stating: "If you understand anything I say here, you will likely be a lawyer, and you will have had your morning cup of coffee."[66]

When Kagan was asked to comment on being named the most "hip" justice, she responded, "It might be a low bar."[67]

Kimble v. Marvel Entertainment[68] was a patent issue involving a Spider-Man toy and whether a license agreement that required royalties beyond the period for the life of the patent was enforceable. In her opinion, Kagan wrote, "The parties set no end date for royalties, apparently contemplating that they would continue for as long as kids want to imitate Spider-Man (by doing whatever a spider can)." Her parenthetical comment was taken from a Spider-Man cartoon show theme song. Kagan, a comic book fan, went on to cite a Spider-Man comic, writing, "What we can decide, we can undecide. But stare decisis teaches that we should exercise that authority sparingly. Cf. S. Lee and S. Ditko, Amazing Fantasy No. 15: "Spiderman," p. 13 (1962) ("[I]n this world, with great power there must also come—great responsibility")."[69]

In *Yates v. U.S.*,[70] a ship's captain threw an undersized fish overboard in violation of a federal officer's instruction and was charged with a crime where he "knowingly alters, destroys, mutilates, conceals, covers up, falsified, or makes a false entry in any record, document, or *tangible object* [our emphasis] with the intent to impede, obstruct, or influence a federal investigation." The issue was whether the fish was a tangible object in the language of the statute; if it was not, the charges against the ship's captain were invalid.

In what was the first citation of Dr. Seuss in Supreme Court history, Kagan wrote in dissent, "A fish is, of course, a discrete thing that possesses physical form. See generally Dr. Seuss, One Fish Two Fish Red Fish Blue Fish (1960). So, the ordinary meaning of the term "tangible object" in Section 1519, as no one here disputes, covers fish (including a too-small red grouper)."[71]

Brett M. Kavanaugh

Born February 12, 1965, in Washington, DC; associate justice, 2018–present. Kavanaugh clerked for Judge Walter King Stapleton of the United States Court of Appeals for the Third Circuit and then for Judge Alex Kozinski of the Ninth Circuit. He then spent a year's fellowship in the Solicitor General's office, followed by a clerkship with Justice Anthony Kennedy, where Neil Gorsuch, whose nomination to the Supreme Court preceded Kavanaugh's, was a co-clerk. He joined the Office of the Independent Counsel and later the White House Counsel's Office under President George W. Bush, who later nominated Kavanaugh to the DC Circuit, where he sat until his elevation to the Supreme Court.

Brett Kavanaugh's close bonds with Neil Gorsuch became clear in a speech Kavanaugh gave at Notre Dame Law School right about the time President Donald Trump nominated Gorsuch to the Supreme Court. Kavanaugh noted that while he was two years ahead of Gorsuch, they both attended high school at Georgetown Prep together; they clerked together for Justice Anthony Kennedy; they worked together in the George W. Bush Administration; both became judges in 2006; both served on the Appellate Rules Committee of the Judicial Conference; and both were among the co-authors of a book on precedent.[72]

Still, the playful rivalry apparently continues. Kavanaugh told the Federalist Society that when he wrote his first opinion for the Court, a 9-0 decision in an arbitration case, "Justice Kennedy sent me the most wonderful note, which I will always cherish." It read, "I like this better than Neil's first opinion."[73]

Kavanaugh was confirmed by a 50-48 vote of the Senate; even closer than the 52-48 vote for Clarence Thomas' confirmation. Justice Stanley Matthews in 1881 was confirmed with a 24-23 vote or 48.94% of Senate votes cast against him; Kavanaugh beat that with 48.98% of Senate votes against him. Matthews had been the closest confirmation of a justice until Kavanaugh.[74]

It was Kavanaugh's habit to carry an index card in his pocket with maxims such as, "Love your friends, live on the sunrise side of the mountain and stay humble."[75]

As with other new justices, Kavanaugh received an assignment to the Court's cafeteria committee. Knowing that Justice Elena Kagan had won big points for introducing a frozen yogurt machine when she joined the committee, Kavanaugh searched for a way to make his mark. He realized that the cafeteria did not serve pizza and declared, "What an outrage."

With the introduction of pizza, Kavanaugh said, "My legacy is secure. It's fine by me if I'm ever known as the pizza justice."[76]

Kavanaugh reported that his arrival on the Court caused Kagan to remark that the Court had changed. She said that casual conversations were now being dominated by sports talk, whereas before, Shakespearean analysis was more standard fare. Kavanaugh said his only comment was, To thine own self be true."[77]

Sonia Sotomayor
Born June 25, 1954, in Bronx, New York; associate justice, 2009–present. Sotomayor served as an assistant district attorney in Manhattan. She was later nominated by President George H. W. Bush to the U.S. District Court for the Southern District of New York and nominated by President Bill Clinton to the U.S. Court of Appeals for the Second Circuit. President Barack Obama nominated Sotomayor to the Supreme Court. She was dubbed the "Savior of Baseball" in 1995 when, as a lower court judge, she ended a 232-day-long players' strike.

Sonia Sotomayor worked as a prosecutor for a while in the Manhattan District Attorney's office. It was not a typical career path for a Yale Law School graduate, and criminal law was not a typical field either. She was an intense worker, venturing into rough neighborhoods to seek witnesses, and, in a case involving the investigation of Chinese counterfeiters, she wore a bulletproof vest to lunch in Chinatown.[78]

Sotomayor is not an early riser. While on the U.S. District Court in New York, she spoke glowingly of a fellow judge who arrived at work each morning at 7 am. Speaking before a group of law students in 1994, she admitted that she would never adopt that schedule. "I am a New Yorker," she said, "and 7:00 am is a civilized hour to finish the day, not to start it."[79]

Sotomayor was surprised as a previously twice confirmed federal judge about the degree of scrutiny she received for her nomination as a Supreme Court justice. She quipped to a friend, "I think they already know the color of my underwear."[80]

New justices often adopt a low profile, but not Sotomayor. Shortly after taking office, the new justice hit the dance floor and showed off her salsa moves at a star-studded event. At a benefit sponsored by the National Hispanic Foundation, Afro-Cuban bandleader Bobby Sanabria invited the justice to the front and asked her to choose her tempo: "rare, medium, and well-done." The justice chose medium and blew the crowd away with her steps as she took her spin with actor Esai Morales. Sanabria wrote the tune for that very occasion, calling it the "Sotomayor Mambo." [81]

Sotomayor's ascension to the Supreme Court also inspired another number. Jazz musician Arturo O'Farrill wrote "Wise Latina Woman" to honor her. The title was a reference to a talk she gave in which she expressed the hope that a "wise Latina Woman with the richness of her experiences would more often than not reach a better conclusion than a white male who hasn't lived that life." The remark became a lightning rod during her confirmation hearings, as opponents seized on it to question her impartiality. After confirmation, it became a catchphrase adopted by supporters. [82]

One week after her hitting the dance floor to salsa, Sotomayor showed up at Yankee Stadium to throw out the first pitch at a game against the Boston Red Sox. The justice's bias was obvious; she wore the jersey of her beloved Yankees for the occasion.[83]

Sotomayor has a fondness for poker – often playing with her law clerks. On her financial disclosure form when she was nominated for the Court, she disclosed that in 2008, she won $8,283 at a Florida casino. [84]

When Sotomayor was asked why the Court was so reluctant to embrace technology, she replied that one reason was tradition; the other was that some of her colleagues didn't know how to use technology.[85]

After Sotomayor went on the Court, she visited Puerto Rico to a heroine's welcome. There she found T-shirts and coffee mugs with her likeness along with the words "wise Latina."

As the Court's first Hispanic woman, she quickly became a celebrity. The Bronx public housing project where she grew up was named the Justice Sonia Sotomayor Houses, and when the New York Yankees—her favorite team—visited the White House after winning the World Series, team officials also showed off their trophy in her chambers.[86] She even pressed the crystal button to lower the ball and led the one-minute countdown to midnight on New Year's Eve in Times Square.[87]

Sotomayor was interviewed for a podcast and in the small audience was a 10-year-old Latina. She asked Sotomayor, "Do you think a girl like me could become president of the United States?" Sotomayor hugged the girl and replied, "Yes, yes." Then she offered four suggestions: (1) Have big dreams; (2) Never let anyone convince you that you can't achieve those dreams; (3) Study; and (4) Work. Before leaving, Sotomayor hugged the child again and said, "I hope to be alive when you become president," because she wanted to be the one to administer the oath of office to her.[88]

In one of the more unusual hearings by a justice, Sotomayor appeared on "Sesame Street" to judge a dispute between Goldilocks and Baby Bear over a broken chair. Her solution to the dispute was for Goldilocks to help fix the chair.[89]

About the Authors

Robert S. Peck is the founder and president of the Center for Constitutional Litigation, PC., and has argued precedent-setting cases in courts throughout the nation, including in the U.S. Supreme Court. He has served as a president of both the U.S. Supreme Court Fellows Alumni Association and the Freedom to Read Foundation, chair of the RAND Institute for Civil Justice, a board member of the National Center for State Courts and the Civil Justice Research Initiative, a member of the House of Delegates of the American Bar Association, and a Leaders Forum member of the American Association for Justice.

Anthony Champagne is Professor Emeritus of Political Science at the University of Texas at Dallas. In 1990-91, he served as a Supreme Court Judicial Fellow (as did Robert Peck). He is the recipient of three university teaching awards and one University of Texas system teaching award. Champagne's teaching and research focused on the Supreme Court, Congressional leadership, and Texas politics.

Endnotes

Chapter 1

[1] One originally named justice, turned down the appointment but then reconsidered. He set out for the Court, then sitting in New York City, from Annapolis, but became ill in Alexandria. He never rode circuit or attended a session of the Court. Because he never actually served, he is never listed among the justices of the Supreme Court. Robert Harrison died at the age of 45, about three months after his unsuccessful trip to New York City. Artemus Ward, Deciding to Leave: The Politics of Retirement From the United States Supreme Court (Albany: State Univ. of New York Press, 2003), p. 31.

[2] Charles Melville Pepper, Every-Day Life in Washington: With Pen and Camera (New York: Klopsch, 1900), p. 15.

[3] Natalie Wexler, *In the Beginning: The First Three Chief Justices,* 154 U. Penn. L. Rev. 1373, 1401-02 (2006).

[4] Robert Schnakenberg, Secret Lives of the Supreme Court (Philadelphia: Quirk Books, 2009), p. 15.

[5] *Ibid.*

[6] *Ibid.*

[7] *Ibid.*

[8] Irving Dilliard, "John Jay," in Leon Friedman & Fred I. Israel, eds., The Justices of the United States Supreme Court 1789-1969: Their Lives and Major Opinions, vol. 1, (New York: Chelsea House Publishers, 1969), p. 9-10 [hereinafter cited as "Friedman & Israel"].

[9] G. Edward White, The American Judicial Tradition (3rd ed.) (New York: Oxford University Press, 2007), p. 10.

[10] *Ibid*, at 19.

[11] *Ibid*, at 10-11.

[12] Natalie Wexler, *supra* note 3, 154 U. Penn. L. Rev. at 1380.

[13] Leon Friedman, "John Rutledge," in Friedman & Israel, *supra* note 8, vol.1, at 44-45.

[14] *Ibid*, at 48; Richard B. Bernstein and Jerome Agel, Of the People, By the People, For the People (New York: Wing Books, 1993), p. 245; Clare Cushman, Courtwatchers: Eyewitness Accounts in Supreme Court History (Lanham, MD: Rowman & Littlefield Publishers, Inc., 2011), p. 5.

[15] *Talbot v. Jansen*, 3 U.S. (3 Dall.) 133, 169 (1795).

[16] Frank H. Easterbrook, *The Most Insignificant Justice: Further Evidence*, 50 U. Chi. L. Rev. 481, 486 n.15 (1983).

[17] Michael Kraus, "Oliver Ellsworth," in Friedman & Israel, *supra* note 8, vol. 1, at 223.

[18] *Ibid*, at 230.

[19] Cushman, *supra* note 14, at 163.

[20] Catherine Drinker Bowen, Miracle at Philadelphia (New York: Little, Brown, 1986 reprint), p. 259.

[21] Clare Cushman, "John Blair, Jr.," in Cushman, Clare, ed., The Supreme Court Justices: Illustrated Biographies, 1789-1995 (Washington, DC: Congressional Quarterly, 1995), p. 25.

[22] Robert R. Bair, & Robin D. Coblentz, *The Trials of Mr. Justice Samuel Chase*, 27 Md. L. Rev. 365, 368 (1967).

[23] Cushman, *supra* note 14, at 1.

[24] *Ibid*.

[25] Bill Kauffman, Forgotten Founder, Drunken Prophet: The Life of Luther Martin (Wilmington, DE: Intercollegiate Studies Institute, 2008), pp. 143-44.

[26] Charles Warren, The Supreme Court in United States History (Boston: Little, Brown & Co., 1922), p. 48 n.1.

[27] Herbert Alan Johnson, in Friedman & Israel, *supra* note 8, at 59, 65; Mary Ann Harrell and Burnett Anderson, Equal Justice Under Law (Washington, D.C.: Supreme Court Historical Soc., 1982), p. 15; Cushman, *supra* note 14, at 2.

[28] Easterbrook, *supra* note 16, at 481.

[29] Wexler, *supra* note 3, at 1387.

[30] Robert M. Ireland, "James Iredell," in Kermit L. Hall, ed., The Oxford Companion to the Supreme Court of the United States (New York: Oxford Univ. Press 1992), p. 441; Willis P. Whichard, "James Iredell: Revolutionist, Constitutionalist, Jurist," in Scott Douglas Gerber, ed., Seriatim: The Supreme Court Before John Marshall (New York: New York Univ. Press, 1998), at 199.

[31] Gerber, *supra* note 30, 29-30.

[32] Wexler, *supra* note 3, 1411-12.

33 Herbert Alan Johnson, "Thomas Johnson," in Friedman & Israel, *supra* note 8, vol. 1, at 150.

34 *Ibid*, at 151-52.

35 Easterbrook, *supra* note 16, at 492. The opinion can be found in *Georgia v. Brailsford*, 2 U.S. (2 Dall.) 402, 405 (1792).

36 David P. Currie, *The Most Insignificant Justice: A Preliminary Inquiry*, 50 U. Chi. L. Rev. 466, 467 (1983).

37 James Sterling Young, The Washington Community 1800-1828 (New York: Harcourt, Brace & World, 1966), p. 77.

38 Ward, *supra* note 1, at 48.

39 *Ibid*, at 933.

40 Andrew Laviano, "James Wilson," in Cushman, *supra* note 21, at 49.

41 Cushman, *supra* note 14, at 7.

42 Robert G. McCloskey, "James Wilson," in Friedman & Israel, *supra* note 8, vol. 1, at 95; Wexler, *supra* note 3, at 1389.

Chapter 2

1 Herbert Alan Johnson, "John Marshall," in Leon Friedman & Fred I. Israel, eds., The Justices of the United States Supreme Court 1789-1969: Their Lives and Major Opinions, vol. 1 (New York: Chelsea House Publishers, 1969), p. 285 [hereinafter cited as "Friedman & Israel"].

2 Robert Schnakenberg, Secret Lives of the Supreme Court (Philadelphia: Quirk Books, 2009), p. 18.

3 *Marbury v. Madison*, 5 U.S. (1 Cranch) 137 (1803).

4 Robert J. Steamer, Chief Justice: Leadership and the Supreme Court (Columbia, S.C.: University of S.C. Press, 1986), p. 42.

5 Clare Cushman, Courtwatchers: Eyewitness Accounts in Supreme Court History (Lanham, Md.: Rowman & Littlefield Publishers, Inc., 2011), p. 13.

6 *Ibid*, at 15.

7 Charles Melville Pepper, Every-Day Life in Washington: With Pen and Camera (New York: Klopsch, 1900), p. 199.

8 This story may be apocryphal, but has been much told over the years. Reportedly, Justice Story is responsible for handing it down. Mary Ann Harrell and Burnett Anderson, Equal Justice Under Law: The Supreme Court in American Life (Washington, DC: Supreme Court Historical Soc. rev. ed. 1994), p. 29. In some versions of the anecdote, rum is the beverage at issue. If it were wine, it probably was the specially bottled wine that Marshall arranged to be delivered to the

Court and which bore the label "The Supreme Court." Cushman, *supra* note 5, at 17.

[9] *Ibid.*

[10] *Ibid.*

[11] Leonard Baker, John Marshall: A Life in Law (New York: Macmillan Publishing Co., 1974), pp. 757-58.

[12] *Ibid*, at 586.

[13] Peter Hay, The Book of Legal Anecdotes (New York: Facts on File, 1989), pp. 288-89.

[14] Harriet Earhart Monroe, Washington: Its Sights and Insights (New York: Funk & Wagnalls, 1903), p. 59.

[15] Artemus Ward, Deciding to Leave: The Politics of Retirement From the United States Supreme Court (Albany: State Univ. of New York Press, 2003), p. 61.

[16] Gerald T. Dunne, Justice Joseph Story and the Rise of the Supreme Court (New York: Simon & Schuster, 1970), p. 346.

[17] Robert D. Ilisevich, "Henry Baldwin," in Clare Cushman, ed., The Supreme Court Justices: Illustrated Biographies, 1789-1995 (Washington, D.C.: Congressional Quarterly, 1995), p. 107.

[18] John Gregory Jacobsen, "Jackson's Judges: Six Appointments Who Shaped a Nation," Ph.D. Dissertation, University of Nebraska (2004), p. 163.

[19] David P. Currie, *The Most Insignificant Justice: A Preliminary Inquiry*, 50 U. Chi. L. Rev. 466, 480 (1983).

[20] Ilisevich, in Cushman, *supra* note 17, at 109.

[21] David J. Garrow, *Mental Decrepitude on the U.S. Supreme Court: The Historical Case for a 28th Amendment*, 67 Univ. of Chi. L. Rev. 995, 1002-03 (2000).

[22] Robert G. Seddig, "Henry Baldwin," in Kermit L. Hall, ed., The Oxford Companion to the Supreme Court of the United States (New York: Oxford University Press, 1992), p. 60.

[23] Jacobsen, *supra* note 18, at 172.

[24] *Trustees of Dartmouth College v. Woodward*, 17 U.S. (4 Wheat.) 518 (1819).

[25] Currie, *supra* note 19, at 466; Irving Dillard, "Gabriel Duvall," in Friedman & Israel, *supra* note 1, at 251 (quoting Ernest Sutherland Bates, The Story of the Supreme Court [Indianapolis: Bobbs-Merrill Co., 1936]).

[26] Currie, *supra* note 19, at 471.

[27] Elliot Spagat, "Book Explores History, Oddities of High Court," St. Louis Post-Dispatch, July 29, 1991, p. 5I.

[28] G. Edward White, *Recovering the World of the Marshall Court*, 33 John Marshall L. Rev. 781, 790 (2000).

[29] Dilliard, "Gabriel Duvall," in Friedman & Israel, *supra* note 1, vol. 1, at 427.

[30] Francis P. Weisenburger, The Life of John McLean: A Politician on the United States Supreme Court (New York: Da Capo Press, 1971), p. 154.

[31] Walker Lewis, Without Fear or Favor: A Biography of Chief Justice Roger Brooke Taney (Boston: Houghton Mifflin Co., 1965), p. 238.

[32] Richard E. Ellis, "Gabriel Duvall," in Kermit L. Hall, ed., The Oxford Companion to the Supreme Court of the United States (New York: Oxford University Press, 1992), p. 241.

[33] Dilliard, in Friedman & Israel, *supra* note 1, at 427.

[34] Donald G. Morgan, Justice William Johnson: The First Dissenter (Columbia, S.C.: University of South Carolina Press, 1954), pp. 50-51.

[35] Donald Morgan, "William Johnson," in Friedman & Israel, *supra* note 1, vol. 1, at 366.

[36] Morgan, *supra* note 34, at 181-82.

[37] Gerald T. Dunne, "Brockholst Livingston," in Friedman & Israel, *supra* note 1, vol. 1, at 396.

[38] Currie, *supra* note 19, at 469.

[39] Lewis, *supra* note 31, at 272.

[40] *Ibid.*, at 525.

[41] Lewis, *supra* note 31, at 272.

[42] Michael B. Dougan, "John McLean," in Hall, *supra* note 22, at 541-42.

[43] *Ibid.*, at 542.

[44] Charles Fairman, *The Retirement of Federal Judges*, 51 Harv. L. Rev. 416 (1938).

[45] William H. Rehnquist, The Supreme Court: How It Was, How It Is (New York: William Morrow and Co., 1987), p. 105.

[46] James Buchanan, "Alfred Moore," in Cushman, *supra* note 17, at 59.

[47] *Marbury v. Madison*, 5 U.S. (1 Cranch) 137 (1803).

[48] Buchanan, *supra* note 17, at 59.

[49] Frank H. Easterbrook, *The Most Insignificant Justice: Further Evidence*, 50 U. Chi. L. Rev. 481, 485 (1983).

[50] R. Kent Newmyer, Supreme Court Justice Joseph Story: Statesman of the Old Republic p. 3 (Chapel Hill, N.C.: University of N.C. Press, 1985).

[51] David Maxey, *The Supreme Court, 1808*, Transactions of the American Philosophical Society (2016), p. 59.

[52] Dunne, *supra* note 16, at 13.

[53] White, *supra* note 28, at 785.

54. *United States v. Crosby*, 11 U.S. (7 Cranch) 115 (1812).
55. Dunne, *supra* note 16, at 91-92.
56. Gerald T. Dunne, Joseph Story, in Friedman & Israel, *supra* note 1, at 435, 442, 445.
57. Lewis, *supra* note 31, at 270-71.
58. Herbert A. Johnson, *Chief Justice John Marshall, 1801-1835*, 1998 Journal of the Supreme Court Historical Society 1, 12-14 (1998).
59. Laura Krugman Ray, *Lives of the Justices: Supreme Court Autobiographies*, 37 Conn. Law Review 233, 248 (2004).
60. Charles Warren, The Supreme Court in United States History, vol. 2, 1836-1918 (Boston: Little Brown & Co., 1926), p. 83.
61. *Ibid.* at 479-81, 484; Earl M. Maltz, *Majority, Concurrence and Dissent: Prigg v. Pennsylvania Decision and the Structure of Supreme Court Making,"* 31 Rutgers L.J. 345, 370 (2000).
62. Linda Greenhouse, Becoming Justice Blackmun (New York: Henry Holt & Co., 2005), p. 247.
63. Elisabeth A. Cawthon, Famous Trials in History (New York: Facts on File, 2012), p. 197; Roger S. Clark, *Steven Spielberg's Amistad and Other Things I Have Thought About in the Past*, 30 Rutgers L.J. 371, 420-21 (1999).
64. The case ended up in the Supreme Court, *United States v. Schooner Amistad*, 40 U.S. (15 Pet.) 518 (1841).
65. Fred L. Israel, "Thomas Todd," in Friedman & Israel, *supra* note 1, vol. 1, at 409.
66. Easterbrook, *supra* note 49, at 490.
67. *Ibid*, at 490 n.36.
68. *Ibid*, at 496.
69. Fred L. Israel, "Robert Trimble," in Friedman & Israel, *supra* note 1, p. 513.
70. Albert P. Blaustein and Roy M. Mersky, "Bushrod Washington," in Friedman & Israel, *supra* note 1, vol. 1, at 247.
71. David A. Faber, *Justice Bushrod Washington and the Age of Discovery in American Law*, 102 W. Va. L. Rev. 735, 749-50 (2000).

Chapter 3

1. *Dred Scott v. Sandford*, 60 U.S. (19 How.) 393 (1857).
2. Sheldon Goldman, Constitutional Law: Cases and Essays (New York: HarperCollins, 2nd ed., 1991), p.78.
3. Walker Lewis, Without Fear or Favor: A Biography of Chief Justice Roger Brooke Taney (Boston: Houghton Mifflin Co., 1965), p. 251.

4. G. Edward White, The American Judicial Tradition (New York: Oxford University Press, 3rd ed. 2007), p. 67-68.
5. Lewis, *supra* note 3, at 37.
6. *Ibid*, at 390.
7. John Gregory Jacobsen, "Jackson's Judges: Six Appointments Who Shaped a Nation," Ph.D. dissertation, University of Nebraska (2004), p. 68.
8. Lewis, *supra* note 3, at 477.
9. *See* Bernard Schwartz, A History of the Supreme Court (New York: Oxford University Press, 1993), p. 104.
10. Catie Edmondson, "House Votes to Remove Confederate Statues from U.S. Capitol," N.Y. Times, Jul. 22, 2020, https://www.nytimes.com/2020/07/22/us/politics/confederate-statues-us-capitol.html.
11. Frank Otto Gatell, "Philip Pendleton Barbour," in in Leon Friedman & Fred I. Israel, eds., The Justices of the United States Supreme Court 1789-69: Their Lives and Major Opinions, vol. 1 (New York: Chelsea House Publishers, 1969), p. 717 [hereinafter cited as "Friedman & Israel"].
12. William Joseph Cibes, "Extra-Judicial Activities of Justices of the United States Supreme Court, 1790-1960," Ph.D. Dissertation, Princeton University (1975), p. 737.
13. Burnett Anderson, "John A. Campbell," in Clare Cushman, ed., The Supreme Court Justices: Illustrated Biographies, 1789-1995 (Washington, D.C.: Congressional Quarterly, 1995), p. 165.
14. Lewis, *supra* note 3, at 290.
15. Steven P. Brown, John McKinley and the Antebellum Supreme Court (Tuscaloosa: Univ. of Alabama Press, 2012), p. 139.
16. "How a Wife Made a Judge," N.Y. Times, May 10, 1896, p. 29.
17. Oscar Sherwin, *Nine Old Men*, 11 Negro History Bulletin 110, 112 (1948).
18. Charles T. Fenn, *Supreme Court Justices: Arguing Before the Court After Resigning from the Bench*, 84 Georgetown L.J. 2473, 2476-80 (1996).
19. John P. Frank, Justice Daniel Dissenting: A Biography of Peter V. Daniel, 1784-1860 (Cambridge, Mass.: Harvard Univ. Press, 1964), p. 164.
20. *Ibid*, at 246; John P. Frank, "Peter V. Daniel," in Cushman, *supra* note 13, at 138.
21. Frank, *supra* note 19, at 231-32.
22. *Ibid*, at 88.
23. *Ibid*, at 165.
24. *Ibid*, at 246.
25. Clare Cushman, Courtwatchers: Eyewitness Accounts in Supreme Court History (Lanham, Md.: Rowman & Littlefield Publishers, Inc., 2011), p. 40.

[26] Frank, *supra* note 19, at 257-258

[27] Charles Fairman, Mr. Justice Miller and the Supreme Court 1862-1890 (Cambridge, Mass.: Harvard Univ. Press, 1939), p. 105.

[28] Artemus Ward, Deciding to Leave: The Politics of Retirement from the United States Supreme Court (Albany: State Univ. of N.Y. Press, 2003), pp. 76-79.

[29] Frank H. Easterbrook, *The Most Insignificant Justice: Further Evidence*, 50 U. Chi. L. Rev. 481, n.40 and accompanying text (1983).

[30] Steven P. Brown, *An Assault on Justice: John McKinley and the Affair at Jackson*, 36 Journal of Supreme Court History 83-95 (2011).

[31] Elliot Spagat, "Book Explores History, Oddities of High Court," St. Louis Post-Dispatch, July 29, 1991, p. 5I.

[32] "The Judge Shatters His Port Light," N.Y. Times, October 6, 1878, p. 9.

[33] Burnett Anderson, "James M. Wayne," in Cushman, *supra* note 13, at 112.

[34] *Ibid*, at 113; Lewis, *supra* note 3, at 274.

[35] *Ibid*.

[36] Vincent J. Capowski, "Levi Woodbury," in Cushman, *supra* note 13, at 147.

[37] David M. O'Brien, Storm Center: The Supreme Court in American Politics (New York: W.W. Norton & Co, 1986), pp. 101-02; Cushman, *supra* note 25, at 31.

Chapter 4

[1] John Niven, Salmon P. Chase: A Biography (New York: Oxford Univ. Press, 1995), pp. 17-18.

[2] Peter Hay, The Book of Legal Anecdotes (New York: Barnes and Noble Books, 1993), p. 27.

[3] Burnett Anderson, "William Strong," in Clare Cushman, ed., The Supreme Court Justices: Illustrated Biographies, 1789-1995 (Washington, D.C.: Congressional Quarterly, 1995), p. 197.

[4] *Hepburn v. Griswold*, 75 U.S. (8 Wall.) 603 (1870).

[5] Niven, *supra* note 1, at 394.

[6] Hay, *supra* note 2, at 282-83.

[7] Herman Belz, *Salmon P. Chase and the Politics of Racial Reform*, 17 Journal of the Abraham Lincoln Association 22-40 (1996).

[8] Harriet Earhart Monroe, Washington: Its Sights and Insights (New York: Funk & Wagnalls, 1903), pp. 64-65.

[9] Louis Filler, "Morrison R. Waite," in Leon Freidman & Fred I. Israel, eds., The Justices of the United States Supreme Court, vol. 1 (New York: Chelsea House Publishers, 1969 [hereinafter cited as "Friedman & Israel 1969"]), pp. 1247-48.

[10] *Ibid.* at 1256.

[11] David T. Pride, "Melville W. Fuller, in Cushman, *supra* note 3, at 247.

[12] Willard L. King, Melville Weston Fuller: Chief Justice of the United States 1888-1910 (New York: MacMillan Co., 1950), p. 40.

[13] Hay, *supra* note 2, at 154-55.

[14] *Ibid*, at 284.

[15] Clare Cushman, Courtwatchers: Eyewitness Accounts in Supreme Court History (Latham, Md.: Rowman & Littlefield Publ. Inc., 2011), p. 145.

[16] King, *supra* note 12, at 134.

[17] *Ibid*, at 126.

[18] Clifton Fadiman, ed., The Little, Brown Book of Anecdotes (Boston: Little, Brown & Co., 1985), p. 226.

[19] *Peake v. City of New Orleans*, 139 U.S. 342 (1891).

[20] King, *supra* note 12, at 161.

[21] Kathleen Shurtleff, "Samuel Blatchford," in Cushman, *supra* note 3, at 239.

[22] Aviam Soifer, "Samuel Blatchford," in Kermit L. Hall, ed., The Oxford Companion to the Supreme Court (New York: Oxford University Press, 1992), p. 78.

[23] Jonathan Lurie, "Joseph P. Bradley," in Cushman, *supra* note 3, at 202.

[24] Anthony Champagne and Dennis Pope, *Joseph P. Bradley: An Aspect of a Judicial Personality*, 6 Political Psychology 481-93 (1985).

[25] Dennis H. Pope, "Personality and judicial performance: A psychobiography of Justice Joseph P. Bradley," Ph.D. dissertation, Rutgers University, 1988, p. 297.

[26] Linda Przybyszewski, *Judicial Conservatism and the Protestant Faith: The Case of Justice David J. Brewer*, 91 The Journal of American History 471, 476 (2004).

[27] Lurie, *supra* note 23, at p. 205.

[28] Edward J. Bander, *Holmespun Humor*, 10 Villanova L. Rev. 503, 505 (1965); James W. Ely, The Chief Justiceship of Melville W. Fuller (Columbia: University of South Carolina Press, 1995), p. 33.

[29] J. Gordon Hylton, *The Perils of Popularity: David Josiah Brewer and the Politics of Judicial Reputation*, 62 Vand. L. Rev. 567, 574 (2009).

[30] Robert M. Warner, "Henry B. Brown," in Cushman, *supra* note 3, at 257.

[31] *Plessy v. Ferguson*, 163 U.S. 537 (1896).

[32] Charles Kent, Memoir of Henry Billings Brown (New York: Duffield & Co., 1915), p. 91.

[33] *Ibid*, at 83.

[34] Trevor Broad, *Justice Henry Billings Brown Part II*, The Supreme Court Historical Society Quarterly, vol. XXVII, at pp. 10-11 (2006).

[35] *Ibid*, at 10.

[36] Richard L. Aynes, *Constricting the Law of Freedom: Justice Miller, The Fourteenth Amendment, and the Slaughter-House Cases - Freedom: Constitutional Law*, 70 Chi.-Kent L. Rev. 627, 666-67 (1994).

[37] Loren P. Beth, John Marshall Harlan: The Last Whig Justice (Lexington: Univ. Press of Kentucky, 1992), p. 135.

[38] Charles Fairman, Mr. Justice Miller and the Supreme Court 1862-1890 (Cambridge, Mass.: Harvard Univ. Press, 1939), p. 106.

[39] Frank H. Easterbrook, *The Most Insignificant Justice: Further Evidence*, 50 U. Chicago L. Rev. 481, 486 (1983).

[40] Raymond J. McKoski, *Reestablishing Actual Impartiality as the Fundamental Value of Judicial Ethics: Lessons from 'Big Judge Davis'*, 99 Kent. L.J. 259, 271 (2010-2011).

[41] "Duffers in Togas," New York Times, May 3, 1885, p. 4.

[42] Carl Brent Swisher, Stephen J. Field: Craftsman of the Law (Hamden, Conn.: Archon Books, 1963 reprint, 1930), p. 31.

[43] David T. Pride, "Stephen J. Field," in Cushman, *supra* note 6, at 187; Roger Roots, *When Lawyers Were Serial Killers: Nineteenth Century Visions of Good Moral Character*, 22 No. Ill. U. L. Rev. 19, 28 (2001).

[44] Garrett Epps, "How Much Care Do Presidents Have to Take?," The Atlantic (Feb. 9, 2016), available at https://www.theatlantic.com/politics/archive/2016/02/take-care-clause/461826/.

[45] Fairman, *supra* note 38, at 298.

[46] Pride, *supra* note 43, at 188-89; Epps, *supra* note 43. *See also Cunningham v. Neagle*, 135 U.S. 1, 52-53 (1890).

[47] *Cunningham v. Neagle*, 135 U.S. 1 (1890).

[48] *Id*. at 98 (Lamar, J., dissenting).

[49] Epps, *supra* note 44.

[50] Willard L. King, Lincoln's Manager: David Davis (Cambridge, Mass.: Harvard Univ. Press, 1960), p. 222.

[51] Hay, *supra* note 2, at 36.

[52] Louis Filler, "Horace Gray," in Friedman & Israel 1969, *supra* note 3, vol. 2, at 1382.

[53] Elbridge B. Davis and Harold A. Davis, *Mr. Justice Horace Gray: Some Aspects of His Judicial Career*, 40 ABA Journal 421, 423 (1955).

[54] Kenneth Turan, "Let Them Entertain You: The Supreme Court: The Best Free Show in Town," Wash. Post, February 2, 1975, p. 10.

[55] Phillip J. Cooper, Battles on the Bench (Lawrence, Kan.: University of Kansas Press 1995), p. 42.

[56] Francis Biddle, Mr. Justice Holmes (New York: Charles Scribner's Sons, 1943), p. 103.

[57] Frank B. Latham, The Great Dissenter: John Marshall Harlan (New York: Cowles Book Co., 1970), pp. 116-17.

[58] Doris Kearns Goodwin, The Bully Pulpit (New York: Simon & Schuster, 2013), p. 503.

[59] E.J. Edwards, Members of the Supreme Court as Human Beings, N.Y. Times, May 15, 1910, p. SM6.

[60] *The Civil Rights Cases*, 109 U.S. 3 (1883).

[61] *Dred Scott v. Sanford*, 60 U.S. 393 (19 How.) 393 (1856).

[62] Malvina Shanklin Harlan, Some Memories of a Long Life, 1854-1911 (New York: The Modern Library, 2001), p. 112-13; Beth, *supra* note 36, at 227-29.

[63] *Pollock v. Farmers' Loan & Tr. Co.*, 157 U.S. 429, *opinion vacated on reargument*, 158 U.S. 601 (1895), *overruled by South Carolina v. Baker*, 485 U.S. 505 (1988).

[64] Beth, *supra* note 37, at 245-46; G. Edward White, The American Judicial Tradition (3d ed.) (New York: Oxford Univ. Press, 2007), p. 110.

[65] King, *supra* note 13, at 131.

[66] Latham, *supra* note 57, at 34-35, 113.

[67] *Ibid*, at 117-18.

[68] Adam Winkler, *A Revolution Too Soon: Women Suffragists and the 'Living Constitution,'* 76 N.Y.U. L. Rev. 1456, 1506-07 (2001); Jack M. Balkin, *How Social Movements Change (or Fail to Change) the Constitution: The Case of the New Departure*, 39 Suffolk U. L. Rev. 27, 45 (2005).

[69] Lewis Laska, *Review of David J. Langum and Howard P. Walthall, "From Maverick to Mainstream: Cumberland School of Law 1847-1997,"* 30 Cumberland L. Rev. 493, 500-01 (1999-2000).

[70] Donald F. Paine, *Book Review: A History of the Federal Court in Jackson*, 47 Tennessee Bar J. 24 (2011).

[71] Harvey Gresham Hudspeth, *Howell Edmunds Jackson and the Making of Tennessee's First Native-Born Supreme Court Justice, 1893-1895*, 58 Tenn. Historical Quarterly 140, 152 (1999).

[72] David T. Pride, "Lucius Q.C. Lamar," in Cushman, *supra* note 6, at 245.

[73] "Another One on Justice Lamar," Wash. Post, May 9, 1888, p. 4.

[74] Louis Filler, "Stanley Matthews," in Friedman & Israel 1969, *supra* note 3, vol. 2, at 1354.

75. *Ibid*, at 1356.
76. William Robert Wantland, "Jurist and Advocate: The Political Career of Stanley Matthews, 1840-1889," Ph.D. dissertation, Miami University, 1994, pp. 185-86.
77. *Ibid*, at 193.
78. Fairman, *supra* note 38, at 417.
79. Michael A. Ross, Justice of Shattered Dreams: Samuel Freeman Miller and the Supreme Court during the Civil War Era (Baton Rouge: Louisiana State Univ. Press, 2003), p. 1.
80. *Ibid*, at 211.
81. Cushman, *supra* note 15, at 42.
82. *Ibid*, at 419.
83. Charles Melville Pepper, Every-Day Life in Washington: With Pen and Camera (New York: Klopsch, 1900), pp. 201-02.
84. Ross, *supra* note 79, at 255-56.
85. Burnett Anderson, "Rufus W. Peckham: 1896-1919," in Cushman, Clare, ed., The Supreme Court Justices: Illustrated Biographies, 1789-2012 (Washington: CQ Press, 2013), pp. 250-251.
86. William H. Rehnquist, The Supreme Court: How It Was, How It Is (New York: William Morrow & Co., 1987), p. 207.
87. *Pollack v. Farmer's Loan & Trust Co.*, 157 U.S. 429 (1895).
88. King, *supra* note 12, at 157.
89. Anderson, *supra* note 3, at 200.
90. Fairman, *supra* note 38, at 105.
91. Matthew Hofstedt, *Afterword: A brief history of Supreme Court messengers*, 39 Journal of Supreme Court History 259 (2014).

Chapter 5

1. *Lochner v. New York*, 198 U.S. 45 (1905).
2. William O. Douglas, The Court Years, 1939-1975: The Autobiography of William O. Douglas (New York: Random House, 1980), p. 10.
3. Clare Cushman, "Edward Douglass White," in Clare Cushman, ed., The Supreme Court Justices: Illustrated Biographies, 1789-1995 (Washington, D.C.: Congressional Quarterly, 1995), at 272.
4. Paul R. Baier, *Edward Douglass White: Frame for a Portrait*, 43 La. L. Rev. 1000, 1002 (1983).

5. Vincent P. Mikklesen, *Fighting for Sergeant Caldwell: The NAACP Campaign Against 'Legal' Lynching after World War I*, 94 The Journal of African American History 464, 480 (2009).

6. Sheldon M. Novick, Honorable Justice: The Life of Oliver Wendell Holmes (Boston: Little, Brown & Co., 1989), at 419, n. 27.

7. Todd C. Peppers, Ira Brad Matetsky, Elizabeth R. Williams, and Jessica Winn, *Clerking for 'God's Grandfather': Chauncey Belknap's Year with Justice Oliver Wendell Holmes, Jr.*, 43 Journal of Supreme Court History 257-293 (2018).

8. Preston Gibson, "The Human Side of the late Chief Justice White," N.Y. Times, May 22, 1921, p. 83.

9. *Ibid.*

10. "Chief Justice White: His Devotion to Duty Illustrated," N.Y. Times, May 29, 1921, p. 26.

11. Phillip J. Cooper, Battles on the Bench (Lawrence, Kan.: University Press of Kansas, 1995), p. 1.

12. Bruce Allen Murphy, The Brandeis/Frankfurter Connection: The Secret Activities of Two Supreme Court Justices (New York: Oxford Univ. Press, 1982), at pp. 76-77.

13. Peppers, *et al., supra* note 7, at 257-93.

14. Joseph Lash, From the Diaries of Felix Frankfurter (New York: W.W. Norton, 1975), pp. 313-14.

15. Judith Ann Schiff, "Life After the White House: Far from Retiring, William Howard Taft Took on the Law School," Yale Alumni Magazine (Apr. 1993), http://archives.yalealumnimagazine.com/issues/93_04/oldyale.html.

16. Charles O. Galvin, *Tax Policy—Past, Present, and Future*, 49 SMU L. Rev. 83, 89 n. 33 (1995); Carl Anthony Sferrazza, "Dog-Paddle Diplomacy," Washington Post, August 18, 1985.

17. Clifton Fadiman, ed., The Little, Brown Book of Anecdotes (Boston: Little, Brown & Co., 1985), p. 532; Paul F. Boller, Jr., Presidential Anecdotes (New York: Oxford University Press, 1981), p. 216.

18. Alpheus Thomas Mason, The Supreme Court from Taft to Warren (Baton Rouge: Louisiana State Univ. Press, 1968), p. 52.

19. Robert Schnakenberg, Secret Lives of the Supreme Court (Philadelphia: Quirk Books 2009), p. 75.

20. William Howard Taft letter to Helen (Nellie) Taft, Dec. 26, 1920, Gus Karger papers, Cincinnati Historical Society.

21. Mason, *supra* note 18, at 52.

22. *Ibid.*

23. David Schroeder, "More Than a Fraction: The Life and Work of Justice Pierce Butler," Ph.D. dissertation, Marquette University (2009), p. 146.

[24] David J. Garrow, *Mental Decrepitude on the U.S. Supreme Court: The Historical Case for a 28th Amendment*, 67 U. Chi. L. Rev. 995, 1016 (2000); Robert Post, *The Supreme Court Opinion as Institutional Practice: Dissent, Legal Scholarship and Decisionmaking in the Taft Court*, 85 Minn. L. Rev. 1267, 1326, n. 186 (2001).

[25] Brad Snyder, *The Judicial Genealogy (and Mythology) of John Roberts: Clerkships From Gray to Brandeis to Friendly to Roberts*, 71 Ohio St. L.J. 1149, 1158 (2010).

[26] *Muller v. Oregon*, 208 U.S. 412, 419 (1908).

[27] Philippa Strum, Louis D. Brandeis: Justice for the People (Cambridge, Mass.: Harvard University Press, 1984), pp. 362-63; Paul L. Rosen, The Supreme Court and Social Science (Urbana, Ill.: Univ. of Ill. Press. 1972, p. 78; Melvin I. Urofsky, 'To Guide the Light of Reason': *Mr. Justice Brandeis—An Appreciation*, 81 American Jewish History 365, 375-76 (1994).

[28] Strum, *supra* note 27, at 293.

[29] Melvin L. Urofsky, *The Great War, the Constitution, and the Court*, 44 Journal of Supreme Court History 257 (2019).

[30] Alpheus Thomas Mason, Brandeis: A Free Man's Life (New York: Viking Press, 1946), pp. 536-37; *cf.* Drew Pearson and Robert S. Allen, The Nine Old Men (New York: Doubleday, Doran and Co., 1936), p. 176.

[31] Philippa Strum, *Louis D. Brandeis*, in Cushman, *supra* note 3, at 334.

[32] Strum, *supra* note 27, at 355.

[33] *Ibid*, at 355-56.

[34] *Ibid*, at 362.

[35] *Ibid.*, at 371.

[36] *Ibid.*, at 354-55.

[37] *Ibid.*, at 352.

[38] David P. Bryden & E. Christine Flaherty, *The "Human Resumes" of Great Supreme Court Justices*, 75 Minn. L. Rev. 635, 654 (1991).

[39] William Reilly, *Pierce Butler*, in Cushman, *supra* note 3, at 352.

[40] David R. Stras, *Pierce Butler: A Supreme Technician*, 62 Vand. L. Rev. 695, 708-14 (2009).

[41] David Schroeder, *Joining the Court: Pierce Butler*, 35 Journal of Supreme Court History 144-165 (2010).

[42] Peter Hay, The Book of Legal Anecdotes (New York: Facts on File, 1989), p. 237.

[43] Schroeder, *supra* note 41, at 164.

[44] Douglas, *supra* note 2, at 16.

[45] *Ibid*, at 164.

[46] Philip E. Urofsky, ed., *The Diary of Wm. O. Douglas*, 1995 J. of Sup. Ct. History 80, 86.

47 Robert J. Steamer, Chief Justice: Leadership and the Supreme Court (Columbia, S.C.: Univ. of South Carolina Press, 1986), p. 61.

48 "John Clarke of Ohio," N.Y. Times, March 23, 1945, p. 18.

49 Carl Wittke, *Mr. Justice Clarke in Retirement*, 1 Case Western Res. L. Rev. 28, 38 (1949); "Justice Clarke Out of Supreme Court; to Work for League," N.Y. Times, Sept. 5, 1922. p. 1.

50 Justin Crowe and Christopher F. Karpowitz, *Where Have You Gone, Sherman Minton? The Decline of the Short-Term Supreme Court Justice*, 5 Perspectives on Politics 425, 432 (2007).

51 Kathleen Shurtleff, *William R. Day*, in Cushman, *supra* note 3, at p. 293.

52 "Notes from the Capital: William R. Day," 102 Nation 216-17 (Feb. 24, 1916).

53 *Hammer v. Dagenhart*, 247 U.S. 251 (1918), *overruled by, United States v. Darby*, 312 U.S. 100 (1941).

54 *Id.* at 275.

55 David J. Danelski and Joseph S. Tulchin (eds.), The Autobiographical Notes of Charles Evans Hughes (Cambridge: Harvard University Press, 2013), p. 171.

56 "McKinley Heirs in Suit: Nephew, Niece and Sisters Want Estate Held by Brother's Children, N.Y. Times, Apr. 9, 1911, p. 1.

57 Hay, *supra* note 42, at 286.

58 Catherine Drinker Bowen, Yankee from Olympus (New York: Little, Brown & Co., 1944), p. 194.

59 G. Edward White, Justice Oliver Wendell Holmes: Law and the Inner Self (New York: Oxford Univ. Press, 1993), pp. 465-66.

60 Francis Biddle, Mr. Justice Holmes (New York: Charles Scribner's Sons, 1943), p.30.

61 Edward J. Bander, *Holmespun Humor*, 10 Vill. L. Rev. 503 (1965).

62 *Ibid.*

63 *Northern Sec. Co. v. United States*, 193 U.S. 197 (1904).

64 Richard H. Wagner, *A Falling Out: The Relationship Between Oliver Wendell Holmes and Theodore Roosevelt*, 27 Journal of Supreme Court History 114-37 (2002).

65 Gary J. Aichele, Oliver Wendell Holmes, Jr., in Cushman, *supra* note 3, at 289.

66 Wagner, *supra* note 64, at 114-37.

67 Bander, *supra* note 61, at 503.

68 Biddle, *supra* note 60, at 12.

69 *Ibid*, at 7.

70 Hay, *supra* note 42, at 73.

71. Felix Frankfurter oral history by Charles C. McLaughlin, June 19, 1964, John F. Kennedy Presidential Library, Boston, Massachusetts.
72. Merlo J. Pusey, Charles Evans Hughes, vol 1 (New York: MacMillan Co., 1952), p. 285.
73. Novick, *supra* note 6, at 249.
74. Danelski and Tulchin, *supra* note 55, at 171-72.
75. Laura Krugman Ray, *Lives of the Justices: Supreme Court Autobiographies*, 37 Conn. L. Rev. 233, 282 (2004).
76. Bander, *supra* note 61, at 507.
77. Loren P. Beth, John Marshall Harlan: The Last Whig Justice (Lexington: Univ. Press of Kent., 1992), p. 174.
78. *Danovitz v. United States*, 281 U.S. 389, 397 (1930).
79. Bander, *supra* note 61, at 503.
80. Schroeder, *supra* note 41, at 146.
81. Biddle, *supra* note 60, at 144.
82. Pusey, *supra* note 72, vol. 1, at 285.
83. Bander, *supra* note 61.
84. *Ibid*, at 97.
85. *Ibid*.
86. *Ibid*, at 96.
87. Anderson, *supra* note 3, at 318.
88. *Ibid*, at 319.
89. "Justice J. R. Lamar Dies in Washington," N.Y. Times, Jan. 3, 1916, p. 13.
90. "Why Lamar and Lehmann Were Made Peace Delegates," N.Y. Times, May 24, 1914, p. 44.
91. Beth, *supra* note 77, at 176.
92. *Ibid*.
93. James O'Hara, "Joseph McKenna," in Cushman, *supra* note 3, at 283-84.
94. *Ibid*., at 284.
95. *Ibid*., at 285.
96. Nina Totenberg, "Fourth-Oldest Supreme Court Justice May Retire," NPR Morning Edition, Jan. 3, 1994.
97. Barry Cushman, *Inside the Taft Court: Lessons from the Docket Books*, 2015 Supreme Court Rev. 345 (2015)
98. Totenberg, *supra* note 96.
99. Cooper, *supra* note 11, at 107.

[100] *Standard Oil Co. v. United States*, 221 U.S. 1 (1911).

[101] *United States v. American Tobacco Co.*, 221 U.S. 106 (1911).

[102] Urofsky, *supra* note 46, at 93.

[103] James E. Bond, I Dissent: The Legacy of Justice James Clark McReynolds (Fairfax, Va.: George Mason Univ. Press, 1992), p. 43.

[104] Cooper, *supra* note 11, at 11, 93, 105.

[105] *Ibid*, at 154.

[106] Kim Eisler, A Justice for All (New York: Simon & Schuster, 1993), p. 60.

[107] Milton C. Handler, *Clerking for Justice Harlan Fiske Stone*, 1995 Journal of Supreme Court History 113, at 119.

[108] *Ibid*, at 99.

[109] Bond, *supra* note 103, at 84; Charles T. Fenn, *Supreme Court Justices: Arguing before the Court after Resigning from the Bench*, 84 Geo. L.J. 2473, 2489 (1996).

[110] William O. Douglas, Go East, Young Man (New York: Random House, 1974), p. xiv-xv.

[111] Urofsky, *supra* note 46, at 93.

[112] Paul T. Heffron, "William H. Moody," in Cushman, *supra* note 3, at 296.

[113] *Ibid*, at 298.

[114] *Ibid*, at 325.

[115] *Ibid*.

[116] Cooper, *supra* note 11, at 108.

[117] *West Coast Hotel v. Parrish*, 300 U.S. 379 (1937).

[118] Cushman, *supra* note 97, at 108.

[119] *Ibid*, at 140.

[120] Cooper, *supra* note 11, at 116; Michael Ariens, *A Thrice-Told Tale, Or Felix the Cat*, 107 Harv. L. Rev. 620, 646 (1994).

[121] Lewis L. Laska, *The Fake Law School: How Today's Written Tennessee Bar Exam Grew From Scandal and Disarray*, 53 Tennessee Bar J. 12, 14 (2017).

[122] David Burner, "Edward Terry Sanford," in Leon Friedman & Fred I. Israel (eds.), The Justices of the United States Supreme Court 1789-1969: Their Lives and Major Opinions, vol. 3, (New York: Chelsea House Publishers, 1969), p. 2204.

[123] *Ibid*.

[124] Barry Cushman, *Rethinking the New Deal Court*, 80 Virginia Law Rev. 201, 214 (1994).

[125] Jay S. Bybee, "George Sutherland," in Cushman, *supra* note 3, at 349.

[126] Douglas, *supra* note 2, at 12-13.

127. Howard Ball & Phillip J. Cooper, Of Power and Right: Hugo Black, William O. Douglas, and America's Constitutional Revolution (New York: Oxford University Press, 1992), p. 76.
128. David T. Pride, "Willis Van Devanter," in Cushman, *supra* note 3, at 314; Danelski and Tulchin, *supra* note 55, at 171.
129. Douglas, *supra* note 2, at 11. Chief Justice Charles Evans Hughes claimed to have made a similar remark. *See* Danelski and Tulchin, *supra* note 54, at 171.

Chapter 6

1. William E. Leuchtenburg, The Supreme Court Reborn: The Constitutional Revolution in the Age of Roosevelt (New York: Oxford Univ. Press, 1995), p. 119.
2. Merlo J. Pusey, Charles Evans Hughes, vol. 1 (New York: MacMillan Co., 1952), p. 80.
3. *Ibid.*, vol. 2, at 425.
4. C. A. Przybyszewski, "Charles Evans Hughes," in William D. Pederson and Norman W. Provizer, eds., Great Justices of the U.S. Supreme Court: Ratings & Case Studies (New York: Peter Lang Publishing, Inc., 1993), p. 174.
5. Pusey, *supra* note 2, vol. 1, at 324.
6. Peter Hay, The Book of Legal Anecdotes (New York: Barnes & Noble Books, 1989), p. 84.
7. Pusey, *supra* note 2, vol. 2, at 635.
8. Charles T. Fenn, *Supreme Court Justices: Arguing Before the Court After Resigning from the Bench*, 84 Georgetown L.J. 2473, 2485 (1996).
9. Pusey, *supra* note 2, vol. 2, at 664.
10. *Ibid.*, at 666.
11. *Ibid.*, at 668.
12. Erwin N. Griswold, Ould Fields, New Corne (Eagan, Mn.: West Academic Publishing, 1992), p. 92 n.25.
13. Pusey, *supra* note 2, vol. 2, at 786.
14. *Ibid*, at 362-63.
15. Hay, *supra* note 6, at 28.
16. David O'Brien, Storm Center: The Supreme Court in American Politics (New York: W.W. Norton, 1986), p. 115.
17. Bernard Schwartz, Super Chief: Earl Warren and His Supreme Court (New York: New York Univ. Press, 1983), p. 28.

[18] Phillip J. Cooper, Battles on the Bench: Conflict Inside the Supreme Court (Lawrence, KS: University Press of Kansas, 1995), p. 94.

[19] Clare Cushman, Courtwatchers: Eyewitness Accounts in Supreme Court History (Lanham, MD: Rowman & Littlefield, 2011), p. 209.

[20] *Ibid*, at 224.

[21] *Ibid*.

[22] John Henry Hatcher, "Fred M. Vinson," in Clare Cushman, ed., The Supreme Court Justices: Illustrated Biographies, 1789-1995 (Washington, DC: Congressional Quarterly, 1995), p. 421.

[23] William O. Douglas, The Court Years, 1939-1975: The Autobiography of William O. Douglas (New York: Random House, Inc., 1980), pp. 225-26.

[24] Cooper, *supra* note 18, at 95.

[25] Bernard Schwartz, A History of the Supreme Court (New York: Oxford Univ. Press, 1993), p. 253.

[26] *Plessy v. Ferguson*, 163 U.S. 537 (1896).

[27] *Brown v. Board of Education*, 347 U.S. 483 (1953).

[28] Cooper, *supra* note 18, at 31.

[29] *Ibid*, at 63.

[30] *Ibid*, at 61.

[31] *Ibid*, at 105.

[32] *Ibid*, at 148.

[33] *Ibid* at 149.

[34] Leuchtenburg, *supra* note 1, at 190.

[35] *Ibid*, at 377.

[36] *Youngstown Sheet & Tube Co. v. Sawyer*, 343 U.S. 579 (1952).

[37] David McCullough, Truman (New York: Simon & Schuster, 1992), p. 901; Charles C. Hileman *et al.*, Supreme Court Law Clerk's Recollections of October Term 1951, including the Steel Seizure Cases, 82 St. John's L. Rev. 1239, 1278-79 (2008).

[38] Roger K. Newman, Hugo Black: A Biography (New York: Pantheon, 1994), p. 485.

[39] Clifton Fadiman, ed., The Little, Brown Book of Anecdotes (Boston: Little, Brown & Co., 1985), p. 65.

[40] Bob Woodward & Scott Armstrong, The Brethren (New York: Simon & Schuster, 1979), p. 80.

[41] Hugo Black, Jr., My Father: A Remembrance (New York: Random House, 1975), p. 184.

[42] Hunter R. Clark, Justice Brennan: The Great Conciliator (Birch Lane Press: New York 1995), p. 203.

[43] *Tinker v. Des Moines Indep. Commun. Sch. Dist.*, 393 U.S. 503 (1969).

[44] Dennis J. Hutchinson, *Hugo Black Among Friends*, 93 Mich. L. Rev. 1885, 1886-87 (1995).

[45] Howard Ball and Phillip J. Cooper, Of Power and Right: Hugo Black, William O. Douglas, and America's Constitutional Revolution (New York: Oxford University Press, 1992), pp. 304-08.

[46] Jennifer M. Lowe, "Harold H. Burton," in Cushman, *supra* note 22, at 418.

[47] *Ibid.*, at 420.

[48] "Harold H. Burton is Dead at 76; High Court Justice for 13 Years; Truman Appointee in '45 Was Regarded as Unifying Influence in Divided Period—Ex— Cleveland Mayor and Senator," N.Y. Times (Oct. 29, 1964), p. 35.

[49] Cooper, *supra* note 18, at 173; Cushman, *supra* note 22, at 147.

[50] Nancy Bunch, *Governor James Byrnes*, 28 Supreme Court Historical Society Q. 8 (2007).

[51] David Robertson, Sly and Able: A Political Biography of James F. Byrnes (New York: W.W. Norton, 1994), pp. 519-22, 536-37.

[52] Andrew L. Kaufman, Cardozo (Cambridge: Harvard University Press, 1998), p. 125.

[53] Andrew L. Kaufman, "Benjamin Cardozo and His Law Clerks," in Todd C. Peppers and Artemus Ward (eds.), In Chambers: Stories of Supreme Court Law Clerks and Their Justices (Charlottesville: Univ. of Virginia Press, 2012), p. 89.

[54] Kaufman, *supra* note 52, at 144.

[55] Kaufman, *supra* note 53, at 95.

[56] Fadiman, *supra* note 39, at 101.

[57] Hay, *supra* note 6, at 31.

[58] "Books of the Times: The Judge The Philosopher The Golfer The Disciple," N.Y. Times, Apr. 12, 1940, p. 26.

[59] *Ibid.*

[60] McCullough, *supra* note 37, at 901.

[61] *Youngstown Sheet & Tube Co. v. Sawyer*, 343 U.S. 579 (1952).

[62] Ball and Cooper, *supra* note 45, at 133.

[63] *Roth v. United States*, 354 U.S. 476 (1957).

[64] Kim Issac Eisler, A Justice for All (New York: Simon & Schuster, 1993), p. 142.

[65] William O. Douglas, Go East, Young Man: The Early Years (New York: Random House, 1974), p. 7.

66 *Ibid*, at 60.
67 *Ibid*, at 149-50.
68 James F. Simon, Independent Journey: The Life of William O. Douglas (New York: Harper & Row, 1980), p. 119.
69 Douglas, *supra* note 65, at 7-8.
70 *Ibid*, at 55.
71 *Ibid.*, at 466.
72 *Remembrances of William O. Douglas on the 50th Anniversary of his Appointment to the Supreme Court*, Journal of Supreme Court History, pp. 104, 107-08 (1990).
73 *Ibid*, at 104-05.
74 Douglas, *supra* note 23, at 182.
75 *Hazel-Atlas Co. v. Hartford-Empire Co.*, 322 U.S. 238 (1944).
76 Douglas, *supra* note 23, at 182.
77 *Ibid*, at 197.
78 Cathleen H. Douglas, *William O. Douglas: The Man*, in Yearbook 1981, Supreme Court Historical Soc., p. 9.
79 Ball and Cooper, *supra* note 45, at 146-47.
80 McCullough, *supra* note 37, at 637.
81 John C. Jeffries, Jr., Justice Lewis F. Powell, Jr. (New York: Charles Scribner's Sons, 1994), p. 255.
82 Cushman, *supra* note 22, at 194.
83 Cooper, *supra* note 18, at 72-73.
84 *Ibid*, at 110.
85 Douglas, *supra* note 65, at xiii.
86 Cooper, *supra* note 18, at 37.
87 Jeffries, *supra* note 81, at 254.
88 Woodward and Armstrong, *supra* note 40, at 399.
89 James F. Simon, The Antagonists: Hugo Black, Felix Frankfurter and Civil Liberties in Modern America (New York: Simon and Schuster, 1989), p. 24.
90 Joseph Lash (ed.), From the Diaries of Felix Frankfurter (New York: W.W. Norton, 1975), p. 10.
91 *Ibid.*, at 15; Simon, *supra* note 89, at 42.
92 *Ibid.*
93 Chalmers M. Roberts, "Felix Frankfurter's 'Happy Hot Dogs,'" Wash. Post, Jul. 10, 1988, available at https://www.washingtonpost.com/archive/

entertainment/books/1988/07/10/felix-frankfurters-happy-hot-dogs/f36a5e60-9fe8-45be-b4f5-f66655ddb88c/.

[94] *Ibid*, at 45.

[95] *Ibid*, at 50.

[96] Simon, *supra* note 89, at 66.

[97] *Nurbo Co. v. Bethlehem Shipbuilding Corp.*, 308 U.S. 165 (1939).

[98] Melvin I. Urofsky, *The Court at War, and the War at the Court*, 1 J. of S. Ct. History 1, 85 (1996).

[99] Susan David de Maine, *Access to the Justices' Papers: A Better Balance*, 110 Law Library Journal 185, 187-88 (2018).

[100] Hay, *supra* note 6, at 293.

[101] Douglas, *supra* note 23, at 40.

[102] Cooper, *supra* note 18, at 9.

[103] *Ibid*, at 53.

[104] Lash, *supra* note 90, at 76.

[105] Douglas, *supra* note 65, at 332.

[106] *Adamson v. California*, 332 U.S. 46 (1947).

[107] Richard L. Aynes, *Charles Fairman, Felix Frankfurter, and the Fourteenth Amendment*, 70 Chi.-Kent L. Rev. 1197, 1223 (1995).

[108] David Jackson, "Judge's fight for gender equity praised," The Dallas Morning News, Jun. 15, 1993, at 1; Todd Peppers and Beth See Driver, "Half Clerk, Half Son: Justice Felix Frankfurter and His Law Clerks," in Todd C. Peppers and Artemas Ward, eds., In Chambers: Stories of Supreme Court Law Clerks and Their Justices (Charlottesville: University of Virginia Press, 2012), p.142.

[109] Peppers and Driver, *supra* note 108, at 148.

[110] Kimberly Greenfield, Jason S. Fleming, and Terri Ann Smith, "The Influence of Justice Frankfurter on Justice Reed: Friendship and Argument," a paper written for a poster presentation at the annual meeting of the American Political Science Association, Washington, D.C., September 4, 1993.

[111] Ball and Cooper, *supra* note 45, at 87.

[112] Eisler, *supra* note 64, at 192.

[113] James M. Marsh, "Robert H. Jackson," in Cushman, *supra* note 22, at 408.

[114] Robert H. Jackson, *Advocacy before the Supreme Court: Suggestions for Effective Case Presentations*, 37 A.B.A Journal 801 (1951).

[115] Louise Arbour, "The Rule of Law and the Reach of Accountability," in Cheryl Sanders and Katerine Le Roy, eds., The Rule of Law (Annandale, Aus.: Federation Press, 2003), at 104.

[116] John M. Ferren, Salt of the Earth, Conscience of the Court: The Story of Justice Wiley Rutledge (Chapel Hill, NC: Univ. of North Carolina, 2004) p. 227.

[117] Robert Schnakenberg, Secret Lives of the Supreme Court (Philadelphia: Quirk Books, 2009), p. 118.

[118] John Q. Barrett, A Rehnquist Ode on the Vinson Court, 11 Green Bag 2d 289, 303 (circa 1953).

[119] Max Lerner, Nine Scorpions in a Bottle (New York: Arcade, 1994) p. 167.

[120] Cushman, *supra* note 22, at 432.

[121] Douglas, *supra* note 65, at 418.

[122] Douglas, *supra* note 23, at 247.

[123] Ed Cray, Chief Justice: A Biography of Earl Warren (New York: Simon & Schuster, 1997), p. 266.

[124] *Past Presidents Reflect of their Years of Service*, 40 Res Gestae 42, 42 (Sept. 1996).

[125] Ferren, *supra* note 116, at 224-25.

[126] *United States v. Darby*, 312 U.S. 100 (1941).

[127] J. Woodford Howard, Mr. Justice Murphy: A Political Biography (Princeton: Princeton University Press, 1968), pp. 266-67.

[128] Cooper, *supra* note 18, at 108.

[129] *Schneiderman v. United States*, 320 U.S. 118 (1943).

[130] Urofsky, *supra* note 98, at 5.

[131] Cooper, *supra* note 18, at 107.

[132] Douglas, *supra* note 23, at 10.

[133] *Ibid*, at 24-25.

[134] *Ibid*, at 26.

[135] *Mortensen v. United States*, 322 U.S. 369 (1944).

[136] Douglas, *supra* note 23, at 25.

[137] John P. Frank, "Frank Murphy," in Leon Friedman & Fred L. Israel, The Justices of the United Supreme Court: Their Lives and Major Opinions, vol. iv (New York: Chelsea House Publishers, 1997), p. 1251.

[138] Brannon P. Denning, "Review Article, 'The Birth of the Modern Constitution: The United States Supreme Court,' in William M. Wiecek, Oliver Wendell Holmes Devise History of the Supreme Court of the United States," vol. 12 (New York: Cambridge University Press, 2006," 99 Law Library Journal 621, 629 (2007).

[139] Artemas Ward, Deciding to Leave: The Politics of Retirement from the United States Supreme Court (Albany: State Univ. of New York Press, 2003), p. 148.

[140] *Norman v. Baltimore & O.R. Co.*, 294 U.S. 240 (1935); *Perry v. United States*, 294 U.S. 330 (1935); *Nortz v. United States*, 294 U.S. 317 (1935).

[141] *Humphrey's Executor v. U.S.*, 295 U.S. 602 (1935).

[142] Leuchtenburg, *supra* note 1, at 64.

[143] Greenfield, Fleming and Smith, *supra* note 110.

[144] *Ibid.*

[145] Benjamin C. Mizer, *The Bureaucratic Court*, 105 Mich. L. Rev. 1301, 1305 (2007).

[146] *Brown v. Board of Education*, 347 U.S. 483 (1954); Frederick P. Aguirre, et al., *Mendez v. Westminster: A Living History*, 2014 Mich. St. L. Rev. 401, 418 (2014).

[147] Ball and Cooper, *supra* note 45, at 77.

[148] Ferren, *supra* note 116, at 59.

[149] *Ibid*, at 115.

[150] *Minersville Sch. Dist. v. Gobitis*, 310 U.S. 586 (1940), *overruled by West Virginia St. Bd. of Educ. v. Barnette*, 319 U.S. 624 (1943).

[151] Ferren, *supra* note 116, at 188; Irving Brant, *Mr. Justice Rutledge-The Man*, 25 Ind. L.J. 424, 436 (1950).

[152] Cushman, *supra* note 22, at 413; Laura Krugman Ray, Lives of the Justices: Supreme Court Autobiographies, 37 Conn. L. Rev. 233, 216 (2004).

[153] *Shelley v. Kraemer*, 334 US 1 (1948).

[154] Ray, *supra* note 152, at 232.

[155] Dillard Stokes, "3 Justices Retire from Racial Case," Wash. Post, Jan. 16, 1948, p. 1.

[156] Ferren, *supra* note 116, at 230.

[157] *Ibid*, at 231.

Chapter 7

[1] *Brown v. Board of Education*, 347 U.S. 483 (1954).

[2] *Marbury v. Madison*, 5 U.S. (1 Cranch) 137 (1803).

[3] Philip B. Kurland, *Earl Warren, The "Warren Court," and the Warren Myths*, 67 Mich. L. Rev. 353, 357 (1968).

[4] Ed Cray, Chief Justice: A Biography of Earl Warren (New York: Simon & Schuster, 1997), p. 20.

[5] *Ibid*, at 53.

[6] Bernard Schwartz, Super Chief: Earl Warren and His Supreme Court (New York: New York Univ. Press, 1983), p. 335.

[7] Cray, *supra* note 4, at 188-89.

[8] *Ibid*, at 17.

9. *Ibid*, at 20.
10. *Ibid*, at 213.
11. David A. Kaplan, "Judging Why Earl Warren Was Hailed as 'Super Chief,'" N.Y. Times, sec. 2 (Dec. 24, 1989), at p. 26.
12. Schwartz, *supra* note 6, at 24.
13. Kim Eisler, A Justice for All (New York: Simon & Schuster, 1993), p. 159. Eisenhower is also quoted as saying that Warren's appointment was "the biggest damn fool thing I ever did." Cray, *supra* note 4, at 10, 337. There is some dispute to whether Eisenhower actually said this, though he may have come to adopt it after the fact. *See* Seth Stern and Stephen Wermiel, Justice Brennan: Liberal Champion (New York: Houghton Mifflin Harcourt, 2010), p. 138-39; Theo Lippman Jr. "Anecdotes are dangerous to biographers and truth Mistakes: When essential little stories are distorted, vast damage is done," Baltimore Sun, Sept. 7, 1997, available at https://www.baltimoresun.com/news/bs-xpm-1997-09-07-1997250003-story.html#:~:text=Dwight%20Eisenhower%20was%20quoted%20once%20again%20in%20som,the%20whole%20thing%20on%20gossip%20and%20Brennan%27s%20biographers.
14. Cray, *supra* note 4, at 337.
15. Schwartz, *supra* note 6, at 280-81.
16. Cray, *supra* note 4, at 392.
17. Phillip J. Cooper, Battles on the Bench (Lawrence: Univ. Press of Kansas, 1995), pp. 162-63.
18. Schwartz, *supra* note 6, at 766.
19. *Ibid*, at 770.
20. Max Wiener, "Brennan, Son of Irish Immigrant, Is Known as Moderate Liberal," Wash. Post, Sept. 30, 1956, p. B3.
21. Eisler, *supra* note 13, at 35.
22. *Ibid*, at 36.
23. *Ibid*, at 99; Hunter R. Clark, Justice Brennan: The Great Conciliator (Birch Lane Press: New York 1995), p. 10.
24. David G. Savage, Turning Right: The Making of the Rehnquist Supreme Court (New York, John Wiley & Sons, 1992), p. 125; Eisler, *supra* note 13, at 103.
25. Garry Jenkins & Robert Clark, *Welcome Address*, 43 N.Y.L. Sch. L. Rev. 9, 10 (1999); Schwartz, *supra* note 6, at 205; Clark, *supra* note 23, at 103.
26. *Jencks v. United States*, 353 U.S. 657 (1957).
27. Stern and Wermiel, *supra* note 13, at 127-30.
28. Richard Arnold, *A Remembrance: Mr. Justice Brennan, October Term 1960*, Journal of Supreme Court History, 1991, pp. 5, 7.

[29] Bob Woodward and Scott Armstrong, The Brethren: Inside the Supreme Court (New York: Simon & Schuster, 1979), pp. 279-80.

[30] Eisler, *supra* note 13, at 264.

[31] Laura Kalman, Abe Fortas (New Haven, Conn.: Yale Univ. Press, 1990), p. 9.

[32] *Ibid*, at 12-13.

[33] *Ibid*, at 42.

[34] *Ibid*, at 60-61.

[35] *Gideon v. Wainwright*, 372 U.S. 335 (1963).

[36] William E. Leuchtenburg, *The Supreme Court Reborn* (New York: Oxford Univ. Press, 1995), p. 256.

[37] Kalman, *supra* note 31, at 192.

[38] Kathleen Shurtleff, "Arthur J. Goldberg," in Clare Cushman (ed.), The Supreme Court Justices: Illustrated Biographies, 1789-1995 (Washington, DC: Congressional Quarterly, 1995), at 468.

[39] In Memoriam, Remarks of Professor David Feller, Proceedings of the Bar and Officers of the Supreme Court of the U.S., 110 S.Ct. 390, 393-94 (Oct. 15, 1990).

[40] Abner J. Mikva, *In Memoriam: Arthur J. Goldberg, 1908-1990*, 84 Nw. U. L. Rev. 811, 813 (1990).

[41] Stephen Breyer, *Clerking for Justice Goldberg*, Journal of the Supreme Court History, 1990, pp. 4, 6.

[42] Robert Schnakenberg, Secret Lives of the Supreme Court (Philadelphia: Quirk Books, 2009), p. 132.

[43] Louis R. Cohen, *A Biography of the Second Justice Harlan* (book review), 91 Mich. L. Rev. 1609, 1610 (1993).

[44] William T. Coleman, Jr., *Mr. Justice Thurgood Marshall: A Substantial Architect of the United States Constitution for our Times*, 101 Yale L.J. 7, 10 (1991).

[45] Carl T. Rowan, Dream Makers, Dream Breakers: The World of Justice Thurgood Marshall (Boston: Little, Brown & Co., 1993, p. 341.

[46] *Ibid*.

[47] *Cohen v. California*, 403 U.S. 15 (1971).

[48] Woodward & Armstrong, *supra* note 29, at 133.

[49] Dennis Drabelle, "Harlan Prodigious Dissenter," Wash. Post, Feb. 25, 1992, p. E2.

[50] Clare Cushman, Courtwatchers: Eyewitness Accounts in Supreme Court History (New York: Rowman & Littlefield Publishers Inc., 2011), p. 245.

[51] Ralph K. Winter, *TM's Legacy*, 101 Yale L. J. 25, 28 (1991).

[52] Elena Kagan, *For Justice Marshall*, 71 Tex. L. Rev. 1125, 1126 (1993).

[53] *Cooper v. Aaron*, 358 U.S. 1 (1958).

[54] Robert L. Carter, *A Tribute to Thurgood Marshall*, 105 Harv. L. Rev. 33, 37 (1991).

[55] Mark Tushnet, *Thurgood Marshall: The Inner-Directed Personality*, 26 Valparaiso U. L. Rev. xxxi, xxxiii (1991).

[56] Kagan, *supra* note 52, at 1126-27.

[57] Winter, *supra* note 51, at 29.

[58] Rowan, *supra* note 45, at 286.

[59] *Ibid*, at 296.

[60] Woodward and Armstrong, *supra* note 29, at 199.

[61] *Ibid*, at 59.

[62] Rowan, *supra* note 45, at 415; Owen Fiss, *A Tribute to Thurgood Marshall*, 105 Harv. L. Rev. 49, 52 (1991).

[63] Deborah L. Rhode, "Thurgood Marshall and His Clerks," in Todd C. Peppers and Artemus Ward (eds.), In Chambers: Stories of Supreme Court Law Clerks and their Justices (Charlottesville: Univ. of Virginia Press, 2012), p. 317.

[64] Rowan, *supra* note 45, at 390.

[65] Woodward and Armstrong, *supra* note 29, at 59.

[66] *Brown v. Board of Education*, 347 U.S. 483 (1954).

[67] Derek Anthony West, *A Tribute To Justice Thurgood Marshall*, 44 Stan. L. Rev. 1209, 1210 (1992).

[68] Anthony M. Kennedy, *The Voice of Thurgood Marshall*, 44 Stan. L. Rev. 1221, 1223 (1992).

[69] *Perry v. Louisiana*, 498 U.S. 38 (1990).

[70] Scott Brewer, *Justice Marshall's Justice Martial*, 71 Texas L. Rev. 1121, 1122-23 (1993).

[71] Kennedy, *supra* note 68, at 1233.

[72] James E. Di Tullio and John B. Schochet, *Saving This Honorable Court A Proposal to Replace Life Tenure on the Supreme Court with Staggered, Nonrenewable Eighteen-Year Terms*, 90 Va. L. Rev. 1093, 1103 (2004).

[73] Brewer, *supra* note 70, at 1121.

[74] Robert S. Marsel, *The Constitutional Jurisprudence of Justice Potter Stewart: Reflections on a Life of Public Service*, 55 Tenn. L. Rev. 1, 15 (1987).

[75] Cray, *supra* note 4, at 360.

[76] *Clemons v. Board of Educ.*, 228 F.2d 853 (6th Cir. 1956).

[77] In Memoriam, Remarks of William P. Rogers, Proceedings of the Bar and Officers of the Supreme Court of the United States, 105 S.Ct. 19, 22 (Oct. 20, 1986).

[78] Lloyd Cutler, *Mr. Justice Stewart: A Personal Reminiscence*, 95 Harv. L. Rev. 11, 13 (1981).

[79] Laurence H. Tribe, *Justice Stewart: A Tale of Two Portraits*, 95 Yale L.J. 1328, 1332 (1986).

[80] *Katz v. United States*, 389 U.S. 347, 351 (1967) (Stewart, J., concurring).

[81] Tribe, *supra* note 79, at 1330 (1986).

[82] Cushman, *supra* note 50, at 114.

[83] *Jacobellis vs. Ohio*, 378 U.S. 184, 197 (1964) (Stewart, J., concurring).

[84] Byron R. White, *Remembering Potter Stewart*, 21 Litigation 3, 57 (Fall 1994).

[85] Potter Stewart, *A Retirement Press Conference (June 19, 1981)*, 55 Tenn. L. Rev. 21, 25 (1987).

[86] Eisler, *supra* note 13, at 218.

[87] Gil Kujovich, "Potter Stewart," in Cushman, *supra* note 38, at 460.

[88] John C. Jeffries, Jr., Justice Lewis F. Powell, Jr. (New York: Charles Scribner's Sons, 1994), p. 542.

[89] Dennis J. Hutchinson, The Man Who Once Was Whizzer White: A Portrait of Justice Byron R. White (New York: The Free Press, 1998), p. 34.

[90] Dennis J. Hutchinson, *The Man Who Once Was Whizzer White*, 103 Yale L.J. 43, 44 (1993).

[91] U.S. Court of Appeals for the Tenth Circuit, "Byron Raymond White," http://www.ca10.uscourts.gov/education/byron_white_html.php.

[92] Hutchinson, *supra* note 89, at 55-56.

[93] Paul Tagliabue, *A Tribute to Byron White*, 112 Yale L.J. 999, 1001 (2003).

[94] David M. Ebel, *A Tribute to Justice Bryon R. White*, 107 Harv. L. Rev. 8, 10 (1993).

[95] Stanley Kay, "The Highest Court in the Land," Sports Illustrated (Jul 25, 2018), available at https://www.si.com/nba/2018/07/25/supreme-court-building-basketball-court.

[96] Hutchinson, *supra* note 89, at 1.

[97] Rhesa H. Barksdale, *A Tribute to Justice Byron R. White*, 107 Harv. L. Rev. 3, 5 (1993).

[98] Pierce O'Donnell, *The Hands of Justice: A Law Clerk Fondly Remembers Byron R. White*, 33 Washburn L. J. 12, 13 (1993).

[99] *Ibid*, at 16.

[100] David M. Ebel, "Law Clerk Recollections of Justice Byron R. White – The Man Behind the Legend," U.S. Court of Appeals for the Tenth Circuit, http://www.ca10.uscourts.gov/education/byron_white_html.php.

[101] *New York v. Ferber*, 458 U.S. 747 (1982).

[102] Hutchinson, *supra* note 89, at 403-04.

[103] William H. Rehnquist, The Supreme Court: How It Was, How It Is (New York: William Morrow & Co., 1987), p. 257.

[104] "This Honorable Court," PBS, Oct. 1988.

[105] Erwin N. Griswold, *Reflections on Justice White*, 58 U. Colo. L. Rev. 339, 346 (1987).

[106] Hutchinson, *supra* note 90, at 54-55.

[107] Kevin J. Worthen, *Shirt-Tales: Clerking for Byron White*, 1994 B.Y.U. L. Rev. 349, 350.

[108] Cushman, *supra* note 50, at 95.

[109] *Bar and Bench Meet to Present Memorials to the Late Byron R. White*, 28 Supreme Court Historical Society Q. 5, 10 (2002).

[110] Kimberly Strawbridge Robinson, "Gorsuch Doesn't Give a 'Fig' What You Think, Just Like Mentor," Bloomberg Law, Jul. 27, 2020.

[111] "Former Justice Whittaker of Supreme Court Is Dead," N.Y. Times, Nov. 27, 1973, p. 44.

[112] William O. Douglas, Go East, Young Man: The Early Years (New York: Random House, 1974), p. 250.

[113] Charles E. Whittaker, *Some Reminiscences*, 43 Neb. L. Rev. 352, 353 (1963).

[114] *Ibid*, at 355.

[115] *Meyer v. United States*, 364 U.S. 410 (1955).

[116] Douglas, *supra* note 112, at 173-74.

Chapter 8

[1] *Roe v. Wade*, 410 U.S. 113 (1973).

[2] *United States v. Nixon*, 418 U.S. 683 (1974).

[3] *Miranda v. Arizona*, 384 U.S. 436 (1966).

[4] *Dickerson v. United States*, 530 U.S. 428 (2000).

[5] Bob Woodward and Scott Armstrong, The Brethren: Inside the Supreme Court (New York: Simon & Schuster, 1979), p. 173.

[6] Douglas D. McFarland, *Chief Justice Warren E. Burger: A Personal Tribute*, 19 Hamline L. Rev. 1, 16 n.45 (1995).

[7] *Ibid*, at 22.

[8] J. Michael Luttig, *In Memoriam: Warren E. Burger*, 109 Harv. L. Rev. 1, 3 (1995).

[9] Woodward & Armstrong, *supra* note 5, at 22-23.

[10] Mark Cannon, *A Tribute to Chief Justice Warren E. Burger*, 100 Harv. L. Rev. 984, 987 (1987).

[11] *Ibid*, at 986.

[12] David Savage, Turning Right: The Making of the Rehnquist Supreme Court (New York: John Wiley & Sons, 1992), p. 16.

[13] J. Harvie Wilkinson III, Serving Justice, A Supreme Court Clerk's View (New York: Charterhouse, 1974), p. 169.

[14] Fred Barbash, "Justice Powell Rebuts Media Reports on Court, Wash. Post, May 2, 1980, p. A2.

[15] John C. Jeffries, Jr., Justice Lewis F. Powell, Jr. (New York: Charles Scribner's Sons, 1994), p. 545.

[16] *Bowsher v. Synar*, 478 U.S. 714 (1986).

[17] Eyewitness account of co-author Robert S. Peck.

[18] "Checkered Past," The Nat'l Law Journal (Jan. 15, 2007), p. 12, col. 2.

[19] John A. Jenkins, The Partisan: The Life of William Rehnquist (New York: Public Affairs, 2012), p. 9.

[20] "Rehnquist Honored for Weather Work," FindLaw (Oct. 25, 2001), http://news.findlaw.com/ap/o/1110/10-25-2001/20011025105022050.html.

[21] John G. Roberts, Jr., *William H. Rehnquist: A Remembrance*, 31 Vermont L. Rev. 431, 433 (2007).

[22] *Oliphant v. Suquamish Indian Tribe*, 435 U.S. 191 (1978).

[23] *Ex Parte Kenyon*, 14 F. Cas. 353 (W.D. Ark. 1878).

[24] Barton H. Thompson, Jr., *Chief Justice William H. Rehnquist: Prizing People, Place, and History*, 58 Stanford L. Rev. 1695, 1699-1700 (2006).

[25] Donald E. Boles, Mr. Justice Rehnquist, Judicial Activist (Ames, Iowa: Iowa State Univ. Press, 1987), p. 5.

[26] John W. Dean, The Rehnquist Choice (New York: The Free Press, 2001), p. 86.

[27] Tony Mauro, Rehnquist's Paper Trail, Nat'l L.J. 1, 12 (Aug. 24, 2009).

[28] CBS News, The Saturday Early Show, "Newly released documents detail the late Chief Justice William Rehnquist's addiction to prescription painkillers, Jan. 6, 2007; Robert Schnakenberg, Secret Lives of the Supreme Court (Philadelphia: Quirk Books, 2009), pp. 196-97.

[29] Emily Bazelon, "The Place of Women on the Court," N.Y. Times Magazine, July 7, 2009.

[30] Woodward & Armstrong, *supra* note 5, at 279.

[31] Jan Crawford Greenburg, "William Rehnquist," Chicago Tribune, Sept. 5, 2005.

[32] David G. Savage, "Former Rehnquist Clerks Recall his Wit, Warmth," L.A. Times, Sept. 7, 2005.

[33] John G. Roberts, Jr., *A Tribute to William H. Rehnquist*, 106 Colum. L. Rev. 487, 488 (2006).

[34] *Ibid*, at 488.

[35] Brad Snyder, *The Judicial Genealogy (and Mythology) of John Roberts: Clerkships From Gray to Brandeis to Friendly to Roberts*, 71 Ohio St. L.J. 1149, 1224 (2010).

[36] Michael K. Young, *Croquet, Competition, and the Rules: A More Personal Reflection on the Jurisprudence of Chief Justice William H. Rehnquist*, 106 Columbia L. Rev. 498 (2006).

[37] Ruth Bader Ginsburg, *In Memoriam: William H. Rehnquist*, 119 Harvard L. Rev. 6, 7 (2005); Charles Fishman, "U.S. Supreme Court Justice Rehnquist to Sit as Judge in a Civil Rights Trial," Wash. Post (May 12, 1984), available at https://www.washingtonpost.com/archive/local/1984/05/12/us-supreme-court-justice-rehnquist-to-sit-as-judge-in-a-civil-rights-trial/d8ab359a-7d7d-44d6-bf5d-b0acfc198d50/.

[38] Christopher Henry, "William H. Rehnquist," in Leon Friedman and Fred L. Israel (eds.), The Justices of the United States Supreme Court: Their Lives and Major Opinions, vol. V (New York: Chelsea House Publishers, 1997), p. 1675.

[39] Maureen E. Mahoney, *In Memoriam: William H. Rehnquist*, 119 Harv. L. Rev. 25, 27 (2005).

[40] "Sworn Testimony: Rehnquist Remembered," Legal Times, Sept. 13, 2005 (recollection of Robert Bennett).

[41] Robert J. Guiffra, Jr., *In Memory of William H. Rehnquist: A Tribute to Chief Justice William H. Rehnquist*, 58 Stanford L. Rev. 1678, 1681 (2006).

[42] Roberts, *supra* note 21, at 435.

[43] Anthony M. Kennedy, *William Rehnquist and Sandra Day O'Connor: An Expression of Appreciation*, 58 Stanford L. Rev. 1663, 1664 (2006).

[44] Jeffries, *supra* note 15, at 532; Charles Lane, "Altered Circumstances, and a Little Less Pomp," Wash. Post, Oct. 30, 2001, at A9.

[45] Francis Biddle, Mr. Justice Holmes (New York: Charles Scribner's Sons, 1943), p. 108.

[46] Joan Biskupic, "Justices Ready to Revise and Compromise," USA Today, Jun. 3, 2002, p. 3A.

[47] *Forsyth County v. Nationalist Movement*, 505 U.S. 123 (1992).

[48] Tony Mauro, "Avowed Racist Flies Solo in Speech Case," Legal Times, Apr. 13, 1992.

[49] Roberts, *supra* note 33, at 488.

[50] *Fogerty v. Fantasy, Inc.*, 510 U.S. 517, 519 n.2 (1994).

[51] John Q. Barrett, *A Rehnquist Ode on the Vinson Court (Circa Summer 1953)*, 11 Green Bag 2d 289, 293-94 (2008).

[52] "Chief Justice Shows His Stripes,", Wash. Times, Jan. 18, 1995, at A15.

53 Schnakenberg, *supra* note 28, at 197.
54 Kerri Martin Bartlett, *Memories of a Modest Man: A Tribute to Chief Justice William H. Rehnquist*, 106 Columbia L. Rev. 490, 491-92.
55 Joan Biskupic, "How the last chief justice handled an impeachment trial of the President of the United States," CNN, Dec. 1, 2019.
56 Tony Mauro, "Justice Annoyed," Legal Times, Dec. 20, 1999.
57 "O'Connor Recalls Humor, Expert Guidance of Chief Justice," The Third Branch 2, 3 (Sept. 2005).
58 Tony Mauro, "Sad Tone Tinges Supreme Court Concert," Legal Times, Jun. 20, 1994, at 8.
59 Kim Eisler, A Justice for All (New York: Simon and Schuster, 1993), p. 220.
60 Joan Biskupic, An Ideological Odyssey Nears End, Wash. Post, Apr. 7, 1994, A1, A10, col. 1; Pamela S. Karlan, *Justice Harry Blackmun: From Logic to Experience*, 83 Georgetown L.J. 1 (1994).
61 Tinsley Yarbrough, Harry A. Blackmun: The Outsider Justice (New York: Oxford University Press, 2008), p. vii.
62 Clare Cushman, Courtwatchers: Eyewitness Accounts in Supreme Court History (New York: Rowman & Littlefield Publishers, Inc., 2011), p. 101.
63 Jeffries, *supra* note 15, at 252.
64 Woodward & Armstrong, *supra* note 5, at 224.
65 Biskupic, *supra* note 60.
66 Phillip J. Cooper, Battles on the Bench (Lawrence, KS: Univ. Press of Kansas, 1995), p. 165.
67 Biskupic, *supra* note 60.
68 Linda Greenhouse, "Justice Blackmun's Odyssey: From Moderate to a Liberal," N.Y. Times, Apr. 7, 1994, at A1, A24.
69 Harold Hongju Koh, *A Tribute to Justice Harry A. Blackmun*, 108 Harv. L. Rev. 20 (1994).
70 Yarbrough, *supra* note 61, at 154.
71 Mark Schneider, *Justice Blackmun: A Wise Man Walking the Corridors of Power, Gently*, 83 Georgetown L.J. 11, 11 (1994).
72 *Roe v. Wade*, 410 U.S. 113 (1973).
73 *Flood v. Kuhn*, 407 U.S. 258 (1972).
74 Eyewitness account of co-author Robert S. Peck of Harry Blackmun, lecture to law students at Yale Law School, during the Spring 1990 semester.
75 Woodward & Armstrong, *supra* note 5, at 190.
76 *Ibid*, at 191.

77 *Ibid*, at 192.

78 Yarbrough, *supra*, note 61, at 333.

79 *Ibid*, at 339.

80 Malcolm Gladwell, "Judge Breyer's Life Fashioned Like His Courthouse," Wash. Post, Jun. 26, 1994, available at https://www.washingtonpost.com/archive/politics/1994/06/26/judge-breyers-life-fashioned-like-his-courthouse/ed3cc454-180c-43fc-a4be-e16e166213a0/.

81 Tony Mauro, "Courtside: Breyer and Brevity," Legal Times, Sept. 30, 1996, p. 12.

82 Stuart E. Eizenstat, "When the GOP approved a lame-duck nominee," Wash. Post, March 17, 2016, p. A19.

83 David Margolick, "Man In the News: The Supreme Court; Scholarly Consensus Builder; Stephen Gerald Breyer," N.Y. Times, May 14, 1994, p. 1.

84 Joan Biskupic, "Supreme Court Follies Brighten Drab Routine," Wash. Post, Feb. 21, 1995, at A13, col. 3.

85 *Ibid*.

86 Debra Cassens Weiss, "Sotomayor Now Court's Junior Justice--and 'Doorkeeper and Secretary,'" ABA J. (Aug. 10, 2009), https://www.abajournal.com/news/article/sotomayor_now_courts_junior_justice--and_doorkeeper_and_secretary.

87 Cushman, *supra* note 62, at 104.

88 Richard Leiby, "The Reliable Source: The Justice, the Actress and the Purloined Book," Wash. Post, Feb. 5, 2004, at C3.

89 "Justices Breyer and Souter Reminisce on Law School and High Court Experience," Harvard Law School Alumni Pursuits, Nov. 4, 2001, p. 1.

90 Susan Dominus and Charlie Savage, "The Quiet 2013 Lunch That Could Have Altered Supreme Court History," N.Y. Times, Sept. 25, 2020.

91 Stephanie B. Goldberg, *The Second Woman Justice: Ruth Bader Ginsburg Talks Candidly About a Changing Society*, 79 ABA J. 40, 42 (Oct. 1993).

92 Nina Totenberg, "A 5-Decade-Long Friendship That Began With A Phone Call," Sept. 19, 2020, https://www.npr.org/2020/09/19/896733375/a-five-decade-long-friendship-that-began-with-a-phone-call.

93 Margaret Carlson, "The Law According to Ruth," Time, Jun. 28, 1993, p. 38.

94 *Ibid*.

95 Mark Sherman, "Ginsburg, a feminist icon memorialized as the Notorious RBG," Wash. Post, Sept. 18, 2020, available at https://www.washingtonpost.com/politics/courts_law/ginsburg-a-feminist-icon-memorialized-as-the-notorious-rbg/2020/09/18/a000bc88-fa10-11ea-85f7-5941188a98cd_story.html.

96 Linda Greenhouse, "Ruth Bader Ginsburg, Supreme Court's Feminist Icon, Is Dead at 87," N.Y. Times, Sept. 19, 2020, at A1, https://www.nytimes.com/2020/09/18/

us/ruth-bader-ginsburg-dead.html?action=click&module=Spotlight&pgtype=Homepage; Carlson, *supra* note 93, at 40.

[97] Linda Hirshman, Sisters in Law (New York: Harper Collins, 2015), p. 21.

[98] Greenhouse, *supra* note 96.

[99] Ruth Bader Ginsburg, "Lighter Side of Life at the United States Supreme Court" (Mar. 13, 2009), available at http://supremecourtus.gov/publicinfo/speeches/sp_03-13-09.html.

[100] "Oversexed," ABA Journal at 45 (Mar. 1994).

[101] Cushman, *supra* note 62, at 132.

[102] Goldberg, *supra* note 91, at 43.

[103] Totenberg, *supra* note 92.

[104] Laura Collins-Hughes, "After the Play, a Supreme Encore from Ruth Bader Ginsburg," N.Y. Times, Jul. 30, 2018.

[105] "Hearsay," Trial, at 80 (July 2009).

[106] Robert Barnes and Michael A. Fletcher, "Ruth Bader Ginsburg, Supreme Court justice and legal pioneer for gender equality, dies at 87," Wash. Post., at A1, Sept. 19, 2020, https://www.washingtonpost.com/local/obituaries/ruth-bader-ginsburg-dies/2020/09/18/3cedc314-fa08-11ea-a275-1a2c2d36e1f1_story.html.

[107] Jessica Gresko, "A rapper, an elevator and an elephant: stories Ginsburg told The Post and Courier," Sept. 20, 2020, available at https://www.postandcourier.com/ap/a-rapper-an-elevator-and-an-elephant-stories-ginsburg-told/article_a64b1ac0-fb5a-11ea-9521-8707ddc02fc3.html.

[108] Robert Barnes, "Stay or go?," Wash. Post Magazine, Oct. 6, 2013, at 8, 13.

[109] "Hearsay," *supra* note 105, at 80.

[110] Richard Binder, "Voir Dire," Nat'l Law J., at 3 (Jun. 6, 2016).

[111] Totenberg, supra note 92.

[112] Andrew Hamm, "Sotomayor Promotes New Law Clerk Hiring Plan at ACS Convention," SCOTUSBLOG (Jun. 8, 2018, 6:07 PM), http://www.scotusblog.com/2018/06/sotomayor-promotes-new-law-clerk-hiring-plan-at-acs-convention/.

[113] "Supreme Court Justice Ginsburg Speaks at Yale," Boston Globe, Oct. 19, 2012.

[114] "Justice never sleeps? Well, this one does," Wash. Post, February 14, 2013.

[115] Kendall Breitman, "Ginsburg: I Wasn't '100 Percent Sober' at SOTU, Politico (Feb. 13, 2105), available at https://www.politico.com/story/2015/02/ruth-bader-ginsburg-napping-alcohol-sotu-115172.

[116] John Rappaport, Twitter, Sept. 21, 2020, 3:56 p.m.

[117] Totenberg, *supra* note 92.

[118] Barbara A. Perry, "'The Supremes': Essays on the Current Justices of the Supreme Court of the United States" (New York: Peter Lang Publishing, Inc., 1999), p. 74.

[119] David G. Savage, Turning Right: The Making of the Rehnquist Court (New York: John Wiley & Sons, Inc., 1992) p. 170.

[120] Douglas Jehl, "A Product of Two Sides of Town: Judge Kennedy's Roots in Sacramento Go Deep," L.A. Times, December 14, 1987.

[121] Robert Barnes, "Supreme Court justices return to Harvard Law to celebrate bicentennial," Wash. Post., October 27, 2017, p. A8.

[122] Sonja R. West, *The Monster in the Courtroom*, B.Y.U.L. Rev. 1953, 1957 n.21 (2012).

[123] Joan Biskupic, "When Court is Split, Kennedy Rules," Wash. Post, Jun. 11, 1995, at A14, col. 1.

[124] *Planned Parenthood v. Casey*, 505 U.S. 833 (1992).

[125] Biskupic, *supra* note 123.

[126] Dahlia Lithwick, "A Supreme Court of One," Wash. Post, July 2, 2006, p. B1.

[127] Evan Thomas, "O'Connor's Rightful Heir?," Newsweek, Jan. 29, 2006, available at https://www.newsweek.com/oconnors-rightful-heir-108621.

[128] John G. Roberts, Jr., *In Tribute: Justice Anthony M. Kennedy*, 132 Harv. L. Rev. 1-3 (2018).

[129] Peter William Huber, "Sandra Day O'Connor," in Clare Cushman, ed., The Supreme Court Justices: Illustrated Biographies, 1789-1995 (Washington, D.C.: Cong. Quarterly, 1995), p. 506.

[130] Perry, *supra* note 118, at 42.

[131] Geoffrey R. Stone, *Review of The Chief: The Life and Turbulent Times of Chief Justice John Roberts by Joan Biskupic and First: Sandra Day O'Connor by Evan Thomas*, 133 Harv. L. Rev. 1010, 1012 (2020).

[132] Kathleen M. Sullivan, *A Tribute to Justice Sandra Day O'Connor*, 119 Harv. L. Rev. 1251, 1251 (2006).

[133] Stephen J. Wermiel, *The Jurisprudence of Justice Sandra Day O'Connor; O'Connor: A Dual Role -- An Introduction*, 13 Women's Rts. L. Rep. 129, 131 (1991).

[134] Perry, *supra* note 118, at 43-44.

[135] Ed Magnuson, "The Brethren's First Sister," Time, Jul. 20, 1981, available at http://www.time.comtime/magazine/printout/0,8816,954833.html.

[136] Evan Thomas and Stuart Taylor Jr., "Queen of the Center," Newsweek, Jul. 11, 2005.

[137] *Ibid*.

[138] Perry, *supra* note 118, at 48.

[139] A.E. Dick Howard, *The Changing Face of the Supreme Court*, 101 Va. L. Rev. 231, 244 (2015).

[140] Wermiel, *supra* note 133, at 132-33.

[141] Stone, *supra* note 131, at 1022.

[142] Viveca Novak and Michael D. Lemonick, "The Power Broker," TIME, Jul. 3, 2005.

[143] Ruth Bader Ginsburg, *A Tribute to Justice Sandra Day O'Connor*, 119 Harv. L. Rev. 1239, 1241 (2006).

[144] *Roe v. Wade*, 410 U.S. 113 (1973).

[145] *Webster v. Reproductive Health Servs.*, 492 U.S. 490 (1989).

[146] *Id.* at 532 (Scalia, J., concurring).

[147] Phillip J. Cooper, Battles on the Bench (Lawrence, KS: Univ. Press of Kansas, 1995), p.121.

[148] Thomas and Taylor, *supra* note 136.

[149] Stone, *supra* note 131, at 1031.

[150] Robert Barnes, "Justices Discuss a Changing Court," Wash. Post, Sept. 4, 2009, at A21.

[151] Joan Biskupic, "A New Page in O'Connors' Love Story," USA Today, Feb. 19, 2009, available at https://abcnews.go.com/TheLaw/Politics/story?id=3858553&page=1; Evan Thomas, First: Sandra Day O'Connor (New York: Random House, 2019), p. 387.

[152] Sullivan, *supra* note 132, at 1255.

[153] Lynne Duke, "From Court to Jester," Wash. Post, Jan. 28, 2007, pp. D1, D6.

[154] Jeffries, *supra* note 15, at 24.

[155] Lewis F. Powell III, *Justice and Mrs. Lewis F. Powell, Jr.: A Son's Perspective*, 33 Univ. of Richmond L. Rev. 1,4 (1999).

[156] Jeffries, *supra* note 15, at 107-08.

[157] *Ibid*, at 189.

[158] *Ibid*, 1-9.

[159] Woodward & Armstrong, *supra* note 5, at 162.

[160] Jeffries, *supra* note 15, at 232.

[161] *Ibid*, at 268fn.

[162] Barrett McGurn, America's Court: The Supreme Court and the People (Golden, Colo.: Fulcrum Publishing, 1997), p. 124.

[163] *Brewer v. Williams*, 430 U.S. 387 (1977).

[164] Jeffries, *supra* note 15, at 402.

[165] *Bowers v. Hardwick*, 478 U.S. 186 (1986).

[166] *Lawrence v. Texas*, 539 U.S. 558 (2003).

[167] Adam Liptak, "Exhibit A for a Major Shift: Justices' Gay Clerks," N.Y. Times, Jun. 8, 2013, available at nytimes.com/2013/06/09/us/exhibit-a-for-a-major-shift-justices-gay-clerks.html?smid=pl-share.

[168] Jeffries, *supra* note 15, at 15.

[169] Joan Biskupic, American Original: The Life and Constitution of Supreme Court Justice Antonin Scalia (New York: Sarah Crichton Books, 2009), p. 88.

[170] Alex Kozinski, *My Pizza with Nino: The Jurisprudence of Antonin Scalia*, 12 Cardozo L. Rev. 1583, 1584-85 (1991).

[171] Adam Liptak, "Antonin Scalia, Justice on the Supreme Court, Dies at 70," N.Y. Times, Feb. 13, 2016.

[172] Cushman, *supra* note 62, at 155.

[173] Charles Evans Hughes, The Supreme Court of the United States (New York: Columbia Univ. Press 1936), p. 68.

[174] *Atkins v. Virgina*, 536 U.S. 304 (2002).

[175] *Id.* at 338 (Scalia, J., dissenting).

[176] *Id.* at 347 (Scalia, J., dissenting).

[177] *King v. Burwell*, 576 U.S. 473 (2015).

[178] *Glossip v. Gross*, 576 U.S. 863 (2015).

[179] "Groundhog Day," (Columbia Pictures, 1993); *Glossip*, 576 U.S. at 893 (Scalia, J., concurring).

[180] *Id.* at 894.

[181] *Id.* at 895.

[182] *Id.* at 898.

[183] *Id.*

[184] *Id.* at 899.

[185] *Maryland v. Wilson*, 519 U.S. 408 (1997).

[186] *Wal-Mart Stores, Inc. v. Dukes*, 564 U.S. 338 (2011).

[187] Tony Mauro and Marcia Coyle, "Protests & Pileups," Nat'l L.J. (Apr. 4, 2011).

[188] Debra Cassens Weiss, "Scalia: Music Improves his Disposition, But Loud Rock Would Spur Confession," ABA Journal News (Jan. 15, 2010).

[189] Tony Mauro, "High Court Returns to a Busy Schedule," Nat'l L.J. (Jan. 11, 2010).

[190] Weiss, *supra* note 188.

[191] *Cty. of Sacramento v. Lewis*, 523 U.S. 833, 861 & n.1 (1998) (Scalia, J., concurring).

[192] Katie Glueck, "Scalia: The Constitution is 'dead,'" Politico, Jan. 29, 2013, https://www.politico.com/story/2013/01/scalia-the-constitution-is-dead-086853.

[193] Dana Milbank, "Scalia Showing His Softer Side, Wash. Post (Mar. 15, 2005), p. A2 col. 2.

[194] Antonin Scalia and Bryan A. Garner, Making Your Case: The Art of Persuading Judges (St. Paul: Thomson West, 2008), p. 183.

[195] Dan Slater, "Law Blog Chats with Scalia, Part III: When Clients Win in Spite of their Lawyers," Wall St. J. Law Blog, May 30, 2008, 9:05 pm ET.

[196] "Hearsay," ABA Journal, Dec. 2013, p. 12, col. 2.

[197] Ruth Marcus and Joe Pichirallo, "Seeking Out the Essential David Souter," Wash. Post (Sept. 9, 1990), at A1.

[198] *Ibid.*

[199] "Marshall Says He Never Heard of Bush's Nominee," N.Y. Times (July 27,1990), at A12.

[200] Dahlia Litwick, "Justice Heartbreaker," Slate (May 1, 2009), www.slate.com/id/2217431/.

[201] Jeffrey Rosen, "The Stealth Justice," Wash. Post (May 2, 2009), at A19, col. 2.

[202] Kermit Roosevelt, "Justice Cincinnatus," Slate (May 1, 2009), www.slate.com/id/2217434/pagenumb/all/

[203] *Bd. of Educ. of Kiryas Joel Vill. Sch. Dist. v. Grumet,* 512 U.S. 687, 708 (1994).

[204] Cushman, *supra* note 62, at 130.

[205] Barnes, *supra* note 150.

[206] Mark Sherman, "Souter bids fond, emotional farewell to judges," The Press-Enterprise (Riverside, CA), May 5, 2009.

[207] "Souter Returns to Granite State," Nat'l L.J. at 1 (Aug. 17, 2009).

[208] Stone, *supra* note 131, at 1026.

[209] Phillip Rucker, "Quiet New Hampshire Home Is Where Souter's Heart Has Always Been," Wash. Post, May 3, 2009, p. A1.

[210] Charles Lane, "John Paul Stevens, longtime leader of Supreme Court's liberal wing, dies at 99," Wash. Post (Jul. 16, 2019), available at https://www.washingtonpost.com/local/obituaries/john-paul-stevens-longtime-leader-of-supreme-courts-liberal-wing-dies-at-99/2019/07/16/701232a2-a829-11e9-86dd-d7f0e60391e9_story.html?utm_term=.4389d8a3fd47.

[211] Rosemary Simota Thompson, *Stevens: Chicago's Native Son,* 24 Chicago Bar Ass'n Record 30, 31-32 (2010).

[212] Yarbrough, *supra* note 61, at 13.

[213] Lauraann Wood, "How Deep Chicago Roots Kept Stevens Grounded," Law 360 (Jul. 17, 2019).

[214] Cara Bayles, "'May I Just Ask': Era of Civility Passes with Justice Stevens," Law 360 (July 17, 2019).

[215] Christopher L. Eisgruber, *John Paul Stevens and the Manners of Judging,* 1992/1993 Ann. Surv. Am. L. XXIX, xxx (1993).

[216] Howard Kurtz, "Passing Judgement on Dave Barry," Wash. Post, Sept. 21, 1991, https://www.washingtonpost.com/archive/lifestyle/1991/09/21/passing-judgement-on-dave-barry/075a42c6-333f-4c43-87ed-f2f28f850a82/.

[217] Samuel Spital, Dedication; Justice John Paul Stevens, 44 Loy. L.A. L. Rev. 813, 827 (2011).

[218] Lane, *supra* note 210.

[219] John Greenya, Silent Justice: The Clarence Thomas Story 32 (Ft. Lee, N.J.: Barricade Books, Inc., 2001).

[220] *Ibid*, at 42.

[221] Stanley Kay, "The Highest Court in the Land," Sports Illustrated (Jul. 25, 2018), available at https://www.si.com/nba/2018/07/25/supreme-court-building-basketball-court.

[222] Tony Mauro, "Justices Kennedy, Thomas Discuss 'Bush v. Gore,' Minority Law Clerks at 11th Circuit Conference," American Lawyer Media (May 21, 2001).

[223] Robert Barnes, "Justices who graduate from Yale Law School hold court," Wash. Post, Oct. 25, 2014.

[224] Mauro, *supra* note 56.

[225] Adam Liptak, "Reticent on the Bench, but Effusive About It," N.Y. Times, Nov. 1, 2016, p. A15.

[226] *Ibid*.

[227] Adam Liptak, "A Sign of Court's Polarization: Choice of Clerks," N.Y. Times, Sept. 7, 2010, p. A1.

Chapter 9

[1] Jo Becker and Brian Faler, "Who Knew about John Roberts? In 1985, Maybe He Did," Wash. Post, Aug. 23, 2005, at A4.

[2] "Inadmissible: Chief Justice Roberts' Krispy Kreme Caper," Nat'l L.J. (Mar. 15, 2010).

[3] Robert Barnes, "Court Views Work of Potential Picks, Wash. Post. (May 24, 2009), at A3.

[4] Robert Barnes, "New Justices Take the Podium, Putting Personalities on Display," Wash. Post, A15 (Nov. 20, 2006).

[5] *Richmond Newspapers, Inc. v. Virginia*, 448 U.S. 555, 604 (1980) (Rehnquist, J., dissenting).

[6] *Sprint Commc'ns Co., L.P. v. APCC Servs., Inc.*, 554 U.S. 269 (2008).

[7] *Id.* at 301 (Roberts, C.J., dissenting).

[8] Bob Dylan, *Like A Rolling Stone*, on Highway 61 Revisited (Columbia Records 1965).

9. *FCC v. AT&T Inc.*, 562 U.S. 397 (2011).
10. Oral Argument in *FCC v. AT&T Inc.*, at p. 35 (Jan. 19, 2011), https://www.supremecourt.gov/oral_arguments/argument_transcripts/2010/09-1279.pdf.
11. Ibid.
12. Ibid, at p. 36.
13. *FCC v. AT&T Inc.*, 562 U.S. 397, 402-03 (2011) (internal citations omitted).
14. *Id.* at 410.
15. *Nichols v. United States*, 136 S. Ct. 1113 (2016).
16. Tony Mauro and Marcia Coyle, "Thomas Ends Silence, Lights Out, and RBG's Name is Flubbed," Nat'l Law J., May 9, 2016, at 17, 20.
17. Sandra Day O'Connor, Out of Order: Stories from the History of the Supreme Court (New York: Random House, 2013), at 117.
18. *Briscoe v. Virginia*, 559 U.S. 32 (2010) (per curiam).
19. Debra Cassens Weiss, "Supreme Court Word of the Day: Orthogonal," ABA Journal Weekly (Jan. 12, 2010).
20. Brad Snyder, *The Judicial Genealogy (and Mythology) of John Roberts: Clerkships From Gray to Brandeis to Friendly to Roberts*, 71 Ohio State Law Journal 1149, 1217 (2010).
21. Jeff Mason, "Obama takes oath again after inauguration mistake," Reuters, January 21, 2009.
22. Adam Liptak, "Justices Return to School and Speak of Lessons Learned," N.Y. Times, Oct. 26, 2014, p. 18.
23. Robert Barnes, "Supreme Court justices return to Harvard Law to celebrate bicentennial," Wash. Post, Oct. 27, 2017, p. A8.
24. Robert Barnes, "Justices who graduate from Yale Law School hold court," Wash. Post, Oct. 25, 2014.
25. Mark Sherman, "Supreme Court Justice Samuel Alito takes on critics, defends Citizen United," The Christian Science Monitor, Nov. 17, 2012.
26. Daniel J. Wakin, "A Prosecutor Known for His Common Sense and Straightforward Style," N.Y. Times, Nov. 2, 2005, p. 24.
27. Rebecca Riddick, "The High Court's Junior Justice Speaks Out," Daily Business Review (Jan. 29, 2007), http://www.law.com/jsp/law/LawArticleFriendly.jsp?id=1169806056396.
28. Barnes, *supra* note 4, at A15.
29. Paul Hagen, "Alito Is One Phillies Fan Whose Opinions Really Matter," Phila. Inquirer (Apr. 13, 2010), https://www.inquirer.com/philly/sports/phillies/20100413_Alito_is_one_Phillies_fan_whose_opinions_really_matter.html.

[30] Clare Cushman, Courtwatchers: Eyewitness Accounts in Supreme Court History (Lanham, MD: Rowman & Littlefield Publishers, Inc., 2011), p. 103.

[31] C-SPAN, "The Supreme Court: Home to America's Highest Court," TV, Oct. 14, 2009.

[32] Rebecca Riddick, "The High Court's Junior Justice Speaks Out," Daily Business Rev. (Jan. 29, 2007), available at http://www.law.com/jsp/law/LawArticleFriendly.jsp?id=1169806056396.

[33] *Brown v. Entertainment Merchants Ass'n*, 564 U.S. 768 (2011).

[34] Oral Argument Transcript, *Brown v. Entertainment Merchants Ass'n*, No. 08-1448 https://www.oyez.org/cases/2010/08-1448.

[35] Adam Liptak, "Justices Return to School and Speak of Lessons Learned," New York Times, Oct. 26, 2014, p. 18.

[36] *Ibid.*

[37] *Ibid.*

[38] Margaret Talbot, "Amy Coney Barrett's Long Game," The New Yorker, February 7, 2022.

[39] *Ibid.*

[40] Aaron Parsley, "Amy Coney Barrett Talks 'Overwhelming' Start, Home Life 'Balance' and Collegiality Among Justices," People, Apr. 6, 2022, available at https://people.com/politics/supreme-court-justice-amy-coney-barrett-family-life-hopping-fences-heels-pizza-work-cafeteria/.

[41] Justice Amy Coney Barrett," University of Minnesota Law School, C-Span, October 16, 2023

[42] Kalvis Golde, "Gorsuch, Speaking to Students on Constitution Day, Honors Ginsburg," SCOTUSblog, Sept. 17, 2020, at https://www.scotusblog.com/2020/09/gorsuch-speaking-to-students-on-constitution-day-honors-ginsburg/.

[43] Terry A. Maroney, *(What We Talk About When We Talk About) Judicial Temperament*, 61 B.C. L. Rev. 2085, 2014 (2020).

[44] Neil M Gorsuch, *Anthony M. Kennedy*, 132 Harv. L. Rev. 3, 4-5 (2018).

[45] *Masterpiece Cakeshop, Ltd. v. Colorado Civil Rights Comm'n*, 138 S.Ct. 1719 (2018).

[46] Transcript of Oral Argument at 12, *Masterpiece Cakeshop, Ltd. v. Colo. Civil Rights Comm'n*, 138 S. Ct. 1719 (2018) (No. 16-111), https://www.supremecourt.gov/oral_arguments/argument_transcripts/2017/16-111_f29g.pdf, at 41.

[47] Adam Liptak, "Gorsuch Rejects Doubts Over Rule of Law Today," N.Y. Times, Jun. 4, 2017, p. 17.

[48] Ann E. Marimow and Aaron C. Davis, "Possible Supreme Court nominee, former defender, saw impact of harsh drug sentence first hand," Wash. Post, January 30, 2022.

49. Marc Fisher, Ann E. Marimow, and Lori Rozsa, "How Ketanji Brown Jackson found a path between confrontation and compromise," Wash. Post, February 25, 2022.

50. Monica Dunn, "Who is Ketanji Brown Jackson, the incoming Supreme Court justice? And the inside story behind her name," ABC News, June 29, 2022.

51. Susan Svrluga, "Justice Ketanji Brown Jackson Shares 'Survivor' Lessons with Law Grads," Wash. Post, May 20, 2023, available at https://www.washingtonpost.com/education/2023/05/20/ketanji-brown-jackson-american-university/

52. Molly Callahan, "Supreme Court Justice Ketanji Brown Jackson to 2023 BU LAW Graduates: 'Anything Is Possible,'" BU Today (May 21, 2023), available at https://www.bu.edu/articles/2023/supreme-court-justice-ketanji-brown-jackson-speaks-to-2023-bu-law-graduates/.

53. Elena Kagan, *For Justice Marshall*, 71 Texas L. Rev. 1125, 1126 (1993).

54. Stanley Kay, "The Highest Court in the Land," Sports Illustrated (Jul. 25, 2018), https://www.si.com/nba/2018/07/25/supreme-court-building-basketball-court.

55. Robert Barnes, "Supreme Court justices return to Harvard Law to celebrate bicentennial," Wash. Post, Oct. 27, 2017, p. A8.

56. *Holder v. Humanitarian Law Project*, 561 US 1 (2010).

57. Oral Argument Transcript, *Holder v. Humanitarian Project*, at 49, available at https://www.supremecourt.gov/oral_arguments/argument_transcripts/2009/08-1498.pdf.

58. Oral Argument Transcript, *United States v. Comstock*, No. 08-1224, at 26 (Jan. 12, 2010), available at https://www.supremecourt.gov/oral_arguments/argument_transcripts/2009/08-1224.pdf.

59. Manu Raju, "Kagan: I spent Christmas at a Chinese restaurant," Politico Now Blog, June 29, 2010.

60. "Supreme Court Justice Elena Kagan speaks at University of Minnesota, Stein Lecture Series" MPR News, Oct. 23, 2019.

61. Elena Kagan, *A Conversation with Associate Justice Elena Kagan*, 91 U. Colo. L. Rev. 749, 760 (2020).

62. *Ibid*, pp. 769-70.

63. Lauren Holter, "Justice Kagan Got SCOTUS A Frozen Yogurt Machine: A Woman After Our Own Hearts," Refinery 29 (Jul. 21, 2017), https://www.refinery29.com/en-us/2017/07/164579/scotus-frozen-yogurt-machine-elena-kagan.

64. Sarah Hedgecock, "11 Wacky Supreme Court Facts: Frozen Yogurt Justice, Scalia and Ginsburg Friendship & More," The Daily Beast (Jun. 26, 2012), https://www.thedailybeast.com/11-wacky-supreme-court-facts-frozen-yogurt-justice-scalia-and-ginsburg-friendship-and-more.

65. *Smith v. Bayer Corp.*, 564 U.S. 299 (2011).

66. Ruth Bader Ginsburg, "A Survey of the 2010 Term: Presentation to the Otsego County Bar Association," Jul. 22, 2011, available at https://www.supremecourt.gov/publicinfo/speeches/viewspeech/sp_07-22-11.

67. Hayley Sanchez, "Justice Elena Kagan in Boulder: It's Less About Partisanship and More 'Ways of Looking at the Constitution,'" CPR News, Oct. 23, 2019.

68. *Kimble v. Marvel Entertainment*, 576 U.S. 446 (2015).

69. Joe Patrice, "Justice Kagan Cites Precedential Authority of Comic Book," Above the Law, Jun. 22, 2015.

70. *Yates v. U.S.*, 574 U.S. 528 (2015).

71. David Lat, "This Citation by Justice Kagan Looks a Little Bit Fishy," Above The Law, Feb. 25, 2015.

72. Brett M. Kavanaugh, *Statutory Ambiguity and Constitutional Exceptions*, 92 Notre Dame L. Rev. 1907, 1908 (2017).

73. Jimmy Hoover, "Kavanaugh Cracks Jokes, Thanks Allies in First Major Speech," Law 360 (Nov. 15, 2019).

74. Kristine Phillips, "'Moral dry-rot': The only Supreme Court justice who divided the Senate more than Kavanaugh," Wash. Post, October 8, 2018.

75. Kavanaugh, *supra* note 72.

76. Hoover, *supra* note 73.

77. *Ibid.*

78. Michael Powell, Serge F. Kovaleski, and Russ Buettner, "To Get to Sotomayor's Core, Start in New York," N.Y. Times, Jul. 10, 2009, p. 1.

79. Alec MacGillis, Amy Goldstein, and Robert Barnes, "Ethnicity and Gender Play Prominent Roles in Sotomayor's Speeches," Wash. Post, June 5, 2009, available at: https:washingtonpost.com/wp-dyn/content/article/2009/06/04/AR2009060403265.html.

80. James Warren, "Sonia Sotomayor on Dating, Deciding, and Being the Newest Supreme Court Justice," The Atlantic, March 7, 2011, available at https: theatlantic.com/politics/archive/2011/03/sonia-sotomayor-on-dating-deciding-and-being-the-newest-supreme-court-justice/.

81. Jesse J. Holland, "Sotomayor adds celebrity to Supreme Court," NBC News, November 17,2009, available at: https: nbcnews.com/id/wbna33975806/.

82. *Ibid.*

83. Jack Curry, "Justice Sotomayor Throws Out First Pitch, N.Y. Times, September 26, 2009, available at: https: archive.nytimes.com/bats.blog.nytimes.com/2009/09/26/justice-sotomayor-throws-out-first-pitch/.

84. Debra Cassens Weis, "Sotomayor Can Thank Mom for Hitting Casino Jackpot," ABA J., May 29, 2019, available at: https: abajournal.com/news/article/sotomayor-can-thank-mom-for-hitting-casino-jackpot/.

[85] Liptak, *supra* note 35.

[86] Robert Barnes, "With Justice Sotomayor, a first year that stands apart; High court's newest member finds her own way of fitting in as she does a job she loves," Wash. Post, Jul. 25, 2010, p. A01.

[87] Emma G. Fitzsimmons, "Sotomayor to Lead Countdown to New Years in Times Square, N.Y. Times, Dec. 30, 2013, p. 16.

[88] Jorge Ramos, "What Sonia Sotomayor Told a 10-Year Old Girl," N.Y. Times, Aug. 7, 2020.

[89] David G. Savage and Ian Duncan, "Supreme Court justices engage in eclectic pursuits beyond the bench," Wash. Post, Feb. 21, 2012, p. A13.

Printed in the USA
CPSIA information can be obtained
at www.ICGtesting.com
CBHW021953191024
15901CB00051BA/779

9 781950 544530